P9-DEK-972

"Phil Kenneson is one of our best bright young minds writing for the church today. His astute and faithful critique of our consumerist culture is both incisive and life-giving for Christians. The insights in this book name well the challenge before the North American church. Yet he moves beyond critique to offer a biblical, hopeful word as well as specific, practical things we can do to be more faithful disciples in a culture that wants us only to be more aggressive consumers."
WILLIAM H. WILLIMON, *Duke University*

" 'The way, the truth and the life,' he said. Pray tell me then why Christian doctrine has been overwhelmed by *truth* questions alone. How he lived, the way he walked, put holy fire in his words.
Kenneson's *Life on the Vine* has the simplicity of truth.
Taking seriously the questions of young adults about the good news and the church that proclaims it allows them to see why the Way and the Life can still call for ultimate commitment of everything we are and could be. This is a book for young energy and aged wisdom.
As old as Scripture, as fresh as the coming millennium."
FREDERICK W. NORRIS, *Emmanuel School of Religion*

"Phil Kenneson has provided us the uncommon gift of making 'real' our Christian discipleship in the midst of a culture whose 'reality' principles are often intractably antagonistic to our faith. In many ways, the advanced industrial and technological culture of American capitalism has colonized our minds, hearts and behaviors.
Life on the Vine is telling diagnosis of our spiritual ills.
What is more rare and welcome, it is a practical, prophetic, Scripture-based prescription for reanimating our lives in the Spirit, bearing the Spirit's gifts, which not only challenge culture but glorify God.
I will pray through this book for my annual eight-day retreat."
JOHN F. KAVANAUGH, S.J., *Saint Louis University*

"Phil Kenneson is not an optimist—he is too insightfully realistic about the sick state of Christian life in North America. Nor is Kenneson a pessimist— he has too much trust in the power of the Holy Spirit to transform God's people.
Instead, through *Life on the Vine* he offers a forthright and superbly hopeful prophetic call. His challenges are coupled with meaty biblical reflections, astute cultural analysis and sound suggestions for positive responses.
I pray that many will hear what the Spirit is saying to the church through this outstanding book."
MARVA J. DAWN, *author of* Reaching Out Without Dumbing Down

"An exciting, accessible, important book. Kenneson understands the challenges
the Christian church needs to face in relation to American culture.
His disarmingly wise and well-developed reflections call us to transformed
and enlivened Christian discipleship. Don't miss it."
L. GREGORY JONES, *Duke University*

"Kenneson gracefully explores the tensions between Christian virtue
and middle-class life in the bull market. Probing Paul's list of fruits of the Spirit
in Galatians, he walks us through the obstacle course of the comfortable:
consumer culture, enslavement to productivity, the lure of aggression and more.
It is an *Imitation of Christ* for our wealthy and frenetic age, filled with carefully
crafted spiritual exercises that cut to the quick of our impatient and loveless age:
insightful, down-to-earth, compassionate."
ELLEN CHARRY, *Princeton Theological Seminary*

"There are just so many things Phil Kenneson does well in *Life on the Vine*.
In exploring the social and cultural obstacles to the life of discipleship—
and more important, what we do about them—he shows his command
of Scripture, social analysis and pastoral realities. Kenneson writes so clearly
and so well that he moves ideas and concerns once discussed only within the
scholarly guild into the everyday life and dialogue of the church.
But behind Kenneson's smooth prose stands the hard edge of gospel truth
and a sophisticated critique of contemporary politics, economics and culture.
This is an essential book for pastors, Christian educators of all kinds,
parents and anyone who would 'seek first the kingdom of God' in our day."
MICHAEL L. BUDDE, *DePaul University*

Life *On* *The* Vine

Cultivating

the Fruit

of the Spirit

in CHRISTIAN

COMMUNITY

PHILIP D. KENNESON

InterVarsity Press
Downers Grove, Illinois

InterVarsity Press
P.O. Box 1400, Downers Grove, IL 60515
World Wide Web: www.ivpress.com
E-mail: mail@ivpress.com

©1999 by Philip D. Kenneson

Published in the United States of America by InterVarsity Press, Downers Grove, Illinois.

All rights reserved. No part of this book may be reproduced in any form without written permission from InterVarsity Press.

InterVarsity Press is the book-publishing division of InterVarsity Christian Fellowship/USA, a student movement active on campus at hundreds of universities, colleges and schools of nursing in the United States of America, and a member movement of the International Fellowship of Evangelical Students. For information about local and regional activities, write Public Relations Dept., InterVarsity Christian Fellowship/USA, 6400 Schroeder Rd., P.O. Box 7895, Madison, WI 53707-7895.

Scripture quotations, unless otherwise noted, are from the New Revised Standard Version of the Bible, *copyright 1989 by the Division of Christian Education of the National Council of the Churches of Christ in the USA. Used by permission. All rights reserved.*

Cover photograph: SuperStock

ISBN 0-8308-2219-4

Printed in the United States of America ♽

Library of Congress Cataloging-in-Publication Data

Kenneson, Philip D.
  Life on the vine : cultivating the fruit of the spirit in
Christian community / Philip D. Kenneson.
    p. cm.
  Includes bibliographical references.
  ISBN 0-8308-2219-4 (paper : alk. paper)
  1. Fruit of the Spirit. I. Title.
BV4501.2.K434 1999
234'.13—dc21   99-36493
                                                                CIP

17	16	15	14	13	12	11	10	9	8	7	6	5	4
12	11	10	09	08	07	06	05	04	03				

In loving memory of my parents,
Edwin A. Kenneson and Kathryn E. Kenneson,
who, along with the other saints
of Jesus Christ at Traders Point Christian Church,
introduced me to life on the vine.

Thanks be to God.

CONTENTS

INTRODUCTION
Being Known by Our Fruit

You will know them by their fruits. Are grapes gathered from thorns, or figs from thistles? In the same way, every good tree bears good fruit, but the bad tree bears bad fruit. A good tree cannot bear bad fruit, nor can a bad tree bear good fruit. Every tree that does not bear good fruit is cut down and thrown into the fire. Thus you will know them by their fruits. (Mt 7:16-20)

The fruit of the Spirit is love, joy, peace, patience, kindness, goodness, faithfulness, gentleness and self-control. There is no law against such things. And those who belong to Christ Jesus have crucified the flesh with its passions and desires. If we live by the Spirit, let us also be guided by the Spirit. (Gal 5: 22-25)

Every year seniors at the college where I teach undertake an intense investigation of what it might mean at the close of the second millennium for Christians to live as the body of Christ in the midst of a culture like ours. What makes this task so invigorating and exciting is that these young men and women genuinely desire to be disciples of Jesus Christ; what makes the task so demanding and challenging is that the culture within which the church finds itself is changing so rapidly that reflection on our present context hardly ever seems to keep pace.

In my relatively short tenure as a teacher I have found that Christians in the United States are understandably of a divided mind when it comes to evaluating their home turf. "It is the best of places; it is the worst of places." On one side stand all the seemingly self-evident advantages of being a

Christian in the United States. Foremost in many minds is the presence of religious freedom, a freedom that some believe so crucial to their way of life that it obliges them to pledge unconditional loyalty to that system of government that has secured this freedom in the past and that continues to protect it in the present. Moreover, since many peoples around the globe have not been afforded this opportunity to worship freely, many thoughtful and sincere Christians conclude that there can be no better place to be a Christian than in the United States of America.

Yet there are also many Christians in this country who acknowledge that there is a fly in the ointment. These Christians, though perhaps equally grateful for the freedoms this nation affords, also recognize that there is much about its dominant culture that makes living the Christian faith difficult. For example, Christians often complain about attacks on their cherished beliefs by the "cultural elite" or about the removal of prayer from schools or about the moral decline of the entire country; these all suggest that at least some Christians recognize that some things are not as they might be. Moreover, these Christians often lament the fact that Christianity has lost its privileged status within the so-called public arena. If this status could be regained (it is argued) and if Christianity could be reinstalled at the center of public life, all would be well.

But all would not be well. Whatever Herculean efforts might be undertaken to elevate some form of Christianity back to a privileged position would be for naught if that form of Christianity turned out to be seriously defective—or worse, if it turned out to be Christianity in name only. We need to remind ourselves that Jesus never suggested that we should evaluate the health of his people by how much power they wielded or how much privilege they amassed. Rather, Jesus insisted that his followers would be identifiable as his followers by their *fruit*.

Evaluating the health of Christian communities means more than simply assessing their political clout or their ability to influence public policy. We must take a hard look at the ways in which we allow the dominant culture to shape our daily lives. As Christians in this society, we often have a dangerous habit of believing that what is wrong in our contemporary situation can be limited to what is going on "out there." Whenever we think this way, we are like a patient whose sickness has been misdiagnosed. It's agony enough to wrestle with an *anonymous* illness, but it's pure torture to wake up one day and discover that the doctors have been fighting the *wrong thing,* especially if, as a result of their ill-advised treatments, you not only remain sick but grow worse. Moreover, as long as the ailment remains misidentified, not only is the likelihood of full recovery slim, but the possibility of further harm increased. I submit that many contemporary Christians find themselves in an analogous position. We rightly sense that something is seriously wrong with the church, but we cannot quite put a finger on it. When a diagnosis of the church's illness *is* made, it's often superficial, resulting in a treatment plan that wreaks more havoc and spawns more frustration than the original condition.

This book is written from the conviction that the church in the United States is seriously ill. The aim of the book is to help the church to name accurately and honestly what ails it. Like most diagnostic work, this book offers both judgment and hope: judgment upon certain bad habits of thinking and acting that have contributed to our sickness; and hope that if, by the grace of God, we might be led to establish new patterns of thinking and acting, God might breathe new life into us so that we might bear good fruit before the world.

Some readers will likely question my insistence that the church is seriously ill. After all, they might ask, haven't the latest polls consistently shown that the United States is as religious as ever? Yes, but though it is relatively easy to tabulate the answers people give to such innocuous questions as "Do you believe in an afterlife?" it is much more difficult to discern whether Christians in the United States are consistently bearing the fruit of the Spirit. Indeed, although I would not want to dismiss entirely statistics that show how many people attend worship on a semi-regular basis, I would not want these numbers to give us a false sense of security, a false sense that things are going well with the church in the United States. Again Jesus did not suggest that we would be known by our answers to opinion polls, but by our fruit.

What the following chapters suggest is that it is quite possible for the church to be both growing and yet not bearing the fruit of the Spirit. What is happening in many cases is that the church is simply cultivating at the center of its life the seeds that the dominant culture has sown in its midst. As a result, the seeds that the Spirit has sown are all but being choked out, and the fruit that is being brought to harvest has little or no likeness to the Spirit's fruit. Said another way, the church that is being cultivated in the United States looks suspiciously like the dominant culture rather than being an alternative to it. In *theory* this mimicking of the surrounding culture might not be a problem, for there is no inherent reason that human cultures must be pitted against the ways of God; however, given that (as I will argue in this book) the dominant culture bears so little resemblance to the reign that God is bringing, this mimicking turns out to be a serious problem in *practice.* Moreover, until we are honest enough to make this painful admission, it seems unlikely that we will be in a position to do much about it.

My hope is that this book will help provoke a serious conversation among Christians in the United States not only about some of the difficulties of embodying the gospel within this culture but also about what directions we might want to move. I have focused my attention throughout this book on the churches in the United States and on the dominant culture within which most of them exist, because this is my own context. Because this dominant culture is propagated by institutions and practices that extend beyond the boundaries of the United States, many of the issues discussed in these pages have parallels in cultures outside the United States. Thus although I expect that much of what I say here will resonate with readers outside this particular context, I leave to others the task of discerning where adjustments for different contexts need to be made.

I am well aware that this book raises more questions than it answers, but I am increasingly convinced that this is not something for which one should apologize. Indeed, I firmly believe that no more important task faces the contemporary church than beginning to ask the right questions.

Like most books, this one would not have been possible without the support and help of people too numerous to name. Yet I consider it a privilege to thank at least some of them for their insights and suggestions at various stages. I am first of all indebted to the hundreds of college seniors at Milligan

College who during the past seven years have explored with me the interplay between Christian faith and the dominant culture of the United States. Their enthusiastic willingness to embark on this investigation each semester continues to inspire and instruct me. I am also indebted to a much smaller group of students who during the spring of 1995 worked through some very early drafts of this material in a seminar setting. Not only did this group think hard and well with me about these important matters, they also managed each week to work through my hastily written and often-incoherent drafts, always encouraging me by identifying something in what I had written that seemed worth saving and expanding. Because this group provided much of the impetus and inspiration for what is now a much revised (and I hope much improved) version, I consider it a privilege to thank them for all of their encouragement and assistance: Monica Click Bird, Christie Dick, Laura Beth Eaton, Brian Free, Stephen Harvey, Jonathan Huddleston, Rebecca Lewis, Robert Marmion, Lisa Morrison, Dasen Ritchey, Linda Street and Tabitha Travis. One final member of this seminar, Miriam Perkins, deserves special thanks for plowing through the manuscript a second time more recently, offering again her invaluable perspective and insight.

The following group of trusted friends also offered feedback at different stages, and their comments and suggestions proved immensely helpful: Margaret and A. K. M. Adam, Steve and Melinda Fowl, Allan and Betsy Poole, Craig and Margaret Farmer, Teresa Hittner, Jean Corey, Lee Magness, Susan Higgins, Frederick Norris, Jonathan Wilson, Sherry Boles, Stan Hauerwas and Kim Kenneson. I am especially grateful to David Cunningham, whose careful reading and editorial work improved both the argument of the book and its readability. Rodney Clapp, my editor at IVP, has been throughout these many years a constant source of encouragement, a discerning reader, a notable exemplar of patience and a good friend.

All the persons named above are partly responsible for the shape of this book. Even more importantly, they are also partly responsible for the shape of my life. Although both this book and my life fall short of what these dear friends would have them be, I give unceasing thanks to God for their faithful and life-giving presence. This book is about cultivating the fruit of the Spirit in Christian community, and in addition to those saints mentioned above, I am grateful to several other brothers and sisters in Christ for being instruments of God's abiding grace and presence. This book is dedicated to my parents, who along with the rest of the saints at Traders Point Christian Church in Indianapolis, Indiana, introduced me to life in the Spirit. Although I am far from being wholly transformed into the image of Christ, I am eternally grateful to these saints who set my feet on the right path.

Most recently, I have become mindful again of how powerful an influence children are in our lives. Thus I consider it a special privilege to thank our five children—Chassy, Peter, Andrew, Katie and Sarah Ann—for the unspeakable joy and irreplaceable perspective they have brought to my life. Kim, my wife of over sixteen years, has also shaped my life beyond measure. She, more than anyone else, knows how far short my life falls of the vision of the Christian life set forth in these pages. For her faithfulness, encouragement and abiding presence in my life these many years, I give her and God great thanks.

ONE
Dying on
the Vine?

I am the true vine, and my Father is the vinegrower. He removes every branch in me that bears no fruit. Every branch that bears fruit he prunes to make it bear more fruit. (Jn 15:1-2)

Then he told this parable: "A man had a fig tree planted in his vineyard; and he came looking for fruit on it and found none. So he said to the gardener, 'See here! For three years I have come looking for fruit on this fig tree, and still I find none. Cut it down! Why should it be wasting the soil?' He replied, 'Sir, let it alone for one more year, until I dig around it and put manure on it. If it bears fruit next year, well and good; but if not, you can cut it down.'" (Lk 13:6-9)

The Spirit is the lifeblood of the church, the vivifying force that makes its very existence possible. Without the Spirit the church is either an empty and lifeless shell or a horrific monstrosity animated by some spirit other than the Spirit of the risen Jesus. Of course, it's not always easy to tell which spirit animates the church; nevertheless, Jesus suggests that one way to discern a plant's pedigree is to examine its fruit. If the Spirit of Christ genuinely animates the church, then it should be bearing the fruit of that Spirit. If some other spirit animates it, then we would expect it to be bearing different fruit. Therefore, one of the critical questions we need to address to the contemporary church is not simply "Is it bearing fruit?" Rather, we need also to ask the more pointed question, "Is the fruit that the church is bearing the fruit of the Spirit?"

I do not presume to render a judgment on this matter for every congregation throughout the United States. Nevertheless, one might offer a few generalizations while recognizing that there are exceptions. Many churches, especially so-called mainline Protestant churches, have over the past few decades experienced a decline in numbers, vitality and intensity of commitment. Other churches—especially more conservative, evangelical or Pentecostal ones—have shown signs of vitality and growth. Presently, some of these churches seem to be growing numerically by riding the current wave of user-friendliness. The long-term effects of such strategies for attracting "seekers" remain unknown, but some wonder whether the majority of people attracted by these methods will be interested in making the difficult transition from "self-interested seeker" to "other-interested disciple."

Yet even if all churches in the United States were holding their own numerically, there would still be plenty of reason for concern. As Christians we affirm that Jesus Christ is Lord and Savior, but what effect does such an affirmation have on our everyday lives? There seems to be little evidence, for example, that divorce rates differ for Christians and non-Christians, just as there seems to be little evidence that Christian teenagers are less likely than their non-Christian counterparts to be sexually active outside of marriage. Moreover, though the church is largely silent on the matter, spouse and child abuse seem as rampant inside the church as they do outside it. Thus although many Christians in this country continue to insist that they believe things that "make them different," it's often difficult to determine where that difference lies. Even if the church in the United States is not completely barren of the Spirit's fruit, it hardly seems to be producing a bountiful harvest of such fruit as love, patience and kindness.

On this point, however, we must be clear: any concern we might have about our barrenness is inseparable from God's *purposes* for calling us to bear the Spirit's fruit. We do not desire a more plentiful harvest of the Spirit's fruit because our salvation is at stake or because we believe God will love us more if we are more fruitful. Instead, our concern is tied to God's mission in the world. Christians believe that God is in the process of healing and reconciling all of creation. We also believe that God has called us in Jesus Christ to be the first fruits of that reconciliation (2 Thess 2:13; Jas 1:18). In short, God has called us to embody visibly before the world the reconciliation that God desires for *all* of creation. Part of that vocation to the world is to bear the fruit of the Spirit as a testimony to God's continued presence and work in the world. To fail to bear this fruit, therefore, is to fail to provide the world an embodied witness of God's reconciling presence. The church may, of course, continue to *speak* to the world of God's reconciling work, but without the fruit of that work its words will sound hollow and its witness will lack credibility and power.

Returning to Our Roots

Why does the church in this time and place seem to have such difficulty forming disciples who embody in their daily lives the distinctiveness of the Spirit? This important question has no simple answer. Indeed, the issues it raises can be examined in numerous ways and by various approaches. This book probes these crucial matters with the aid of a common biblical metaphor: horticulture. Other metaphors could certainly be employed, and I will have reason to appeal to others along the way as well. Nevertheless, rooting this study in horticultural metaphors has several advantages.

First, it takes full advantage of a pervasive biblical motif. Anyone who has read even portions of the Bible knows that it is replete with horticultural metaphors and images. Indeed, the canonical Scriptures are themselves framed by such images. In Genesis, God creates the first human beings out of the dust of the ground and places them in a garden where they are offered almost unlimited access to its bountiful fruit. Their subsequent disobedience has several consequences, one of which is a curse upon the ground: "In toil you shall eat of it all the days of your life; thorns and thistles it shall bring forth for you" (Gen 3:17-18). The book of Revelation closes by referring back to this event and yet also looking ahead:

> Then the angel showed me the river of the water of life, bright as crystal, flowing from the throne of God and of the Lamb through the middle of the street of the city. On either side of the river is the tree of life with its twelve kinds of fruit, producing its fruit each month; and the leaves of the tree are for the

healing of the nations. Nothing accursed will be found there any more. (Rev 22:1-3)

Between these two instances Scripture is replete with horticultural imagery. Such imagery retains its striking power even in our own age—characterized as it is by microwave ovens and processed food. Who can forget the imagery of the first Psalm, which compares the righteous to trees planted by streams of water that yield fruit in their season and whose leaves do not wither (Ps 1:3)? Or the way in which God repeatedly refers to Israel as a vineyard (Ps 80:8-18; Is 5:1-7; Jer 2:21; 11:16; 12:10; Hos 10:1)? Or the striking prophecy that "a shoot shall come out from the stump of Jesse, and a branch shall grow out of his roots" (Is 11:1)? One of Jesus' most elaborate parables tells of a sower who generously scatters seeds on all kinds of terrain, knowing full well that not every seed will germinate, take root, mature and bear good fruit. Elsewhere, Jesus teaches by speaking of wheat, tares, mustard seeds and vineyards. And in the Gospel of John, Jesus refers to himself as the vine, to his disciples as the branches and to his father as the gardener.

In similar fashion the apostle Paul spends considerable energy in Romans explaining how the Gentiles, a wild olive shoot, have been grafted onto the cultivated olive tree, Israel. Toward the end of his letter to the Galatians, Paul reminds us that we will reap what we sow: "If you sow to your own flesh, you will reap corruption from the flesh; but if you sow to the Spirit, you will reap eternal life from the Spirit" (Rom 6:8). Several verses earlier, Paul has enumerated for us the fruit of the Spirit.

A second important reason for holding on to these biblical metaphors and images is this: these metaphors and images underscore the importance in the Christian life of both work and grace. All farmers know that there is always more work to be done than there is time to do it; nevertheless, these same farmers also understand that much of what happens to the crops is beyond their control. There is much for the farmer to do, but the farmer cannot make the seed sprout, the sun shine or the rain fall. In fact, it is only because the farmer trusts that these good gifts will *continue* to be given that the challenging and risk-filled enterprise of farming is undertaken at all. Grace and effort, gift and work: these must be held together. Unfortunately, Christians often either pit these against each other or emphasize one to the exclusion of the other. The wisdom of the farmer reminds us that both are required, in full measure, in order to grow anything worth harvesting. The same holds for the life of the Spirit. There is always plenty of work to be done, but no one who undertakes that work should do so without realizing that growth in the Spirit is first of all the gift of God.

This crucial relationship between grace and human effort is only one issue that the practice of horticulture helpfully illuminates. Another is the complex *interplay* of factors required to bring to harvest a single piece of fruit. Many factors are involved: the quality of seed, the composition of the soil, the character of surrounding vegetation, and the range and fluctuations of temperature and rainfall. In addition to these "natural" factors, there are those practices of cultivation that also have an impact on the quality of the fruit brought to harvest. These include such activities as tilling, planting, weeding, fertilizing, mulching, staking, pruning, irrigating and harvesting. In several interesting ways this horticultural complexity seems to parallel the *cultural* complexity within which the church is called to bear good fruit. In order to see how this might be the case, we need to understand a little better what we mean when we use the word *culture.*

What Is a Culture?

The word *culture* as commonly used in contemporary English is one of those beguiling words that we employ frequently with little hesitation but that we can't easily define. And we are in good company. Raymond Williams, a widely regarded scholar on the subject, has noted that *culture* is one of the two or three most complicated words in the English language.[1]

The English word derives from the Latin *colere,* which began as an agricultural term meaning to till or take care of a field or garden. Over time its use expanded to include the cultivation or care of other things, such as the body, mental abilities, virtues and even the gods and their temples. Therefore a *colonus* was a farmer or tiller of the land, and a *colonia* a farm, estate or settlement; as a result, the word could also be used more generally to refer to any habitation (compare our words *colonist* and *colony*). The emphasis on care and honor of the gods accrued to the past participle *cultus,* which forms the root for our English word *cult.*

Later, the word *culture* began to be used as a synonym for "civilization." Consequently, to be "cultured" was to be "civilized." According to this usage, some people had culture while others did not, or at least there were various gradations, a belief still embodied in the contemporary distinction between "high" and "low" culture. Such a distinction trades on the value of what those making the distinction consider to be the self-evident superiority of a certain range of activities, usually of an artistic sort. Thus a "person of culture" is well-acquainted with the subtleties of music, literature, theater, painting and sculpture.

A broader concept of "culture," informed by anthropology, refers to a particular way of life, whether of a specific people, group or period. At its most basic level, culture in this sense is a set of expectations that guide and shape a people's life. Anyone who has traveled to a different culture—whether that culture was located in a different country or a different section of town—knows the uncomfortable feeling of not knowing either what can be expected of other people or what is expected of them. This more abstract use of "culture," a usage that assumes that *everyone* and *everything* around us is embedded within *some* culture, has only arisen in the West during the past one hundred years or so. This more anthropological concept of "culture" is the one I employ throughout this book.

Even though the word *culture* has had a quite tortuous development, I think it helpful to keep in mind several words that share the same root. A culture, as a way of life or a set of expectations, is always *cultivated;* it never simply happens. Even though cultures, simply by being what they are, always appear "natural," they are always human creations, nourished and sustained by certain habits of thought and action. A culture is also a habitable space, a *colony* where certain ways of thinking and acting are assumed, cherished and routinely reproduced. As such a culture is a kind of embodied argument about what reality is like, about the place of humans beings within it and about what is worth doing and why. For this reason every culture is also a kind of *cult*—a form of veneration of or means of giving honor to something or someone.

With this linguistic genealogy in mind, we may move on to a more precise working definition of culture. Because culture is an object of study in multiple disciplines, there are numerous ways of defining it, each of which has its own strengths and weaknesses. Here I want to underscore that cultures are distinguished from one another by those shared *practices, convictions, institutions* and *narratives* that order and give shape to the lives of a particular group of people.

In order to begin unpacking this working definition, conduct the following thought-experiment. Imagine that you are an archaeologist who has just stumbled upon an extinct culture. While digging through its remains, you find a piece of paper with several strange markings, including one that is particularly puzzling: "©1999." You next unearth a smooth piece of granite with the following inscription: "1919-1975, R.I.P." Finally, you dig up an old sign that reads: "Happy Valley Nursing Home." As you seek to make sense of these cultural artifacts, you strive to imagine a way of life in which each of them would have a function. What else would you need to know about this culture before you would be able to understand the place of each of these artifacts within it?

My contention is that these artifacts remain unintelligible apart from the practices, convictions and institutions that shaped the life of that culture. For example, the practice of assigning a copyright is inseparable from certain convictions about intellectual property, ownership and fairness, as well as certain institutions that are authorized to assign them. Similarly, an institution like a cemetery only "makes sense" within a culture's practice of burying the dead and its specific convictions about death and dead bodies, just as a nursing home only "makes sense" when embedded within a specific practice of taking care of the elderly and when framed by specific convictions about aging, productivity, necessary care and convenience. So identifying a culture's distinctive practices, convictions and institutions is indispensable to any attempt at understanding that culture. However, simply locating or naming these features is insufficient. To understand why a culture engages in *these* activities, establishes *these* institutions or holds *these* convictions, we must also assume a story about that culture and what it cares about, hopes for and places its trust in.

A central component of any cultural heritage is the stories its advocates tell and retell. This is why explaining the cultural significance of any of the above artifacts requires locating them within a larger framework, a framework that invariably takes narrative form. The story lines of such narratives usually involve embedding certain stories within an overall scheme that lends all of them, when taken together, a particular meaning. By telling stories human beings seek not only to explain the world around them but also to explain their own place within it. This means that two people who appear on the surface to be engaged in similar cultural practices might understand themselves to be doing quite different things. For example, two male war veterans, the first, a white veteran of World War II and the second, an African-American veteran of the Vietnam War, might find their affinity as war veterans overshadowed by the way they narrate (and therefore understand) their service to their country. The veteran of World War II, standing in a long line of veterans in his family, might locate his service primarily in terms of his and his family's unflagging devotion to their country. In contrast, the Vietnam veteran may understand his tour of duty as a glaring example of the white majority's willingness to exploit his people for its own benefit. In short, practices and artifacts do not narrate themselves, but are only given meaning within larger narrative frameworks. A crucial task in understanding any culture, therefore, is discerning the ways in which people tell—and therefore order—their stories.

Part of what makes people who they are is that certain stories are considered most determinative, thereby forming for them a framework within which other stories find their place and meaning. Apart from some larger narrative ordering, individual actions alone tell us little or nothing. This helps explain why we often misunderstand other people's actions or are ourselves misunderstood. We each narrate not only our own lives but also the lives of others. The less we know someone, the more dependent we are on stereotypical plot lines. We observe certain patterns of action, locating them at every point within some story that seems to make sense of them. When somebody acts in a way that violates that story line, we either adjust our story line (and hence our view of them) or we seek to find out why they weren't "being themselves." This point was brought home to me several years ago when I began hearing rumors that a certain professor on campus was having an affair with one of the college coeds. The incriminating evidence: from time to time the professor was seen putting his arm around this coed and giving her a kiss. What was particularly disturbing about these rumors was that they were about me! You can imagine my surprise. Or more to the point, you can imagine the surprise of those people telling this story when they learned that this coed happened to be my daughter! Although I don't really blame those students for locating my actions within the narrative they did, I hope they learned, as I have on more than one occasion, that an unknown piece of the narrative often holds an important key to understanding a perplexing action.

In sum, cultures are enormously complex webs of convictions, practices, institutions and narratives that give shape and meaning to the material realities of people's everyday lives. If we wish to understand what makes any given culture tick, we must be willing to become a student of that culture's intricacies. Just as farmers must understand all the variables that influence the growth of their crops, so students of culture must be willing to explore the various and complex relationships that structure any given culture.

Why Study Cultures?

Different people have different reasons for being students of culture, reasons that are themselves integral elements of some culture. For example, cultural anthropologists study cultures not only because they desire to understand them but also because their research positions at universities demand such work. Christians, I believe, have their own reasons for attending closely to cultures, reasons that should flow from their self-understandings *as* Christians.

Christians desire to be faithful to their calling as disciples of Jesus Christ. As a result, their loyalty and allegiance is first of all to Christ, a commitment that makes relative all other loyalties and allegiances. Being a disciple of Christ requires a willingness to locate one's story within the wider, more-encompassing narrative of God's ongoing relationship with Israel and the church through Jesus Christ. This task is complicated by many factors, not the least of which is that we find ourselves surrounded by a cacophony of cultural voices. These clashing voices continually encourage us to construct our identities according to the assumptions embodied in their stories, practices, convictions and institutions. As a result, my self-understanding or identity often seems like little more than a hodgepodge of competing roles and narratives, all of which make some claim on me and assure me that they hold an important key to my real identity.

To illustrate what a powerful hold these various narratives have on our lives, imagine for a moment that you are traveling in a foreign country. Imagine further that you have struck up a conversation (in English, most likely!) with a resident of this foreign country, who after a short time asks you to tell her a little about yourself. What do you tell her? Who are you? More than likely you begin by telling her that you're from the United States and perhaps even that you're from a particular region, state or city. From there you most likely tell her about your occupation, including how long you've been doing this kind of work and what aspirations you have for the future. After exhausting this story line you probably talk about your family, beginning with (depending on your age and marital status) either your spouse and children or your parents and siblings. From here you might discuss your reasons for traveling, your hobbies, your taste in books or music, your favorite foods. Then, realizing that you might be hogging the conversation by talking only about yourself, you politely inquire about your new acquaintance's life and sit back to listen attentively, assured that she now knows as much about you as most of your acquaintances in the States do.

Perhaps I am wrong about this. Perhaps your imaginary conversation goes differently. But in any case, where in all of this does one mention that one is a Christian? Why does it seem that this is somehow inappropriate to bring up unless one is asked about it specifically? Part of the reason is that the dominant culture around us assumes that religious convictions are "private" and therefore not an appropriate subject for polite conversation. How is it that we learned this, even though no one has likely ever told us so explicitly?

This is the shaping power of culture. But is it really only politeness and a desire not to seem pushy that keeps us from mentioning this? Or is it also that we believe that these other story lines are much more compelling, much more determinative, of who we are? If so, how did we learn that we should consider these stories as more determinative of our identities? This is the shaping power of culture.

Most of us, of course, dwell in the midst of a number of cultures at any one time. Because the boundaries of cultures are rarely delineated sharply, we often find ourselves moving among groups of people with quite different sets of convictions, practices, institutions and narratives. We do not, however, usually find ourselves equally at ease in all of them. This usually goes back to matters of expectations. The cultures where I feel most "at home" are normally the ones where I best understand what is expected of me and what I can expect of other people. This is one of the reasons that many college students find it so threatening to leave the safe confines of academic life and enter the so-called real world. Even when they were unhappy with their college lives, they were secure in knowing what was expected of them. Indeed, the shaping power of an institution like a college lies precisely in its ability to instill over time a certain set of expectations that can be assumed by all involved. Those who come to understand those expectations, conform to them and perhaps even exploit them usually end up being "successful" within academic culture. Those who fail to conform don't.

Yet academic culture is not the only kind of culture that attempts to squeeze people into its mold. Because all cultures do this to some degree, the question is never simply *whether* we are being molded, but more importantly, into *whose image* are we being shaped. In the pages that follow I often refer to what I call "the dominant culture." In using this phrase I mean to call attention to the following phenomenon. Even though most of us over the course of a week or month move in and out of a number of different cultures, most of these cultures also have some striking similarities. For example, most will likely place a high value on individual achievement, competitiveness, productivity, efficiency, self-sufficiency, youth, the "cutting edge" and the satisfaction of desire. Those who allow their lives to be molded by these values will likely "succeed" in those societies where this dominant culture reigns. As I try to show in the following pages, these pervasive values are promoted by the powerful institutions of mass culture, including the educational and economic systems as well as mass media. This explains why the above values are held in high esteem far beyond the borders of the United States. Because the institutions of mass culture reach beyond our borders, so do their shaping influence.

But what if we come to discern that we are being molded into the image of something far less glorious than the image of Christ? What if we come to believe that the dominant culture's powerful and competing convictions, practices, institutions and narratives have a stranglehold on our day-to-day lives, a stranglehold that threatens to prevent us from producing the fruit of the Spirit? Some Christians might assert that God will transform us in God's own time, and so we should not overly worry about our current situation. Such an attitude seems to suggest that the Spirit does its work in our lives apart from any cooperation from us. But there is considerable evidence in the New Testament to suggest that the Spirit does not work coercively. In addition to Paul's warning against quenching the Spirit (1 Thess 5:19), we have the account of Jesus' inability to work miracles in certain locations because of the people's unbelief. And we have the moving response and consent of Mary the mother of Jesus to the announcement that she will conceive by the Holy Spirit, a response that in the long tradition of the church has been held up as an example of cooperative obedience.

I believe that our call to be "salt" and "light" in the world requires us to understand the dominant cultural forces that are shaping both the church and the world around it. Christians have no choice but to be diligent students of their host cultures. Although Christian missionaries to foreign cultures have recognized this need for some time, Christians in this country have only recently begun to see the necessity for such work here. One critical issue concerns the inability of many Christians to identify the important differences between native flora and flora of God's kingdom. For too long we have wrongly assumed that indigenous plants pose no serious threat to a Christian way of life. As a result, many churches routinely and unwittingly cultivate these indigenous plants, bringing to harvest fruit that bears within it the seeds of some other kingdom. For example, in a society that believes that people can only be motivated by appealing to self-interest, the church is often tempted to present the gospel primarily in such terms. Not surprisingly, the fruit produced by such a "gospel" tastes less like the sweetness of the Spirit and more like the sourness associated with self-concern. Unless we learn to be more discerning, we might find ourselves cultivating and harvesting a different crop than the one for which we've been given responsibility.

How Are We Called to Respond?

The challenges that we face as Christians stem from some of our most pervasive cultural practices, convictions, institutions and narratives. Indeed, there is much about the dominant culture that makes it difficult *for anyone* to nurture a life of virtue, a reality that has been acknowledged by many more people than simply those interested in embodying the life of the Spirit. For example, the popularity of William Bennett's collection of moral stories *The Book of Virtues* suggests that many people are interested in expanding their repertoire of moral exemplars. Bennett's introductory remarks are instructive: "The purpose of this book is to show parents, teachers, students, and children what the virtues look like, what they are in practice, how to recognize them, and how they work."[2] In short, Bennett understands that without stories that show what the life of virtue looks like, those who are unskilled in their practice will have little hope of even recognizing them, let alone embodying them.

But Bennett's anthology also raises at least two important questions, especially for Christians who desire to bear the fruit of the Spirit. First, which virtues should people seek to embody? Bennett's book takes up ten: self-discipline, compassion, responsibility, friendship, work, courage, perseverance, honesty, loyalty and faith. Any list of virtues that is commended, whether Bennett's or Paul's, always invites us to ask why *this* list rather than some other. I defer the question as it relates to Paul's list until the next section. Bennett's list, like all attempts to sketch the contours of the virtuous life at a fairly abstract level, both presupposes and underwrites certain conceptions about what counts for good character. Moreover, even when it is not acknowledged, such lists are always rooted in certain views about what it means to be genuinely human. In short, Bennett believes that a person who desires to lead a good life should embody these ten virtues to the fullest degree possible. Although some Christians might quibble with the inclusion of this or that virtue, most would likely find Bennett's anthology refreshing, particularly given the moral dispositions routinely embodied by much of the population. Indeed, some Christians might note that although Bennett's list is not a perfect match with the nine virtues listed by Paul as the fruit of the Spirit, there does seem to be some overlap.

This brings us to the second important question that Bennett's collection nicely raises. When people agree that a virtue like "loyalty" is to be commended, are these people necessarily commending the same thing? Or more precisely, would all agree about what being loyal demands in this or that specific situation? There is good reason to think they would not. As noted above, our actions· derive their intelligibility from the wider frameworks within which they are narrated. Thus a Christian who is attempting to embody his or her loyalty to Christ may have different convictions about what such loyalty entails and demands than does a worker trying to be loyal to his or her company. Granted there may be some interesting similarities, but it would be naive to assume that because all are using the language of "loyalty" that they are commending the same thing. In a similar way, what a non-Christian in our society might consider "compassionate" may be strikingly different from what a follower of Jesus believes, since non-Christians may not share our reasons for valuing the practice of "suffering with" other people (which is, after all, the root meaning of the word *compassion*).

If Christians cannot and should not assume that everyone will share their convictions, then part of what Christians in the United States need to recover is a healthy sense of their distinctiveness *as* Christians. And perhaps more importantly, we also need to come to a clear understanding that this distinctiveness does not reside simply in our assenting to certain assertions, such as "Jesus is Lord." The principalities and powers arrayed against our Lord presumably believe this as well, at least at the cognitive level, though that hardly qualifies them for being disciples of Jesus. Christians, more than simply being those who have an interesting set of beliefs floating around in their heads, are those who put their trust in this Jesus. Part of what this trust entails is being willing to follow in the footsteps of this Jesus, realizing up front that this narrow path is not likely one that everybody will want to tread.

Christians who are held captive to the way of life propagated by the dominant culture need a way of being liberated from that bondage. What is needed is an alternative set of practices, convictions, institutions and narratives that can both curb the dominant culture's power over our lives and nourish a way of life capable of producing the fruit of the Spirit. To do this, Christians in the United States will need to become more discerning about their host culture. Without such skills at discernment, we will find it impossible to differentiate those elements of our culture that can be employed to the glory of God and those that hold little such promise. Developing skills of discernment must become a high priority for the contemporary church, because for good or ill, our day-to-day practices and activities cultivate the character of our lives. Too often we are pledging allegiance to Christ with our lips while engaging in practices that cultivate a quite different set of loyalties, dispositions and convictions. The predictable result is that we keep on insisting that we are fig trees, yet we bear many of the outward attributes of stinging nettle. Is it any wonder that people looking for figs go elsewhere?

As Christians we have a long way to go in learning to identify and resist the full range of cultural practices that inhibit a life of the Spirit. Many Christians in this country have for some time been vigilant about the dangers of certain (primarily sexually related) practices; however, we have been blind to a whole host of other equally dangerous ones. It's as if we have become so fixated on a particular kind of weed in our garden that we fail even to see the others; we simply wander through our garden being sure to uproot this one particular variety. Although some may argue that such selective weeding is better than nothing, I doubt that those plants being choked out by the remaining weeds feel the same way.

Discovering one day that there are more weeds in your garden than you had previously realized can be demoralizing. It might lead some people to give up gardening altogether. But leaving the field uncultivated means handing it over to the weeds. As a child I always wondered why the tomatoes, green beans and corn always had a much harder time making it than the weeds. If you wanted the vegetables to grow and yield produce, you had to work hard to help them. If you wanted the weeds to take over your garden, you didn't have to do anything but stand back and watch. I can remember more than once weeding the garden and accidentally pulling up a shoot of corn or a young tomato plant. They never grew back. And I can also remember spending countless hours bent over rows and rows of vegetables, uprooting bushels of weeds. They always grew back. I can even remember thinking how unfair this all seemed. But any wise gardener knows that fairness is beside the point. If you care about what's growing in your garden, you have to care more than in word only; you have to log in hours of hard work.

Having said all of this, we must remind ourselves that there are limits to what we can do; we are not in control of the entire process. For the Christian, the good seed that is sown is truly a gift; there is nothing we can do by ourselves to manufacture the seed. Paul's words to the Corinthians are a healthy reminder about our role:

> So neither the one who plants nor the one who waters is anything, but only God who gives the growth. The one who plants and the one who waters have a common purpose, and each will receive wages according to the labor of each. For we are God's servants, working together; you are God's field, God's building. (1 Cor 3:7-9)

The church is God's cultivated field; ultimately, it is God who gives the growth. There is no rigorous method, technique or process that will guarantee the church's faithfulness and fruitfulness. This book should not be read, therefore, as a how-to book for cultivating the fruit of the Spirit. The contemporary church *does* need to understand clearly its mission in the world, but it also needs to remember that God is the one who brings growth and maturity. God has given us plenty to do; fortunately, God has also given us plenty of resources with which to do it. For example, the church's ongoing reflection on Scripture and its embodied life throughout history offer us a wealth of wisdom. Such wisdom might help us understand the composition of our soil, locate some of the rocks in our field and discern the character of those surrounding and competing plants. Such reflection might also help us imagine what it might mean to till, weed, fertilize and nurture those tender plants entrusted to our care, in the hope that they might bear fruit to the glory of God.

Theological reflection that is of service to the church must be *bilingual*, speaking of both theological truths and cultural realities. To be able to speak only one language is to rob the church of the perspective it needs in order to sustain a faithful witness to the world. The church must always be prepared to make critical discernments about itself and about the wider culture in which it participates. Such discernments, when exercised under the guidance of the Spirit, help to prune the unproductive growth from our lives. Without good pruning, trees or vines use all of their available resources simply to sustain their expanding network of branches. For this reason, the farther the branches grow from the main trunk or vine, the less likely they are to bear good fruit. Furthermore, as Jesus remarks in the Gospel, even the branch that is already bearing fruit remains a candidate for pruning, since such activity may spur the production of even more and better fruit.

Most churches in the United States would benefit from a good pruning. Much of our energy and many of our resources are being used to sustain practices, convictions, institutions and narratives that do not necessarily lead to the bearing of good fruit. We have heard hundreds, perhaps even thousands, of sermons and Bible lessons, read countless books, attended numerous seminars. Although there is nothing wrong with such activities, occasionally we forget that participating in them does not necessarily make us fruitful. We may simply be like the wild, unpruned tree that continues to grow, but in a completely undisciplined fashion and with little prospect for bearing fruit. Or to switch metaphors, a person who simply attends regional agricultural conferences and sits in the barn week after week studying farming magazines would not likely be mistaken for a farmer. No doubt such activities could be beneficial, but only if they do more than deepen a person's understanding and knowledge about farming. Learning a little bit about farming and actually bringing good fruit to harvest may require radically different practices.

Why Focus on the Fruit of the Spirit?

One final preliminary matter needs to be taken up. Why focus on the fruit of the Spirit? Isn't there more to the Christian life than embodying love, joy, peace, patience, kindness, goodness, faithfulness, gentleness and self-control? Or as noted above, if any specific set of virtues always presupposes an equally specific view of what it means to be human, what view is being commended here?

Human beings are not God, and so we cannot do all that God does. But we *were* originally created in God's image, and the New Testament affirms that this image is both seen aright and restored anew in the person of Jesus Christ. The Holy Spirit continues this process of restoring all things to God in Christ by working in and through the community of disciples known as the church. Although the Spirit's work is in no way limited to this community, Scripture suggests that God desires to use the church in a special way and so continues to pour out the Spirit upon it to renew and revitalize it for witness and service.

The goal of the Christian life is to be conformed to the image of Christ. Yet God has not called us out of darkness simply for our own sake. God has called us to be a light to the nations. Or as the passage already quoted from the closing chapter of Revelation puts it, "the leaves of the tree are for the healing of the nations" (Rev 22:2). God has called out a people who through their very life together would bear witness to God's character and reconciling mission in the world. That character and mission have been uniquely embodied in the person of Jesus Christ, and it continues to be reflected, even if imperfectly, in the life of that community animated by his Spirit. The fruit that the Spirit desires to produce in our corporate and individual lives, therefore, is not merely a hodgepodge of admirable character traits or virtues that are universally admirable or commendable. Rather, God desires to produce this fruit through the Spirit—and the community of Jesus Christ desires to have this fruit produced in its life—because these dispositions reflect the very character and mission of God.

If the church is to be the community God desires it to be, then it will have to reflect the character and mission of the God it worships. I understand these nine virtues to be the fruit that this community bears when the Spirit is allowed to work in our lives *together* to reflect the character and mission of God. In short, these virtues embody what corporate life in the coming kingdom will entail. This is why in the chapters that follow I attempt to show how each virtue or disposition reflects the character and mission of God. Moreover, when identifying resources that the church might use to cultivate a way of life that embodies these virtues, I have tried to begin by looking to the church's most characteristic activity: its worship. If the community of Jesus Christ is genuinely animated by his Spirit, then the hallmarks of that Spirit's presence should be evident whenever we gather as a people to offer praise and thanksgiving to our God. Understood in this way, our corporate worship life can and should provide a kind of foothold for the Spirit's work, a foothold that can be nurtured and expanded to embrace the rest of our lives.

In the chapters that follow I take up the nine virtues Paul identifies as the fruit of the Spirit in the order in which he lists them in Galatians. Each chapter begins with a biblical exposition of that fruit, followed by an explanation of some of the ways in which the dominant culture inhibits its cultivation. (You are encouraged, of course, to think of others.) Next I examine some of the resources the church has for cultivating the Spirit's fruit in this society. Each chapter concludes by offering questions for reflection, as well as practical suggestions for modest steps that Christians might take both to minimize the impact of these obstacles and to cultivate an alternative way of life that nourishes the Spirit's fruit in our lives. Please do not regard these questions and suggestions as an exhaustive list of possibilities but as an attempt to encourage and enrich your imaginations. I realize that in risking specific suggestions, I likely reveal little more than my own struggles and the poverty of my own imagination. Nevertheless, the risk seems worth taking because cultures always involve us in the particularities of life, and people's interactions with and through cultures are always equally particular. That being said, I should also note that I don't expect that every reader will agree with every detail of my analysis or suggestions. I do hope, however, that those who don't can be urged to follow the impulses of my analysis and to reflect concretely and creatively on the shape of their own faithfulness.

One final note about "possessing" virtues or fruit. If, as I will try to demonstrate, we cannot recognize, nourish, embody or sustain these dispositions *on our own*, then we should probably stop thinking and speaking as if these virtues are somehow our own individual *possessions*. Indeed, such ways of thinking and speaking encourage us to think of possessing these fruit or virtues as a goal to be achieved or an accomplishment to be sought, primarily for our own sakes. But this is to get things backward. Virtues are those dispositions to act in certain ways rather than others that are rooted deeply in the dynamics of any community; they both reflect and sustain that common life. Yet the common life of the Christian community is intended to glorify God, not the community. Thus if a community of Christians discerns that one of its members is bearing the fruit of patience, it will only be because a community of the Spirit exists that has learned to recognize, cherish and nourish that fruit. Nurturing individual fruit in individual lives is not our ultimate goal. Instead, the church is called to embody before the world in all its relationships the kind of reconciled and transformed life that God desires for all of creation. This is a lofty goal and one we would be foolish to think that we could achieve apart from God's powerful working in our lives. But it is precisely this high calling to which we have been called and as an aid to which these reflections are offered.

TWO

Cultivating Love in the Midst of Market-Style Exchanges

My Father is glorified by this, that you bear much fruit and become my disciples. As the Father has loved me, so I have loved you; abide in my love. If you keep my commandments, you will abide in my love, just as I have kept my Father's commandments and abide in his love. (Jn 15:8-10)

If you love those who love you, what credit is that to you? For even sinners love those who love them. If you do good to those who do good to you, what credit is that to you? For even sinners do the same. If you lend to those from whom you hope to receive, what credit is that to you? Even sinners lend to sinners, to receive as much again. But love your enemies, do good, and lend, expecting nothing in return. Your reward will be great, and you will be children of the Most High; for he is kind to the ungrateful and the wicked. Be merciful, just as your Father is merciful. (Lk 6:32-36)

The half-page ad runs regularly in our college newspaper. It is aimed, no doubt, primarily at our students, many of whom live hours from home and often find themselves in need of a little extra cash. In large letters the ad announces: BECOME A PLASMA DONOR AND EARN UP TO $130 PER MONTH. Lest the thought of selling your plasma appear a bit mercenary, the ad immediately informs the reader that the plasma is made into "products" that benefit hemophiliacs, burn victims and cardiovascular patients. The ad closes with what is presumably the company's motto: "Be a Plasma Donor . . . Because Life Is Everybody's Business."

Shortly after the ads began running I asked some students how they thought Christians should think about such matters. Should Christians sell their life-giving bodily fluids to someone who will turn around and make a profit by selling these "products" to people in dire need of them? Given who we are, shouldn't we be willing to be donors in the truest sense, as those who offer a gift? The sheepish looks on several faces suggested that some of them had already pocketed their bonus money for their initial visit. One even approached me later and said that he was embarrassed to admit it, but it had never occurred to him that Christians might refuse to engage in such practices. I suspect he's not the only one.

Cultures like ours encourage us to consider all aspects of our lives in terms of self-interest. How do we cultivate a life marked by God's love—a love that is always directed toward the needs of others—in a culture so thoroughly saturated with self-concern? Before considering what cultivating the practice of Christian love might look like, we need to remind ourselves of the character of that love and its centrality to the life of God and the story of the church.

The Centrality of Love

Most people who know anything about the Christian faith know that love stands at its center. Countless children have memorized "For God so loved the world . . ." (Jn 3:16), being instructed that this one verse summarizes the whole gospel. Most are also familiar with John's simple but profound insistence that "God is love" (1 Jn 4:8). These and other passages of Scripture suggest that love is not simply one virtue among many. We are instructed on numerous occasions that loving God and neighbor sums up the whole law (Deut 6:4-5; Mk 12:28-30; Gal 5:14). Paul, the great advocate of the centrality of *faith* to the Christian life, remarks in his famous "love chapter" that although "faith, hope and love abide," the "greatest of these is love" (1 Cor 13:13). A similar echo is heard in Paul's letter to the Galatians, where he insists that "the only thing that counts is faith made effective through love" (Gal 5:6). And when the Colossians are urged to clothe themselves with compassion, kindness, humility, meekness, patience, forbearance and forgiveness, they are also urged, "above all," to clothe themselves with love, "which binds everything together in perfect harmony" (Col 3:12-14).

Thus that love heads Paul's list of the Spirit's fruit is hardly accidental. Indeed, many Christian thinkers across the ages have insisted that the fruit of the Spirit listed by Paul are not nine separate fruit, of which love is simply the first. Rather, love—as embodied in Jesus Christ and poured into our hearts by the Holy Spirit (Rom 5:5)—most fully reflects the very character of God. Love ought, therefore, to be *the* primary disposition of the Christian life. The eight other virtues or dispositions that follow in Paul's list might best be understood as amplifying and further specifying what is entailed by this way of love. In short, these other eight dispositions, taken together, characterize a life lived in, by and through God's love. In this sense, love is much like light, which, when passing through a prism, breaks into its component colors.[1] Just as these colors neither exist apart from the light nor are something added to the light, so these eight fruit neither exist apart from nor are something added on to love. We might also note that just as each color blends seamlessly into those adjacent to it, so it is difficult (and perhaps even unwise) to draw excessively precise boundaries around these dispositions; they quite naturally seem to blend into each other.

The Character of Love

Much has been written about the poverty of the English language when it comes to terms of endearment. As is commonly known, Greek has at least four different words that are commonly translated into English by the single word *love*. We typically use the word *love* to describe a wide range of sentiments, affections and dispositions toward an equally wide range of objects or people. We use the same word for the physical attraction between a man and a woman, the devotion of parents to their children, the bond between siblings, the affection of close friends, the pride of place given to one's country, the adoration offered to God and even one's personal preferences and tastes. In fact, some may justifiably doubt whether a word that can be applied with ease to both God and pizza can illuminate the character of the Christian life.

Given the centrality of love to both God's character and the story of "God with us," one would like to be able to recapture its potentially powerful resonances. Admittedly, such a recovery will not be easy. But perhaps we can make a start by reminding ourselves of several aspects of God's love that distinguish it from much that we call love.

Scripture delineates several characteristic features of God's love. First, God's love for us is completely unmerited, completely undeserved. Central to the message of the gospel is that God has reached down to us in love despite our rebelliousness. For Christians, the definitive act of God's love is the Son's willingness to empty himself, become a human being and humbly take on the role of the suffering servant in order to reconcile us to God. As Paul argues in Romans, "God proves his love for us in that while we still were sinners Christ died for us" (5:8). Though we see this feature of God's love most clearly in Jesus Christ, much of the Old Testament reminds us that God has always loved deeply. This reminder is offered perhaps most poignantly by the prophet Hosea, who reminds Israel that despite its whoring after false gods and repeated unfaithfulness, God constantly woos God's beloved people. Such passages remind us of a central Christian conviction: God's love is always a gift; we can do nothing to earn it. Paul instructs the Ephesians on this matter in one long but powerful sentence: "But God, who is rich in mercy, out of the great love with which he loved us even when we were dead through our trespasses, made us alive together with Christ—by grace you have been saved—and raised us up with him and seated us with him in the heavenly places in Christ Jesus, so that in the ages to come he might show the immeasurable riches of his grace in kindness toward us in Christ Jesus" (Eph 2:4-7).

A second characteristic feature of God's love for us is its steadfastness. Because God's love for us is unmerited love, there is nothing we can do that can keep God from loving us. Even should we choose to spend eternity separated from God, there is no reason to think that God would thereby stop loving us. Indeed, some have suggested that it is precisely *because* God loves us so much that God refuses to coerce or manipulate us into loving in return. But even as the spurned lover, God's unrequited love remains steadfast. In a passage that is unsurpassed in its tribute to the unrelenting power of God's love, Paul asks the Romans:

> What then are we to say about these things? If God is for us, who is against us? He who did not withhold his own Son, but gave him up for all of us, will he not with him also give us everything else? Who will bring any charge against God's elect? It is God who justifies. Who is to condemn? It is Christ Jesus,

who died, yes, who was raised, who is at the right hand of God, who indeed intercedes for us. Who will separate us from the love of Christ? Will hardship, or distress, or persecution, or famine, or nakedness, or peril, or sword? . . .

No, in all these things we are more than conquerors through him who loved us. For I am convinced that neither death, nor life, nor angels, nor rulers, nor things present, nor things to come, nor powers, nor height, nor depth, nor anything else in all creation, will be able to separate us from the love of God in Christ Jesus our Lord. (Rom 8:31-39) .

Third, God's love for us is suffering love. God does not love us from a distance; rather, God's love is such that it draws God into the very fabric of human life. Christians affirm that God's willingness to suffer with—as well as suffer for—God's people is manifested most supremely in the life, ministry and death of Jesus. Echoing the strains of the so-called Servant Songs of Isaiah (especially Is 53), the apostolic preaching contains an important refrain: this Messiah was a suffering Messiah (Acts 3:18; 8:30-35; 17:3; 26:3, 23; cf. Lk 24:26). The clear message throughout Scripture is that God never stands aloof, insulated from our sufferings. Instead, from the moment of creation God determined to be our God by willingly entering into our struggles, our sufferings. Thus the incarnation represents not a change in plans, but the supreme expression of the lengths to which God is willing to go in order to embody this eternal, steadfast and suffering love.

Finally, God's love knows no bounds. In addition to the boundaries of time and space noted above, God's love transcends those boundaries constructed by human societies. If Jesus reaffirmed what most Jews already knew when he stated that the law was summed up in the command to love God and neighbor, he sounded a distinct and piercing note when he insisted that his followers should love their enemies (Mt 5:43-48; Lk 6:27-36). Both passages make clear that the paradigm for such loving action is God's own character. Because God reaches out in love even to those who set themselves up as God's enemies, so should those who would revere God love their own enemies.

Jesus illustrates the radical nature of this teaching with his parable of the Samaritan (Lk 10:25-37). This story is framed by a lawyer's inquiry about the proper interpretation of the double command to love God and neighbor. The lawyer, "wanting to justify himself," seeks clarification about boundaries: "And who is my neighbor?" Jesus responds by telling the now-familiar story of the Samaritan, who by his willingness to care for the one in need—regardless of cultural boundaries—imitates the boundlessness of God's love. In light of the Samaritan's actions, we see that our tendency to offer our love only to those who meet specific criteria falls far short of God's way of loving. Perhaps Jesus hoped to get the lawyer to see this as well, and so he turned the lawyer's question around at the end of the story, asking not about who properly qualifies for being the *recipient* of love, but about *who acts neighborly*: "Which of these three, do you think, *was a neighbor* to the man who fell into the hands of the robbers?"

The Pattern of Love

After telling the story of the Samaritan and questioning the lawyer about its implications, Jesus speaks these final words: "Go and do likewise" (Lk 10:37). This kind of love, Jesus clearly seems to be saying, is what the command to love one's neighbor actually involves. Because God does not discriminate in loving, so neither can those who seek both to love God wholeheartedly and to pattern their ways after God's ways. John also reminds us that our love is always a response to God's prior action and that our love for God cannot be separated from our love of our fellow human beings:

> We love because he first loved us. Those who say, "I love God," and hate their brothers or sisters, are liars; for those who do not love a brother or sister whom they have seen, cannot love God whom they have not seen. The commandment we have from him is this: those who love God must love their brothers and sisters also. (1 Jn 4:19-21)

Again, the notion that God's people should seek to embody God's loving character is not a minor theme of Christian Scripture. Consider three more examples of God's people being instructed to love as God loves because God had so acted in the past on their behalf:

> When an alien resides with you in your land, you shall not oppress the alien. The alien who resides with you shall be to you as the citizen among you; you

shall love the alien as yourself, for you were aliens in the land of Egypt: I am the LORD your God. (Lev 19:33-34)

Be imitators of God, as beloved children, and live in love, as Christ loved us and gave himself up for us, a fragrant offering and sacrifice to God. (Eph 5:1-2)

We know love by this, that he laid down his life for us—and we ought to lay down our lives for one another. How does God's love abide in anyone who has the world's goods and sees a brother or sister in need and yet refuses to help? Little children, let us love, not in word or speech, but in truth and action. (1 Jn 3:16-18; see also 1 Pet 2:20-25)

These examples, and countless others that could be cited, remind us that *the* defining feature of God's love is its "other-directedness." When we are called to imitate the love of God, we are being called out of ourselves, called to live a life of unconditional concern for the well-being of others. This holds even when Jesus admonishes us to "love our neighbors *as ourselves*" (Mt 22:39; cf. Lev 19:18). This admonition, which is sometimes cited in order to excuse, if not authorize, our penchant for selfish behavior, does nevertheless stand as an important reminder for those whose tendency is toward self-loathing. Such persons need to be reminded that they should not desire anything less for themselves than they do for others: God calls them to desire what is genuinely best for all. Unconditional concern for the well-being of all, including ourselves, is not, of course, the same as pursuing whatever I want, because the call to love oneself is a call to desire for ourselves what God desires for us. Thus even this kind of self-love is manifestly other-directed, for we love ourselves as a response to God's prior act of love.

The entire story of Scripture—from creation to consummation—is a story of God's relentless, other-directed love. But several questions remain, even for those who intensely desire to love as God loves. Is it possible for human beings to love in this way, to be other-directed as God is other-directed? Or perhaps more to the point: if it *is* possible, is this ability to love as God loves a gift or is it a disposition we should attempt to cultivate? With respect to the first question regarding the possibility, we would do well to heed the words of Mother Teresa, who echoes a theme that runs throughout the history of

Christian thinking—that God does not command the impossible:

> "Thou shalt love the Lord thy God with thy whole heart, with thy whole soul and with thy whole mind." This is the commandment of the great God, and he cannot command the impossible. Love is a fruit in season at all times, and within the reach of every hand. Anyone may gather it and no limit is set.[2]

With regard to the second question, Scripture testifies that the ability to love as God loves is both gift and task. Paul tells the Romans that "God's love has been poured into our hearts through the Holy Spirit that has been given to us" (Rom 5:5). Yet Paul sounds a different note after concluding his "love chapter"—a note that often goes unheard as a result of arbitrary chapter divisions—when he challenges the Corinthians to "pursue love" (1 Cor 14:1). Here we have a prime example of that seeming paradox that stands at the center of the Christian life (and horticulture): the fruit is always a gift, but it still requires hard work.

Obstacles to the Life of Love

Many have written about how the word *love* is abused and how, as a result, people don't really understand what genuine love is. But understanding is only part of the problem. Even if we were to *understand* God's love completely, we would still likely be in deep trouble. So the above exposition, like all the ones that follow, must be kept in proper perspective. Gaining a deeper understanding of these virtues is only part of the task. Christians must take a further, riskier step: we must attempt to embody this mark of God's character in this time and place. To do this we must take a closer look at those practices, convictions, virtues and narratives that are native to contemporary life and that impede the development of the Spirit's fruit.

Promoting self-interest. An enormous amount of everyday life in the United States is shaped by economic practices. Few people would disagree that buying and selling goods and services is an integral feature of our daily lives. If this exchange of goods and services was simply an efficient means of securing the basic necessities of life, we might have less cause for concern. But we live and move and have our being within an economic system that impacts nearly every aspect of our lives. The obvious strength of this system is its ability to deliver a tremendous variety of goods and services to vast numbers of people in a relatively cost-effective way. The advantages of such division of labor are obvious to anyone who has considered how different our lives would be if we had to grow our own food, sew our own clothes and build our own homes.

However, the obvious advantages of such a system are only part of the story. Most people who are adept at functioning within such an economic system rarely notice the potentially dangerous features of such systems. For example, even though the market system *could* be viewed as a mechanism for rendering mutual service, little in our society encourages us to do so. Instead, we are encouraged to operate in the marketplace as self-interested parties attempting to secure our own existence in the midst of others doing the same. As a result, we tend to view other people in the marketplace not as unique and splendid people in their own right who warrant our attention, but as actors in *our* drama. In our drama, these people play the part of producers of goods and services for *us,* or of potential customers for *our* goods and services, or of competitors whose own attempts to secure their livelihood may threaten *our* attempts to do the same. Can we really be other-directed when so many of our daily interactions encourage us to be self-interested, to pay attention to others only to the extent that they can benefit us?

Putting a price on everything (and everyone). The cultivation of love is also threatened by the way market relationships demand that we put a price on everything. Because of the complexity of the economy and its specialization, a common register or currency is required. For the system to work, everything that is part of that system must be able to be assessed some "value" in terms of that currency. In short, everything must have a price tag. Raw materials, transportation, manufacturing equipment, human labor, advertising space or even time itself—all must have a dollar figure placed upon them. Only in this way may we leave behind the inefficiencies of bartering systems. To grasp this, one need only imagine what going to the grocery store might involve if we were expected to barter for our food rather than traffic in pieces of paper, metal or plastic.

Few people, I suspect, would want to return to the bartering system. For most of us the idea of trading a bushel of potatoes for a pair of pants, or one's services as a lawyer for a new roof, sounds too complicated and inefficient. But even if we don't want to return to such a cumbersome system, comparing it with our own might highlight some of the latter's pervasive shortcomings. In other words, we may not want to go back, but we should understand as clearly as we can why market exchange systems may inhibit the cultivation of love.

People who are engaged in bartering are still involved in exchanges; however, they are not the same kind of exchanges as those made for money. Bartering requires a level of *direct* human interaction and cooperation that is unnecessary in the abstract market. Moreover, since all goods and services are not first being translated into a common currency, bartering also encourages a measure of give and take between the two parties when determining what counts for a fair exchange. In contrast, when I go to the supermarket and buy a box of corn flakes, I am not expected or encouraged to interact or cooperate with anyone at more than the most superficial level. I have no relationship at all with the people most responsible for making those corn flakes available. And I certainly am not invited to discuss the equity of the store's prices. All that is expected of me is a certain decency as I walk through the checkout line and plop down my $3.89.

The two systems also differ in reach and impact. Bartering, by its very inefficiency and cumbersomeness, works only on a relatively small scale, both with respect to the number of people engaged and the number of goods and services exchanged. Thus bartering is usually found in agrarian economies where most people can provide for themselves at least some of what they need to subsist. Within such economies, bartering is used primarily to acquire those goods and services one cannot provide for oneself. As a result, at least some aspects of life remain outside the exchange system. But this is dramatically different in a highly specialized and efficient market economy like our own. Most people acquire through the market nearly all goods and services required for day-to-day existence, to say nothing of those purchased for comfort and convenience. As a result, it becomes all but "natural" within such a system to expect that everything has a price, that everything is a potential commodity that may be secured in order to enrich my life. Thus in market economies like our own, we learn at an early age that nearly everything is for sale: food, clothing, housing, entertainment, art, physical abilities, expertise, knowledge, insight, image, prestige, health-care, security, time, affection, sex, loyalty and even our bodily tissues and organs.

The sheer pervasiveness of exchange relationships in our daily lives all but guarantees that our thinking will be affected by this mentality far beyond decisions about whether we can afford a new pair of shoes. A few examples may help to make the point.

Market economies place a precise dollar figure on our skills and abilities, which impacts our lives in at least three important ways. First, it is difficult to avoid equating people's worth with what they are paid. We quite naturally assume that a corporate lawyer is more important, has greater worth and should command greater respect than the woman who works in a sweatshop stitching blue jeans. Second, and closely related to the first point, such a system plays down the significance of those persons and things that cannot or do not automatically have a dollar figure assigned to them. Consider a stay-at-home parent, typically a woman, who spends her days working at innumerable unpaid tasks, each of which, if hired out, would immediately become visible within the economic system. But as it stands, this unremuner-ated work and to a large degree the person doing the work remain completely invisible as long as she continues to do the work. Even those persons who are convinced that engaging in such work is vitally important often admit feelings of utter worthlessness. Furthermore, such a system encourages us to think of our skills and abilities not in terms of what they can contribute to the common good of a community, but primarily in terms of the purchasing power they secure for us. How many people have chosen a line of work not primarily because they believed they would enjoy it or because it was a service worth rendering, but because it promised to pay well? As a result, our abilities and talents are transformed into one more commodity to be bought and sold in the marketplace to the highest bidder.

Contracting relationships. Given the pervasiveness of self-interested exchanges, we should not be surprised if market-style thinking impacts some of our most cherished relationships. By evaluating our relationships to everyone and everything on the basis of self-interest, we foster a flinty indifference toward all those people and things that make no promise to enhance our lives. This helps explain why some people are more attached to their cars or homes than they are to other people. Put bluntly, as several recent advertisements have, people are a lot more trouble and a lot less dependable than cars, so why bother? Perhaps such cost-benefit analysis makes good sense when one is running a business, but what are we to think when we hear marriage partners explain that they have terminated a relationship because "the costs were too high"? Or because the relationship was no longer "meeting my needs"? Although many people would resist the notion that they view relationships contractually, this often appears to be what is happening: people agree to continue a relationship only as long as it meets certain needs; once those needs are no longer being met, they feel free to end the relationship. The contract has been broken, and so the relationship is dissolved. Can we hope to cultivate other-directed love in a society that encourages us to view each other as simply objects to be used?

Although we might be hesitant to admit it, the market mentality also affects our lives "inside" the church. This is due not only to the market's pervasiveness but also to the fact that what we do inside the walls of the church building cannot be easily sequestered from the activities we engage in the rest of the week. For example, Christians are not exempt from thinking and acting as if their commitment to Christ is simply one more consumer choice. They often cast themselves, whether knowingly or not, in the role of a consumer, expecting churches to woo them with programs and services that appeal to their particular interests. In response many churches have self-consciously incorporated marketing strategies into their ways of being the church, pitching their programs and services to prospective seekers who are well-versed in such habits of thinking. By blatantly appealing to self-interest, such tactics—no matter how well meaning—neither demonstrate our love for these seekers nor cultivate the habits of thought and action that would nourish Christian love.

Living in a culture like ours also encourages Christians to frame their understanding of the faith primarily in terms of self-interest. (What's in it for me? Plenty! Start with eternal life.) Hence, many people are "converted" less out of their sense that they are estranged from God and other people and their desire to be reconciled, but more out of a sense that they're savvy consumers, knowing a good deal when they see one. Such people, I suspect, have difficulty understanding someone like Paul, who understood that God's plans for reconciliation were cosmic in scope. Rather than being consumed with self-interest, Paul was so sorrowful and anguished over Israel's unbelief that he could wish that he "were accursed and cut off from Christ for the sake of my own people" (Rom 9:3).

Finally, in a culture that encourages us to distinguish ourselves from one another by our consumer choices, where "we are what we consume," we can easily be led to believe that we are Christians simply because we are consumers of "Christian" products. Though Jesus said we would be known as his disciples by our love for one another (Jn 13:35), we often settle for distinguishing ourselves from the wider culture by being consumers of Christian music, books, concerts, seminars, T-shirts, jewelry, plaques, figurines and bumper stickers.

Cultivating Love

Given my comments about the relationship between love and the other eight fruit of the Spirit, I hope that the remainder of this book will be understood as a guide to cultivating love. Here we will only pause to consider briefly those resources that Christians might employ to counter some of the more insidious features of life in a society permeated by market exchanges. As in each of the chapters that follow, we look first to the gathered church to see what resources it offers as we seek to cultivate the fruit of love.

Paying attention to others. We cannot love other people without paying attention to them. Yet the practices and virtues of the marketplace nourish a kind of indifference. To the extent that the marketplace encourages us to see each other at all, it encourages us to see each other as commodities, as objects that may be exploited for our benefit. Too often the freedom of the marketplace is translated into freedom *from each other* or freedom *to exploit each other,* all for the sake of self. But Paul tells the Galatians, "Do not use your freedom as an opportunity for self-indulgence, but through love become slaves to one another (Gal 5:13). If Christians are to cultivate a way of life that resists the commodification of all of life, including the commodification of our relationships with God, other people and the rest of God's creation, then there is perhaps no better place to gain a foothold than in our corporate worship.

At its best, worship schools us in the art of paying attention to others, drawing our focus away from ourselves and redirecting it toward God. We gather to worship first of all not because we desire to be blessed, or because we need our "spiritual batteries charged," or because we believe God will love us more if we "go to church." We gather first of all out of gratitude, as a response to God's prior activity. We gather to give God praise for creating and sustaining the entire cosmos and for creating us in the divine image in order that we might have communion with God and with one another. We gather to give God praise for creating a covenant people, Israel, who would be a light to the nations and through whom all nations would be blessed. We gather to give God praise for sending the Son in the person of Jesus Christ, in order that we might be reconciled to God and the rest of the cosmos. We gather to give God praise for pouring out the Spirit upon the church that we might be the body of Christ for the world.

There are, of course, many more reasons why we might gather to praise God. I hope, however, that the point is clear: in gathering to praise God as God deserves to be praised, we attempt to set aside our self-interestedness and focus our attention on the One who creates and sustains all life. Although none of us succeed completely in leaving behind our preoccupation with self, we should not thereby assume that our worship leaves us unchanged. Every deliberate attempt to pay attention to another *for the sake of the other* is a welcome reminder that all of life need not be sifted through the sieve of self-interest.

Our gathered worship might also remind us that not all relationships must be rooted in self-interested exchanges. We do not offer our praise and thanksgiving to God because God needs it. God is ceaselessly and eternally praised by innumerable hosts whom we simply join when we lift our voices in praise and adoration. This is not to suggest, of course, that God does not take pleasure in our worship. I suspect, however, that the pleasure God takes in our worship is inseparable from its being offered freely, from its character as a gift. We do not gather to praise God with an eye toward what we will receive in return, or in order to keep God pacified for another week. God has entered into relationship with us by making us the recipients of God's boundless generosity and grace; we bring an offering of praise not as an exchange, but as a gift.

Receiving and giving graciously. The above reflections remind us that at the heart of Christian faith and practice is the giving of gifts. God has abundantly given to us; we respond in gratitude by offering gifts to God, and we seek to continue to be avenues of God's grace by giving gifts to one another.

This drama of gift-giving also stands at the heart of Christian worship, most visibly in that central practice of the church: the Lord's Supper. Though the name of this practice varies among Christian traditions, and though it is understood and celebrated in a variety of ways, all Christians who engage in this practice sense that the incomprehensible mystery at the heart of the Eucharist is inseparable from God's other-directed love. This meal celebrates God's love toward us in the past, empowers us for loving service in the present and serves as a foretaste of that final meal when we will celebrate together the consummation of God's reconciling work.

Thus few moments in the life of the church can compare to that moment, as enacted in the liturgy of several traditions, when the elements are presented to the people with these words: "The gifts of God for the people of God." Here we are reminded most powerfully that we are the recipients of gifts beyond measure, and so we gather with open hands, humbly receiving all that God would give to us.

Yet we also come with open hands because God's love calls us to give. From its earliest days, the Lord's Supper has been understood as a call to love our neighbors in visible and tangible ways. There is, for example, evidence in Scripture that at least some of the earliest celebrations of the Lord's Supper were combined with an *agapē* or love feast (Jude 12; cf. 2 Pet 2:13). Indeed,

Paul rebuked the Corinthians (1 Cor 11:17-34) for gathering to celebrate this meal in ways that violated the very Spirit of that gathering. What were they doing? Apparently, the rich Christians were gathering to eat a private meal before the common one; as a result, there was less food to share with the poorer members of the community. This selfish and insensitive behavior not only violated the Spirit of love that stands at the center of the meal, but heightened the social and economic divisions that Christ's love was to overcome. So certain was Paul that these selfish practices were contrary to that gospel the Corinthians were called to embody, that he could insist that regardless of what they believed they were doing, they were not actually eating the Lord's Supper (1 Cor 11:20). It is this violation of the body that Paul has in view when a few verses later he declares that "all those who eat and drink without discerning the body"—that is, without realizing that this community is the body of Christ—"eat and drink judgment against themselves" (11:29).

Paul's words of warning are some of the most sobering in all of Scripture, for they remind us that the ways we *embody* God's love matter more than what we *say that we believe about* God's love. Or perhaps more precisely, the way we embody (or fail to embody) God's love is a surer indicator of what we actually believe than are our words. It is not enough simply to gather around the Lord's Table and mouth pious formalities about love, sacrifice and forgiveness. If these beliefs about God's love are not embodied in the very way we gather, then we would likely be better off not gathering at all (cf. Mt 5:23-24).

In sum, the Eucharist is a powerful reminder that God's grace comes not only in the form of bread and wine but also in the form of flesh and blood. Those people who gather with us to celebrate the Lord's Supper are as much the body of Christ—and hence expressions of God's love and grace—as the elements we receive. To open our hands to the one without opening our hands to the other is to do violence to the very life-giving mystery at the heart of the church's life. Thus when we hear the words "The gifts of God for the people of God," we should be prepared to receive not only these elements but also each other as God's good gifts.

Sustaining stewardship. The presence of social and economic divisions in the Corinthian church reminds us how easily we allow our possessions, as well as the status associated with them, to divide us. Most of us can recall being in situations where we found ourselves uncomfortable because we sensed we didn't belong. How did we know this? By observing such things as the clothes other people were wearing, the cars they were driving, or the houses in which they were living. Whether we liked it or not, we sensed an invisible barrier that seemed to prohibit genuine interaction.

This, of course, is only one role that our material possessions play in cultures like ours. At the heart of the marketplace is the notion of ownership and possession. Each of us knows that the purpose of engaging in self-interested exchanges is to acquire those things we need and desire. Indeed, the consumer mentality in our society actually encourages us to think of our purchases as an expression of our identity: I am what I consume. Or as one recent automobile advertisement impudently intoned: "Is who you are a reflection of what you drive, or is what you drive a reflection of who you are? That depends on what you drive." This intimate link our culture encourages us to forge between one's *self* and one's *stuff* creates potential problems for Christians who believe that God has created all things and has called us to be stewards of them. How might Christian teaching on stewardship serve as a resource for reconceiving our relationship to "our stuff"? Might such teaching help us discover ways in which "our stuff" might be used as a vehicle for expressing Christian love and concern rather than as a means for division and self-indulgence?

This subject obviously deserves more than brief attention, but perhaps a few comments will foster further reflection. First, in order for the Christian concept of stewardship to function as a resource, we must remind ourselves of what it means to be a steward. Too often the concept is used as an excuse to protect our stuff: "Oh, we'd love to feed the homeless in our fellowship hall, but we're called to be good stewards of what God has given us, and all that extra traffic would wear out our new carpet too quickly." In contrast, the concept of stewardship at its best is rooted in the doctrine of creation: God created and sustains all there is. In creating us in God's image and entrusting the rest of the creation to our care, God places us in a privileged position in creation. This privilege, however, entails not the freedom to exploit the rest of creation for our own benefit, but the responsibility to embody God's presence throughout creation.

To be a faithful steward, therefore, is always to act on *behalf* of the one who has called you to this responsibility. For this reason, our acts of stewarding should reflect what God would do if God were acting directly. Moreover, given that Christians believe that God *has* walked among us in the person of Jesus Christ, we are not wrong to imagine how he would respond in circumstances similar to ours. Thus the question we must ask ourselves repeatedly is not, "Since God has given me these resources, how do I protect them?" but "Since God has entrusted these resources to me to do with them what Jesus would do if he were here, what does acting in such a way require in this specific situation?" Because we affirm that God epitomizes other-directed love, it seems plausible that those who act as stewards of this God—and as disciples of God's son—should also act in love. For example, can we imagine Jesus living in relative luxury while those nearby go hungry?

Of course, someone might argue that this is precisely what we *do* see. After all, they might say, if God wanted to end world hunger tomorrow, then God could. Since God doesn't, why should I worry about it? This raises our final consideration: Why does God call us to be stewards in the first place? Doesn't God know the old adage, "If you want something done right, you have to do it yourself"? If God wants all people everywhere taken care of, why doesn't God "just do it"?

This way of thinking makes perfectly good sense as long as one is concerned primarily about the final product. If all God cared about, for example, was *that* people were fed, then presumably God might have chosen to distribute resources more equitably. But God also cares deeply about *the way* people get fed. To see why this might be the case, entertain the following thought-experiment. Imagine that you are going away for the weekend and you need to provide for your five children in your absence. You could, if all you cared about was *that* they were provided for, give each of them a large box of breakfast cereal and instruct each to take care of him or herself in your absence. But you could also make one of the children the steward of the cereal with instructions to make sure that all were provided for, knowing that this would require the children to learn to interact with each other in ways that would be unnecessary in the fend-for-yourself strategy.

What if God has entrusted to some of us much more than we need, not as a sign of God's favor or as a "blessing" to be hoarded, but as a call to reach out to those in need that they might be provided for by the One who loves them most? It may be that too many of us have taken the large box of cereal, written a check for 10 percent of its volume to the church and then gone off to enjoy one heck of a big breakfast. Surely this is not stewardship.

Reflection Questions and Practical Suggestions

The final section of this and subsequent chapters will invite you to think carefully about the ways in which the issues raised throughout the chapter impact your life directly. Since the purpose of this section is to enrich your imagination, not stifle it, please do not limit yourself to these few modest suggestions. When faced with a formidable task, most of us find it helpful to find someplace to start. That's what these final sections are about: starting points. My hope is that each of you will use these simple questions and suggestions as a means to a life of deeper and more profound reflection and embodiment.

☐ This chapter has focused on the other-directedness of love. Reflect on the proportion of time you devote each day to yourself, your concerns and your agenda, compared with how much you devote to the needs and concerns of others. Although most of us will always be "self-centered" in this respect, we should be troubled if the needs of others *always* take a back seat to our own. Consider beginning each day by asking God to give you eyes to see the needs of others, even if this means setting aside your own agenda and preoccupations.

☐ Devote some time to reflecting on your personal relationships and the ways that you view them. Have you ever found yourself evaluating an existing or potential relationship by engaging in a crude form of cost-benefit analysis, weighing the benefits and costs it offered you? Do you think relationships contracted in this way are capable of nurturing other-directed love?

Can you think of any practices you engage in that encourage you to view other people as objects for your own pleasure or benefit? Many cultural commentators have suggested that we live in a "voyeuristic culture," that is, a culture where people derive an inordinate amount of pleasure from watching other peoples' lives. Is it possible that much of the pleasure gained from sordid talk shows, tell-all memoirs, pornography or web cams is related to the fact that such pleasure is secured from a safe distance, without risk of human involvement? If Christians are not free to consume as entertainment another person's troubles, body or life, then perhaps we should make a concerted effort to limit our exposure to those venues that encourage us to do precisely that.

☐ Set aside some time to evaluate honestly whether our cultural habit of viewing most of life through the lens of self-interest has affected the way you view your relationship with God. Have you ever found yourself thinking of your relationship with God or the church in terms of self-interest? Have you ever evaluated these relationships by using something akin to cost-benefit analysis? For example, have you ever been tempted to think about the Christian life primarily in terms of "what's in it for me"? Have you ever ended your relationship with a church because the "cost" of continued involvement was too high?

Most of us will likely answer yes to at least one of the questions above. Our problem, in a nutshell, is that our vision of the Christian life is far too puny. We have been called by God to be partners in God's glorious and cosmic work of reconciliation. God is in the process of bringing healing and resto-ration to all of creation, and we have been called to be agents of that reconciling work. That call from God has the potential to free us from our bondage to our own visions of what life is about, visions that usually entail little more than orchestrating all of life to serve our own narrow interests. What we need is a clearer recognition that central to the salvation or wholeness that God offers us is a salvation from ourselves. God offers us a life saturated in love—in other-directedness—if we are but willing to step aside and allow God's vision for human life to become our vision.

☐ Since market-style economies are here to stay for the foreseeable future,

Christians who must function within them must find creative ways to keep their entire lives from being colonized by market-style thinking. If Christians are to continue to tell the story of God in Christ with integrity—a story that remains incomprehensible apart from the notion of "gift"—then we will need times and places in our lives where the attitudes and practices of the marketplace are kept at bay. What might we do to cultivate a different set of practices and convictions?

We might begin by working hard to keep ourselves from viewing worship as merely another exchange. We need to catch ourselves when we say things like "Well, I didn't get anything out of *that* this morning" and realize that such a mentality reflects our bondage to viewing everything through the lens of self-interest. If we gather primarily to offer God an offering of praise and thanksgiving, then whether or not we are blessed or edified in the process will be of secondary importance.

Christians should also seek to have their friendships rooted in the gracious giving and receiving of gifts, rather than in the calculated exchange of benefits. If you find yourself, for example, devoting considerable energy to "keeping score" with your friends (How much did they spend on me for my birthday?), then you are probably neither giving nor receiving graciously. In a similar way, when someone offers you a gift, resist the urge to reciprocate immediately. Too often our acts of reciprocity are (or at least appear to be) attempts to deflect the gift originally given by transforming the situation into one of exchange.

We also need to reconsider our relationship to "our stuff." What might happen if we began to think of "our possessions" as given to us as resources for furthering God's reign in this place? Would this encourage us to open our eyes to the needs around us? Are we really acting in love when we see someone in need, yet salve our consciences by telling ourselves that we've given God our obligatory tithe and so are "free" to spend *our* 90 percent on ourselves?

Do a word study on the New Testament concept of *koinōnia*. This Greek word, often translated as "fellowship" (but also as "communion," "brother-hood" and "participation"), entails a good deal more than simply being with other people and having a good time. Indeed, there are several places in

Scripture (and in the writings of the early church) where what was implied and apparently practiced was a complete sharing of life, including the sharing of material possessions (Acts 2:42-47; 4:32-35). Even when the word is not explicitly employed, we see the concept at work. Thus a disciple such as Barnabas (Acts 4:36) is willing to sell a parcel of land and bring the money to the apostles in order to take care of pressing needs, not believing that his possessions are strictly "his own."

Some churches are experimenting with some creative ways of helping their members reconceive their relationship to their possessions. For example, I know of churches that maintain a database of people's stuff that they are willing to loan to other people. Some members may have only one or two items on the database, while others may have many. In each case, however, such a practice serves as an important reminder that our stuff is not our own. If we really are stewards, then we have to do everything in our power to make sure that what is done with it pleases and furthers the purposes of the One to whom it all belongs. Moreover, such a practice brings us into relationship with one another in ways that are not necessary when we each have our own stuff.

Finally, we should seek out opportunities to give without expectation of return. For example, those of us who are able should consider *donating* our blood. It's a simple gesture, yet in addition to helping another human being, it may also serve as a reminder that we need spaces in our lives that operate outside the market. There are very few spaces left in our culture that are not framed by self-interested exchanges; Christians should be grateful for those few that remain and should joyfully support them. How tragic it would be if we were known as the people who on Sundays celebrate the new life we have received through the gift of Christ's blood and who then turn around on Monday and sell our blood for a profit to a brother or sister in need.

I pray that, according to the riches of his glory, he may grant that you may be strengthened in your inner being with power through his Spirit, and that Christ may dwell in your hearts through faith, as you are being rooted and grounded in love. (Eph 3:16-17)

THREE
Cultivating Joy in the Midst of Manufactured Desire

My Father is glorified by this, that you bear much fruit and become my disciples. As the Father has loved me, so I have loved you; abide in my love. If you keep my commandments, you will abide in my love, just as I have kept my Father's commandments and abide in his love. I have said these things to you so that my joy may be in you, and that your joy may be complete. (Jn 15:8-11)

When a woman is in labor, she has pain, because her hour has come. But when her child is born, she no longer remembers the anguish because of the joy of having brought a human being into the world. So you have pain now; but I will see you again, and your hearts will rejoice, and no one will take your joy from you. (Jn 16:21-22)

The memory remains so vivid that it could have happened yesterday. Kim and I were in the combination labor and delivery room of our local hospital, anxiously awaiting and painfully aiding the arrival of our first son. I felt intensely helpless, coaching Kim to breathe through the intense pain of the contractions and then to rest between them. Never before had I seen my wife in such agony; her iron grip on my left hand during the contractions was a periodic reminder that our roles in this unfolding miracle were terribly unequal. At one point I actually had to remove my sterling silver wedding band, realizing only later that Kim's clasp on my hand had cracked it.

Yet this is not what either of us remembers most vividly. Kim tells me that she can remember the pain, but only with effort. What she remembers most clearly is how she felt when the doctor laid this tiny, helpless life upon her chest. And what is forever etched on my mind is the expression of unspeakable joy that appeared on Kim's face at this very moment. What both of us felt at this instant, with tears of joy flowing freely down our faces, was as intense and as indescribable as anything either of us has ever experienced. Though neither we nor countless others who have experienced this can fully explain how we felt, when we do try to speak of it, one word inevitably comes to mind: joy, pure joy.

Most of us can remember at least a few times in our lives when we have experienced this kind of intense joy. Is there some connection between such experiences of joy and what Paul identifies as the second fruit of the Spirit?

The Character of Joy
Gaining a deeper understanding of this second fruit of the Spirit is complicated by its overlapping usages. In English we commonly use the same word for the *state* of experiencing joy itself ("Playing in the orchestra gives me such joy"), for the *source* of our joy ("My children are the joy of my life") and for our *expressions* of joy ("When I finally saw her again, I jumped for joy"). Even though New Testament Greek has several different words that are commonly translated as "joy," the word most often used—*chara*—is likewise used in overlapping ways for the state, source and expression of joy. Thus when the star leads the Magi to Bethlehem, they are "overwhelmed with joy" (Mt 2:10), while John the Baptist, when speaking of his joy at the coming of Jesus, notes that the friend of the bridegroom "rejoices greatly at the bridegroom's voice" (Jn 3:29). Moreover, anyone who has studied Paul's letter to the Philippians, which is often referred to as "the epistle of joy," knows that Paul repeatedly urges his brothers and sisters to express their joy, to rejoice.

But what *is* this joy we are called to express? What experience are we trying to convey when we find ourselves reaching for this word? Usually, we employ this word to communicate our intense satisfaction, our sense of well-being and our underlying contentment at having experienced something for which we have earnestly longed, something that we have deeply desired. The object of this longing and desire can of course vary, as can the depth and intensity of our subsequent joy.

To see this more clearly, it may help to compare the experience of joy to other human experiences, such as the experience of pleasure. Joy and pleasure both involve taking delight in something or someone. But the objects of delight, as well as the reasons for delighting in that object, affect the character of that subsequent delight. Enjoying a good meal and enjoying a good conversation are both pleasurable, but they are pleasures of a different kind because their objects are different. Moreover, enjoying a good meal when we are famished is different again from enjoying a good meal prepared by our dearest friend. Each may be the occasion of intense pleasure, but the character of that pleasure will differ to the extent that we are drawn out of our selves. The more that we are drawn out of our selves, the more we likely characterize our delight as *joy* rather than simply *pleasure.*

Hence, unlike pleasure, joy cannot be pursued for its own sake. Joy is the satisfaction that comes when we find that for which we've been looking. So to pursue joy itself is akin to looking for something not because you want to *find* it, but because you want the *pleasure* that accompanies finding it. Such a strategy is bound to fail, however, because joy—as C. S. Lewis well noted—cannot be pursued for its own sake; rather, joy is a byproduct whose "very existence presupposes that you desire not it but something other and outer."[1] Joy is simply one of the consequences of being open to that which is beyond one's self. To pursue joy for its own sake, in order to take delight in one's own delight, is to ignore this crucial "other-directedness" of joy.

This outward movement of joy is perhaps why Scripture so closely links joy and love. By reflecting on the character of God's love as grace, as gift, as we did in the last chapter, we are prepared to see the significance of the etymological connection between the Greek word for "grace" *(charis)* and the New Testament word most commonly translated as "joy" *(chara)*. Both words developed from the same root, and both imply the activity of freely taking delight in something or someone beyond one's self.

Reaching out beyond our selves is only possible if we are able to overcome those innumerable fears that urge us to turn inward and focus exclusively on ourselves. For example, the old adage, "If you don't take care of yourself, no one else will," is not so much a piece of sage advice as it is an excuse for self-centeredness rooted in our fear and mistrust of one another. The Christian life, in contrast, calls us to "fear not." By freeing us from our fears, God frees us to enter into the life of love and joy. As Evelyn Underhill writes: "Real love always heals fear and neutralizes egotism, and so, as love grows up in us, we shall worry about ourselves less and less, and admire and delight in God and his other children more and more, and this is the secret of joy."[2]

Given this connection between love and joy, we should not be surprised when God's love as expressed in God's creative and redemptive work incites a joyful response, both from creation and from God. The book of Job tells us that God's creative activity led the stars to sing and all the heavenly beings to shout for joy (38:7). Isaiah assures Israel that when God delivers them from exile, their response will be one of everlasting joy:

> And the ransomed of the LORD shall return,
>   and come to Zion with singing;
> everlasting joy shall be upon their heads;
>   they shall obtain joy and gladness,
>   and sorrow and sighing shall flee away. (Is 35:10; cf. 52:9)

But Isaiah also makes clear that God's activity of recreating Israel brings joy not only to the people but also to God:

> For I am about to create new heavens
>   and a new earth;
> the former things shall not be remembered
>   or come to mind.
> But be glad and rejoice forever
>   in what I am creating;
> for I am about to create Jerusalem as a joy,
>   and its people as a delight.
> I will rejoice in Jerusalem,
>   and delight in my people;
> no more shall the sound of weeping be heard in it,
>   or the cry of distress. (Is 65:17-19; cf. Is 62:5; Zeph 3:17)

This emphasis on the outward movement of joy is carried over into the New Testament, where healing and restoration of wholeness are an occasion for joy and praise. When Jesus heals a crippled woman, she stands straight up and begins praising God (Lk 13:13). The Samaritan leper who is healed by Jesus returns to thank him, "praising God with a loud voice" (Lk 17:15). When the lame man at the Beautiful Gate is healed, he gets up and goes into the temple, "walking and leaping and praising God" (Acts 3:8). Similarly Philip's healing ministry in Samaria brings "great joy in that city" (Acts 8:8).

The New Testament also testifies that conversion itself is an occasion for joy, both for those converted and for those involved in the harvest. After his encounter with Philip and his subsequent baptism, the eunuch goes on his way rejoicing (Acts 8:39). The Philippian jailer and his entire household rejoiced "that he had become a believer in God" (Acts 16:34). Jesus notes that the fields are ripe for harvesting and that the reaper is gathering "fruit for eternal life;" as a result, both sower and reaper rejoice together (Jn 4:36). Moreover, Luke notes that the conversion of the Gentiles "brought great joy to all the believers" (Acts 15:3).

Joy also characterizes our relationships with other Christians, particularly those whom we have helped to nurture in the Lord. Paul asks the Thessalonians, "For what is our hope or joy or crown of boasting before our Lord Jesus at his coming? Is it not you? Yes, you are our glory and joy!" (1 Thess 2:19-20; cf. 3:9). Paul also calls the Philippians "my joy and crown" (Phil 4:1) and tells the believers in Rome of his deep desire to "come to you with joy and be refreshed in your company" (Rom 15:32; cf. 2 Tim 1:4; Philem 7).

But perhaps most significantly, joy is a defining characteristic of the life of God. The parables of Luke 15 remind us that God also rejoices when those who were lost are found. God has always longed for the reconciliation of all creation. Thus when some parts of that creation are restored to their proper relation to God, God takes great delight. The parables of the lost sheep, the lost coin and the lost son all emphasize in their own way this profound truth: *God* rejoices when those who are estranged are restored. If God's life is marked by such joy, how can the lives of those who are called to embody God's character be any less joyful?

Suffering and Joy

One of the hallmarks of Christian joy is that it can be experienced in the midst of immense sorrow and loss. Here we find one of the great differences between the joy of the Christian community and the joy or happiness that the world knows. Our society often encourages us to believe that joy and happiness are the same thing and that both can only be experienced by *escaping* from the world's cares, afflictions and sorrows. But escaping or avoiding the world of pain and suffering in order to "be happy," in our culture's language, is neither possible nor desirable for the follower of Christ.

Often we define joy or happiness as the *absence* of something undesirable, such as pain, suffering or disappointment. If these undesirable states are absent, we surmise that we are happy. But Christian joy is the proper response to the *presence* of something desirable: God. Granted, there are plenty of times, because of our sinful proclivities, that we do *not* desire God's presence. Yet as Augustine reminds us in his memorable words addressed to God, "You have created us for yourself, and our hearts are restless until they rest in you." If Augustine is correct—that the final resting place of our hearts and our affections is in God—then it follows that true joy and happiness can only be found in God, a point which Augustine himself makes later in the same work:

> O Lord, far be it from me to think that whatever joy I feel makes me truly happy. For there is a joy that is not given to those who do not love you, but only to those who love you for your own sake. You yourself are their joy. Happiness is to rejoice in you and for you and because of you. This is true happiness and there is no other. Those who think that there is another kind of happiness look for joy elsewhere, but theirs is not true joy.[3]

If God is both the source and object of our joy, such joy is not, therefore, necessarily incompatible with sorrow or pain. That this is the case we see from the testimony of Scripture. Although the Old Testament rarely links suffering and joy, except to note that one is often followed by the other (Ps 30:5; Ps 126; Is 16:8-10), the New Testament makes some striking connections between the two. For example, in his parable of the sower, Jesus observes the way in which afflictions and persecutions can have a devastating effect on initially joyful—but inadequately rooted—followers:

> And these are the ones sown on rocky ground; when they hear the word, they immediately receive it with joy. But they have no root, and endure only for a while; then, when trouble or persecution arises on account of the word, immediately they fall away. (Mk 4:16-17)

But suffering does not rob all believers of their joy in the Lord. Indeed, the New Testament contains numerous examples of and admonitions to living joyfully in the midst of suffering. Jesus tells his disciples in his farewell discourse that, like a woman who gives birth, their coming pain at his absence will be replaced by an indestructible joy. This abiding joy—made possible by the Spirit's abiding presence—overflows even in the midst of suffering and persecution. Hence, after being flogged and thrown into prison in Philippi, Paul and Silas pray and sing hymns to God (Acts 16:25). Paul praises the Thessalonians for being an example of living joyfully despite persecution: "And you became imitators of us and of the Lord, for in spite of persecution you received the word with joy inspired by the Holy Spirit, so that you became an example to all the believers in Macedonia and in Achaia" (1 Thess 1:6-7).

Living joyfully *despite* persecution and affliction does not require one to deny the reality of suffering or pain. Suffering and pain, both our own and of others, are real and they can take a toll on even the heartiest Christian faith. Yet people are capable of enduring an enormous amount of pain if they believe that this pain and suffering are not the final word. The writer of Hebrews alludes to this with respect to Jesus, "who for the sake of the joy that was set before him endured the cross, disregarding its shame, and has taken his seat at the right hand of the throne of God" (Heb 12:2). In this way Christian joy is bound up closely with hope: we believe that the pain and suffering that we experience in this life, though real, is not the last word on the matter. Or, as Karl Barth has aptly stated, in the face of human suffering the joy of a Christian stands as a "defiant 'Nevertheless!' "[4]

The New Testament sounds an additional note about joy and suffering, and this note is both more striking and more open to misunderstanding. Several times in Scripture we are told that Christians do and should take joy *in* their suffering. For example, Jesus tells his followers:

> Blessed are you when people hate you, and when they exclude you, revile you, and defame you on account of the Son of Man. Rejoice in that day and leap for joy, for surely your reward is great in heaven; for that is what their ancestors did to the prophets. (Lk 6:22-23)

Or we have the account of Paul and Barnabas who, after being persecuted in Antioch of Pisidia, leave and go to Iconium "filled with joy and with the Holy Spirit" (Acts 13:52). To many people, including many Christians, this sounds disturbingly like some form of masochism. But Scripture does not instruct Christians to rejoice in their pain and suffering in any straightforward way, as if the *source* of our joy is the pain or suffering itself. Rather, Scripture suggests that certain kinds of suffering—particularly suffering that results from being faithful to Christ—can be an *occasion* for joy. So the apostles, after they have been flogged for disobeying the Sanhedrin's order not to teach in the name of Jesus, "rejoiced that they were considered worthy to suffer dishonor for the sake of the name" (Acts 5:41).

A slightly different tack is taken by James, who insists that trials may be the occasion for growth and maturity and thus an occasion for joy: "My brothers and sisters, whenever you face trials of any kind, consider it nothing but joy, because you know that the testing of your faith produces endurance; and let endurance have its full effect, so that you may be mature and complete, lacking in nothing" (Jas 1:2-4).

Finally, this theme of growth and maturity is combined with the admonition to follow joyfully the example of Christ—even in his sufferings—in two other arresting New Testament passages:

> Beloved, do not be surprised at the fiery ordeal that is taking place among you to test you, as though something strange were happening to you. But rejoice insofar as you are sharing Christ's sufferings, so that you may also be glad and shout for joy when his glory is revealed. If you are reviled for the name of Christ, you are blessed, because the spirit of glory, which is the Spirit of God, is resting on you. (1 Pet 4:12-14)

I am now rejoicing in my sufferings for your sake, and in my flesh I am completing what is lacking in Christ's afflictions for the sake of his body, that is, the church. (Col 1:24)

Whatever it may mean to "complete what is lacking in Christ's afflictions," Paul found it to be an occasion for joy. This affirmation, along with the above discussion, should be enough to convince us not only that joy is central to the Christian life but also that the joy of the Christian community—by being determinatively other-directed—is of a different character than the world's joy.

Obstacles to a Life of Joy

If joy requires a willingness to be open to something beyond one's self, then it should come as no surprise that people deeply rooted in the dominant cultural *ethos* have a difficult time experiencing joy. We are encouraged from an early age to seek our own pleasure above all else. Such relentless pursuit of personal pleasure is what the dominant culture means by "the pursuit of happiness." Each of us is urged, in subtle and not-so-subtle ways, to pursue our own individually-defined happiness; in almost every case, we are called to pursue that which promises to give pleasure to each of us as individuals. The dominant culture also has enormous power to form our desires and affections. If one doubts this, simply consider the following questions: Where did we learn to desire what we desire? Where did we learn what we should want out of life? Or what we should wear or eat? Or what we should look like? Or what car to drive or house to buy? Or what we should do with our time? Although most of our desires have complex sources, we would be naive to doubt the significant impact that the dominant culture wields in shaping—and in many cases fabricating—those desires.

Manufacturing desire. Many cultural practices instill in us the desires that direct and give meaning to our lives. One of the most powerful of these practices and the one that may be most responsible for inhibiting the cultivation of Christian joy is the practice of advertising. This complex and multi-tentacled industry spends well over a trillion dollars a year to instill in us certain desires. And given that most advertisers do not consider themselves to be engaging in charity, one might suspect that ads often succeed in eliciting the desired response. In short, if a company like Proctor and Gamble determined that its advertisements for products such as Crest and Prell weren't working, it wouldn't spend three billion dollars a year in television advertising alone (an amount that is nearly 50 percent more than the entire gross national product of our poor neighbor to the south, Haiti).

Nor are the persuasive practices in which advertisers engage limited simply to establishing and maintaining brand loyalty. Instead, advertising both plays on and helps create our contemporary confusions and anxieties about who we are and whether we have worth. Advertisers freely admit that contemporary advertising involves creating a connection between their products and certain images or values. The hoped-for-result is that people will be convinced that consuming a certain product will bring with it the associated and desired image or values. John Kavanaugh writes:

> Friendship, intimacy, love, pride, happiness, and joy are actually the *objects* we buy and consume, much more so than the tubes, liquor bottles, Cadillacs, and Buicks that promise them and bear their names. And since none of these deepest human hopes can be fulfilled in any product, the mere consumption of them is never enough; "more" of the product, or a "new improved" product, is the only relief offered to our human longings. Thus the seller drives us to greater purchasing with even more extravagantly concocted promises: more commodities are the solution to anxiety stimulated by media manipulation. Consumption, consequently, is not just an economic factor. It emerges as a "way of life." It is an addiction.[5]

Thus the line penned by the English poet Lord Byron—"There's not a joy the world can give like that it takes away"—takes on an added poignancy in a culture such as ours that prides itself on creating ever-new but always evanescent desires. And because advertising cultivates the insatiable desire for the new, the improved, the bigger and better, we find ourselves all but incapable of experiencing joy and contentment in our everyday lives.

Although the practice of advertising shapes our experience of desire in powerful ways, it does not act in a cultural vacuum. Rather, this practice (along with others) is interwoven with certain convictions, narratives and dispositions that together shape our experience of desire and our subsequent views of happiness and joy. Several deserve brief mention.

Glorifying the novel. One of the dominant culture's deepest prejudices is that the new is always better than the old. A corollary to this prejudice is that the past should always be viewed with suspicion. This prejudice is codified and passed on in the stories our culture tells of how traditional thinking consistently inhibits individual autonomy, freedom and progress. For a trenchant example of this, we need only consider the powerful hold that a figure like Galileo has over our imaginations. What schoolboy or girl has not heard the story of how the authorities of the church rejected Galileo's discoveries, learning well the lesson that tradition always obstructs progress and innovation?

This desire for the new, however, is not limited merely to a preference for that which is up-to-date and modern; it also extends to the desire for "the new" understood as "different." Hence, we are convinced that if we are to be genuinely happy, our lives will need to be filled with an endless array of new and exciting experiences. As a result, we are convinced that to spend one's life doing the same sorts of things is a sure recipe for boredom and unhappiness. We are taught at an early age that "variety is the spice of life," but increasingly we seem to want the spices to constitute the whole meal. But setting off on a quest for ever-new forms of pleasure is to begin a pilgrimage that is sure to disappoint, since the very character of that search guarantees that one can not be ultimately satisfied. The end result, it seems, is that we find ourselves pursuing pleasure for its own sake, a pursuit that robs us of our ability to experience and express genuine joy.

We do not necessarily drop this desire for the new (and therefore better) when we gather as the church. There is a tendency among many Christians, especially young people, to doubt the worth of the church's two thousand-year-old traditions. Many believe that this "old, boring stuff" automatically inhibits progress and growth. Many don't want the church to do anything that the church has done for a long time; they want everything to be new and different. For example, why would we want to do the same things over and over again in worship week after week, year after year? In many people's minds what the church most needs is a good dose of variety in order to keep people from getting bored. There is of course a legitimate place for new expressions of the Christian faith, but we need to ask ourselves: What makes these new expressions legitimate? Is it simply because they are *new?* Or is it because we discern that they are edifying expressions of *the Christian faith?* If it is the latter, then there must be some appropriate reasons for glancing backward, for otherwise how would we know that this *new* expression was an expression of anything *Christian?* Such discernments call us to evaluate our new expressions against previous expressions in determining whether they are faithful. As a result, Christians have their own reasons for believing that it will not do to jettison the past as so much worthless jetsam.

Craving more. The desire for "more" and "better" does not always simply translate into a desire for the new; the desire for "more" and "better" can also manifest itself in economic terms where *more* means "bigger": a bigger salary, a bigger house, a bigger car, a bigger wardrobe, a bigger assortment of toys. All of this and more is commonly assumed to be "better" and therefore desirable. But in addition to "bigger," *more* also regularly means simply that: "more" (as in "more than one"). If owning one house is good, having a vacation home in addition to that is considered even better; if one car is good, two or three would be better still; if one graduate degree is good, wouldn't two or three be even better? The areas of our lives where we have come to assume that more is necessarily better are legion. We desire to shop at the grocery store with the most variety, because having more choice is better. We desire to upgrade our current computer system, even though the present one works just fine, because we have learned that more speed and more memory capacity are better. We desire to cruise the information superhighway in order to have more information instantly at our fingertips—even if we don't have a context that would allow us to know what to do with the information we already have—because we are sure that having more information is better. The list goes on and on.

In short, we are led to believe that our endless pursuit of "more" will eventually lead to more happiness. Furthermore, because we believe we are entitled to pursue happiness and because our culture defines happiness in terms of what we possess, we believe we are entitled to acquire and accumulate whatever possessions we believe will make us happy. The result, as many of us can well attest, is that our lives (not to mention our closets, garages and attics) are often cluttered with stuff that promised to bring us happiness but didn't and doesn't.

The threat to joy posed by the "more-is-always-better" conviction is obvious. If more is always better, then there is little reason to be thankful for or content with what one presently has. The assumption is that one will be *more* happy and *more* content in the future, because one will *have* more. But once this conviction is established, there is no logical stopping point where one will finally be content at all, for one would always be happier if one had more. The result is that whatever joy and contentment we might experience and express in the present are endlessly deferred.

Breeding anxiety and fear. Rather than joy and contentment, the dominant culture cultivates a way of life marked by the dispositions of anxiety and fear. Advertisers know that in a relatively homogeneous society that offers few opportunities for most people to stand out, many consumers want to distinguish themselves from other people by their peculiar patterns of consumption. But behind this desire to be (triflingly) different lurks a deeper anxiety and fear: the fear of being (substantively) different.

For example, if I buy a new Honda Accord rather than an old Chevrolet Chevette in order to get to and from work, I have distinguished myself from other people in a certain sort of way. At least this is the assumption. But if I choose to walk, ride a bicycle or take the bus to work, I am in danger of being considered "weird." (Don't worry, this is just an example; I drive a car to work just like everyone else.) Though it would never occur to anyone to inquire as to why I bought a new Accord rather than an old Chevette (the reasons are obvious, right?), most people would find it difficult *not* to inquire about my preferred mode of transportation if I arrived by some means other than my own automobile. Or more to the point, even if they *didn't* ask, I would likely feel that I needed to explain myself. And if I did explain myself, I would likely try to do so in a way that showed that I wasn't that different from them after all: "I'd like to drive to work, but our car is in the shop"; or "We're trying to save money for our summer vacation, and this seemed like a reasonable way to pinch pennies"; or "I decided that I needed more exercise than I was getting, so biking seemed like the perfect solution." Each of these responses leaves things pretty much as they are, thereby affirming both my peers and me. What I certainly would not want to say is something like: "Well, our family has decided that owning an automobile isn't as essential as our culture has led us to believe, and so we've decided not to own one in order to free up more resources for kingdom work. Besides, we've found that not owning one makes you dependent on other people in all sorts of surprisingly wonderful ways." Saying *that* would make you truly different; saying *that* would make you a threat; and saying *that* would likely ostracize you from just about everyone you know, including most Christians.

One of the great ironies of consumerism is that it promotes itself as a means to exercise our personal freedom, when in fact it promotes the most insidious forms of homogeneity. We are led to think that we are incredibly free when we go off to buy what *we* desire, but it turns out that we end up buying pretty much what everyone else does. Sure, there are some variations in style, but this is part of the game. What is more significant is the way this freedom is really a form of bondage. How many people feel free *not* to buy a new car every three or four years? (Or not to buy one at all?) How many people feel free *not* to dress in the latest styles or fashions? How many people feel free *not* to look like, talk like, walk like and think like everyone else? In short, how many people feel free *not* to desire what everyone else desires?

The advertising industry feeds on and promotes our fear of being (too) different. We desperately desire to fit in and we fear that we won't. As a result, we spend much of our lives trying to look and dress and talk and consume like other people. But the gospel has good news for us: we no longer have to believe that our worth is contingent upon our ability to produce and market an acceptable image of ourselves for the consumption of those around us. Rather than trying to transform ourselves into the latest image offered to us by Madison Avenue, Christians are free to be transformed into the image of Christ (Rom 8:29; cf. 1 Pet 1:14).

As should be obvious, the mindset described above does not just affect the lives of individual Christians; it also affects the life of the gathered community. When we gather, our thanksgiving is often truncated, because our lives are habituated to feel insatiable desire rather than heartfelt gratitude. Thus even when we do offer thanks, it is often with an eye toward how much *more* thankful we'd be if something really good would happen to us.

Similarly, we are very fearful about appearing to be different from our neighbors, and we are perhaps even more fearful about raising our children to be different. Too often we want them (as well as ourselves) to be successful in the world's eyes and not to stick out too much. The result is that most of us have a thin veneer of Christian conviction that overlays (and hardly challenges) the convictions that we have learned from the wider culture.

Cultivating Joy

Cultivating joy in the midst of a culture that is steeped in manufactured and insatiable desires will not be easy. Yet there is reason to be hopeful, for God has given the church enormous resources on which it may draw. We begin our reflections once again by focusing on the church at worship.

Rejoicing in worship. Desire in itself is not a bad thing. Christians are not called to refrain from desiring, but to desire the right things for the right reasons. In a culture like ours, Christians must carefully examine the sources and objects of our desires. We are frequently tempted to take delight primarily in what this world has to offer, with the result being that our own pleasure and that which promises to deliver that pleasure become our primary objects of delight. Although God certainly wants us to enjoy the goodness of the created order, the created order and its pleasures should not become our idols. Paul notes that humankind has repeatedly turned away from God, worshiping the creation rather than the Creator (Rom 1:22-25). What would it mean to desire God and what God desires, rather than what the world teaches us to desire? How do we learn to desire God like the psalmist did?

> O God, you are my God, I seek you,
> > my soul thirsts for you;
> my flesh faints for you,
> > as in a dry and weary land where there is no water.

So I have looked upon you in the sanctuary,
     beholding your power and glory.
Because your steadfast love is better than life,
     my lips will praise you.
So I will bless you as long as I live;
     I will lift up my hands and call on your name.

My soul is satisfied as with a rich feast,
     and my mouth praises you with joyful lips
when I think of you on my bed,
     and meditate on you in the watches of the night;
for you have been my help,
     and in the shadow of your wings I sing for joy. (Ps 63:1-7; cf. Ps 84)

Elsewhere we are told how David brought up the ark of the covenant to
Jerusalem with rejoicing and that he "danced before the LORD with all his
might" (2 Sam 6:12-14). To those who did not understand the redemption
brought by this God, David's actions no doubt seemed odd. Yet for those of
us who have even greater reason than David did to rejoice and dance before
the Lord, worship ought to be the very character of our lives.

The joy that comes from worship and thanksgiving derives from our
desiring and then experiencing what we were created to do. If our day-to-day
lives fail to be marked by joy, perhaps it is because those lives so seldom testify
to what we believe is the goal or purpose for life. Surely we have not been
called out of darkness into his glorious light in order to bear witness that "He
who dies with the most toys wins." One of the church's traditional responses
to the question of our true purpose has been that our "chief end is to glorify
God and to enjoy him forever" (Westminster Shorter Catechism, Q. 1). This
is our eternal purpose. When we gather for worship, therefore, we are focusing
our attention on that which is our chief end. Such gatherings should be
marked by the joy that comes from doing what we were created to do.

Such gatherings should also be characterized by joy because Christ is
present in our gathering. Christ's presence brings joy: recall that the resurrection accounts are filled with references to joy (Mt 28:8; Lk 24:41; Jn 20:20).
Luke's account of the ascension is similarly instructive: "While he was

blessing them, he withdrew from them and was carried up into heaven. And they worshiped him, and returned to Jerusalem with great joy, and they were continually in the temple blessing God" (Lk 24:51-53).

The Psalms encourage us to make a joyful noise to the Lord (Ps 66:1; 95:1-2; 98:4-6; 100:1).

> But let the righteous be joyful;
>   let them exult before God;
>   let them be jubilant with joy.
>
> Sing to God, sing praises to his name;
>   lift up a song to him who rides upon the clouds—
> his name is the LORD—
>   be exultant before him. (Ps 68:3-4)

Too much of the time there is little joy in our worship. Although reverence and solemnity in worship have their rightful place, our gatherings must also have a strongly celebrative and joyful character. Many of us are more than willing to "shout for joy" when our favorite athletic team prospers, but find it difficult to find anything worth shouting about in the presence of the living God. Perhaps this is why the so-called charismatic movement has struck a chord with so many people. Yet all Christians, rather than just a select group, should be "charismatic," in the sense of being noticeably marked by the grace and joy of the Lord.

The source of our joy as Christians is God and God's reconciling work. Even the Old Testament rings out with psalms of joy to the God who saves. This joy in God's salvation cannot be silenced by the misfortunes of our lives:

> Though the fig tree does not blossom,
>   and no fruit is on the vines;
> though the produce of the olive fails
>   and the fields yield no food;
> though the flock is cut off from the fold
>   and there is no herd in the stalls,
> yet I will rejoice in the LORD;
>   I will exult in the God of my salvation. (Hab 3:17-18)

In the New Testament this joy is focused specifically in the reconciling work of God in Christ. To express this, the early church took those everyday occasions and images of joy and gave them a new, christological focus. Harvesting, getting married, giving birth, finding something lost, sharing a banquet—all are used as ways of expressing the joy that marks our lives on account of Christ. This inseparable connection between our joy and the reconciling work of God in Christ is powerfully expressed in 1 Peter:

> Blessed be the God and Father of our Lord Jesus Christ! By his great mercy he has given us a new birth into a living hope through the resurrection of Jesus Christ from the dead, and into an inheritance that is imperishable, undefiled, and unfading, kept in heaven for you, who are being protected by the power of God through faith for a salvation ready to be revealed in the last time. In this you rejoice, even if now for a little while you have had to suffer various trials, so that the genuineness of your faith—being more precious than gold that, though perishable, is tested by fire—may be found to result in praise and glory and honor when Jesus Christ is revealed. Although you have not seen him, you love him; and even though you do not see him now, you believe in him and rejoice with an indescribable and glorious joy, for you are receiving the outcome of your faith, the salvation of your souls. (1 Pet 1:3-9)

As important as the church's worship is, we must also keep it in proper perspective. When we joyfully praise God, we become participants in a broader, richer, ceaseless worship. Scripture tells us that the throne of God is surrounded by those who engage in the eternal worship of our God. When we gather to worship, therefore, we are joining the heavenly chorus in anticipation of the future and eternal worship that we will freely and joyfully offer.

Although God does not need our worship, it would be wrong to suggest that God does not delight in it. Shakespeare once wrote that "joy delights in joy" (Sonnet 8). I believe that God enjoys our joy. Scripture admonishes us repeatedly to "bless the Lord," which is a strange thing to do for someone who arguably needs nothing that we have to offer. Yet God inhabits the praises of God's people. In a sense, when our joyful worship blesses God it completes a circle of love and joy: God loves and redeems God's people, who respond with joy and adoration, which in turn brings joy to God. Perhaps it is similar to something I frequently experience when I return home from a day at work. As I walk across the yard to the front door, our younger children are often in our living room standing on a wooden stool that sits in front of the large picture window. Their joyful bobbings up and down usually catch my eye long before I am close enough to see their faces. When I am closer and we make eye contact, they usually charge for the door, where they greet me with outstretched arms and ear-to-ear smiles. As I stoop to take them in my arms, I am often deeply moved by the purity and intensity of their joy. Indeed, some of *my* most intense moments of joy have come as a response to theirs. Perhaps God does no less when we joyfully enter into the presence of God to offer our heartfelt worship and adoration.

Nurturing contentment. If our lives were marked by a spirit of joy that flows from authentic praise and thanksgiving, this would affect more than our corporate worship. The habit of expressing our gratitude for God's abundant care seems to place a much-needed check on our covetousness. Can we imagine offering thanks and praise for God's unmerited bounty and at the same time immersing ourselves in the interminable quest for the "new," the "better" and the "different"? I doubt it. Perhaps our insatiable cravings for more and better say more than we know about the depth of our joy and the genuineness of our praise and thanksgiving.

As Christians, our goal is not to quench our desires or even to minimize their intensity. Rather, what must be different is the *object* of our desires and affections. Paul tells the Philippians that he has learned to be content with whatever he has (Phil 4:11). My hunch is that Paul's contentment was made possible not least by the wellspring of joy and thanksgiving that God had sprung at the center of his soul, a joy and thanksgiving that clearly marked all his letters. Because Paul's desires and affections were set on God, the importance of pursuing worldly pleasures faded.

In a similar vein the first letter to Timothy reminds us "There is great gain in godliness combined with contentment, for we brought nothing into this world, so that we can take nothing out of it; but if we have food and clothing, we will be content with these. But those who want to be rich fall into temptation and are trapped by many senseless and harmful desires that plunge people into ruin and destruction" (1 Tim 6:6-9; cf. Heb 13:5; 1 Jn 2:15-17). If there is one phrase that well describes the lives of countless people, including the lives of many Christians, it is simply that: "trapped by many senseless and harmful desires." But God's desire is not that we be trapped by our desires, but that our desires be rightly ordered to God.

Reconceiving tradition. Cultivating a life of joy and contentment in an age such as ours is no easy task. Formidable as it is, it would certainly be even more so were we without one of our greatest resources: the history and traditions of the church across time and space. Unfortunately these immense and rich resources too often lie fallow in our tradition-suspicious culture. In our rush for the new and the better, we ignore much from the church's past that God might use to edify us today. Rather than limit our imaginations to a repertoire of stories defined by our desires for newness and up-to-dateness, we might open up our imaginations to being enriched by what God has done in the lives of Christians across the centuries and around the world. Similarly God has been praised in song in innumerable languages and cultures across the ages. Why limit ourselves to what has been written by middle-class American Christians during the last ten years? (Or for that matter, to what was written by middle-class European and American Christians during the latter half of the nineteenth century?)

I am firmly convinced that one of the greatest obstacles to living the Christian life in contemporary society is an impoverished imagination. Most of us will find it difficult to live a life we cannot imagine. (This, by the way, is the same principle that makes advertising so effective: ads help you imagine what your life would be like with such and such a product.) But how will we imagine a life different from the one we are currently living if we do not immerse ourselves in a different set of narratives that display life and its purposes differently? Here the traditions of the church across time and space offer us wealth beyond measure. By steeping ourselves in the stories of Christians across the ages—by listening to their struggles, their failures, their God-enabled victories—we begin to have our imaginations opened up to new possibilities hidden within our seemingly necessity-driven contexts. Contrary to the spirit of our age, therefore, living faithfully in the present might require us to listen much more attentively to the past.

En-joying children. Finally, let me mention briefly an area that could be the subject of its own book. It seems to me that the cultivation of joy cannot be easily separated from the presence of children. Those who would cultivate joy could do worse than provide themselves with regular opportunities to interact with and care for children. The reasons for this appear to be at least twofold. First, children are a seemingly endless source of joy for others, not least because they are so full of joy. Let's face it: children see the world differently than we do. Although in some cases we might be justified in labeling their views as "childish," more often than not being around children reminds us that our view of the world is unnecessarily jaded. The result: our all-too-pervasive cynicism and deeply-held suspicions rob us of joy.

Another reason for regularly hanging out with children is that such a practice reminds us that joy is not to be equated with trivial notions of pleasure or happiness. Anyone who has changed a dozen diapers, played hide-and-go-seek for the fourth time in an afternoon and helped to settle an intersibling squabble for who-knows-how-many times knows this to be the case. Although it is true that most people do not *en-joy* such necessary activities, it is also the case that joy can pop up in and around these and other such activities without warning. Somehow we rightly suspect, even if we cannot explain why it should be so, that if we were to avoid all of these seemingly unpleasant tasks, we would also be ridding ourselves of countless opportunities to experience deep and abiding joy. It seems that wherever there are children, joy is not far away.

Reflection Questions and Practical Suggestions
How can Christians go about loosening the grip that manufactured desires have on our lives and the ways in which those desires rob our lives of joy? There are of course no simple solutions, but there are some things we *can* do to try and cultivate a life of joy.

☐ Reflect on the way you begin most days. What typically happens in the first ten minutes of your day? In the first hour? Do your mind and your energies, like those of most people, turn immediately to the concerns and pressures of the day ahead? If so, joy may be having a difficult time gaining a foothold in your life. Rather than beginning each day with the frenzy that marks so much of our lives, perhaps we would be wise to spend some quiet moments at the beginning of each day giving thanks to God for life's seemingly simple pleasures and joys. Even a couple of minutes after we first open our eyes, before we get out of bed, might help us gain the perspective we need as we respond to all the seemingly urgent claims on our attention.

□ Make a list of all your deepest desires, being as honest with yourself as you can. After making your list, go back through your list and reflect on each one. For each desire jot down as clearly as you can *why* you desire this. Next, try to discern *how* you came to desire this. What led you to desire this rather than, or more than, something else? Finally, in light of the above discussion and your knowledge of what God desires, try to discern if your longings and desires are appropriate. Where they seem appropriate, give thanks to God for instilling right desires in your heart. Where your desires seem inappropriate, ask God to direct your longings in other directions.

But this raises another important issue: how do you decide what you really need? If we live in a culture that unceasingly manufactures novel desires, how can we trust our own sense of what we need? And if, as Christians, we have even more reasons to suspect the desires of our heart, shouldn't we be less than willing to put stock in our own views about such matters? Likely we have here another good reason why Christians need to be part of a functioning community of faith. What would it mean for us to be the kind of community that would encourage people to have their desires and needs appraised by others within the community of faith? Obviously this would run counter to our culture and would probably feel to many of us like a frontal attack on our personal freedom (and would also likely make us and others who heard about us wonder if we were part of some strange "cult"). But such an admission is only a reminder that our culture encourages each of us to think of our personal freedom as license to consume *whatever* we want to *whenever* we want to; we need be accountable to no one for such decisions but ourselves.

Is it possible that I would think differently about my "needs" if I were encouraged to discuss them with my brothers and sisters in Christ? Such a disciplining of our needs would not deny that we have needs, but it might give us some much-needed (and perhaps even welcome) help in distinguishing legitimate from fabricated needs. Of course, given how strange such a suggestion sounds to most people (including many Christians), I suspect that those who see the wisdom in such a practice might begin modestly. You might seek one or two other Christians that believe such a practice makes sense and begin by submitting to them for discernment some of your own "personal" needs and desires.

☐ If you're like most people, there are at least a few suspect items on your list of desires. You may even have had a difficult time discerning how you came to desire those things. Our desires are shaped in subtle and not-so-subtle ways and so we should be vigilant about the sources we allow to form our desires. We can certainly work to resist some of the impact of fabricated desire by minimizing our exposure to its primary venues. Television remains the advertising medium of choice, not least because of its enormous audience. But it would be a mistake to think that merely zapping the ads would be enough, though this might be a logical place to begin. One problem with such an approach is that it ignores the way in which television has intentionally blurred the line between programming and advertising. This trend is most visible on channels like Home Shopping Network and MTV, but it is not limited to them. In the past, programs routinely either used generic-looking products or attempted to hide the brand names of the products that did appear; however, advertisers now pay handsome sums to have their products appear prominently in sitcoms, soaps and movies.

Yet it would also be a mistake to think that the only desires that are being instilled by television advertising or programming are those for certain products. Rather, what is being aroused in many cases is a desire for desiring, a desire that makes contentment with who one is and what one has all but impossible. Such desire, coupled with our insecurities about who we are, make possible such things as the fashion industry, which routinely informs us that the clothes we bought last year to make a statement are making quite a different statement now that they are "out of style." Since this desire for desiring is aroused as much by programming as it is by advertisements, cutting down on the amount of television you watch is probably a good place to begin. And when you do watch, you should do so with the full awareness that television programmers and advertisers have more to gain if their audiences are not only continually dissatisfied with their lives, but are also looking for novel ways of filling that void.

We might also consider carefully the impact of leafing through the advertising circulars and mail-order catalogs that arrive daily in our mailboxes. How many times have we found ourselves "needing" something immediately after thumbing through these ads and finding out that this or that (previously unnecessary or even unknown) product was "on sale"? I suspect that advertisers are more than happy for us to feel as if we are doing ourselves some favor by buying at a discount something that only minutes before we didn't need at all. Perhaps it would be a small step in the right direction if we determined not to peruse these instruments of desire unless we had already determined what it was that we needed.

☐ Work to expand your and your church's repertoire of stories and songs. For example, you might commit to reading at least one biography or autobiography each year of a Christian from another era or culture. You might also commit to learning at least one song from a culture other than your own. Rather than judging the song on whether you "like" it or whether it fits your "style," determine to appreciate the song for its ability to communicate something vital about the Christian faith.

☐ How long has it been since you have chosen to have regular and sustained interaction with young children? If it's been a while, consider volunteering your services to a school, a church or a neighbor. Rather than insisting that the children see the world through your eyes, do your best to see the world through theirs.

> *Now to him who is able to keep you from falling, and to make you stand without blemish in the presence of his glory with rejoicing, to the only God our Savior, through Jesus Christ our Lord, be glory, majesty, power, and authority, before all time and now and forever. Amen. (Jude 24)*

FOUR
Cultivating Peace
in the Midst of
Fragmentation

Do not let what you eat cause the ruin of one for whom Christ died. So do not let your good be spoken of as evil. For the kingdom of God is not food and drink but righteousness and peace and joy in the Holy Spirit.... Let us then pursue what makes for peace and for mutual upbuilding. (Rom 14:15-17, 19)

For where there is envy and selfish ambition, there will also be disorder and wickedness of every kind. But the wisdom from above is first pure, then peaceable, gentle, willing to yield, full of mercy and good fruits, without a trace of partiality or hypocrisy. And a harvest of righteousness is sown in peace for those who make peace. (Jas 3:16-18)

Toward the end of my graduate work I interviewed for jobs at several academic institutions around the country. One particular year I had the good fortune of being invited to four campuses for the final round of interviews. Being wanted brought a feeling of exhilaration, and the prospect of actually securing a teaching job after so many years of preparation brought its own sense of excitement. But exhilaration and excitement were only part of the story. While flying to my second interview, I was overcome by a profound sense of cultural vertigo. I realized for the first time that I was about to land in the Midwest for a job interview at a state university, that the following week I would be on the West Coast for an interview at a large Catholic university and that shortly thereafter I would be on my way to an Ivy League institution. Moreover, each of these schools had quite different expectations. As I began to consider how each of these very different institutions would size me up, it dawned on me that no one at any of these places had the slightest idea who I was. Sure, they had my résumé, but they didn't really know what made me tick. No one at any of these institutions knew what I cared deeply about and the inner convictions that animated my life. Suddenly I realized that I might be better off if I stopped asking, *What will they think of me?* and began to consider a quite different question: *Who would they* like *me to be?*

This second question structures the lives of many contemporary people. Gone forever are the days when people were in face-to-face relationships with only a small group of people who shared most experiences of life. Instead, the people we live near are rarely the people with whom we work. The people with whom we work are rarely the people with whom we play. And often none of these are the people with whom we worship. And in the electronic age of telephones, faxes and e-mail, we often have contact with countless numbers of people to whom we remain all but anonymous. In short, we regularly find ourselves moving in a dizzying number of settings whose expectations are radically different. The result is often a sense of fragmentation, a disturbing sense that not only our lives but also our very identities are fractured into scores of isolated if not contradictory fragments. How can Christians bear the fruit of peace in a culture that seems to specialize in cultivating fragmentation?

The Character of Peace

Scripture speaks of peace in more encompassing and far richer ways than our common understandings of peace. We tend to define peace primarily in negative terms: as the cessation or absence of conflict. But the concept of peace that pervades Scripture has more positive resonances. Indeed, we would be less likely to mute those resonances if we were to substitute for the word *peace,* the word *wholeness* or even *salvation.* Listen to the prophet Isaiah, who by means of Hebrew parallelism aligns peace and salvation: "How beautiful upon the mountains are the feet of the messenger who announces peace, who brings good news, who announces salvation, who says to Zion, 'Your God reigns' " (Is 52:7; cf. Rom 10:12-15).

The Hebrew concept of peace, or *shalom,* informs both the Old and New Testaments. *Shalom* (or *eirēnē* in the New Testament) refers to the state of well-being, wholeness and harmony that infuses all of one's relationships. Such a view of peace is inherently social; to be at peace only with oneself is not to experience *shalom* in all its fullness. Perhaps this is why Scripture rarely speaks of peace as a purely mental state, as serenity or "peace of mind." Peace is not something confined within one's psyche; instead, peace is a way of life. In this regard, Scripture more than once speaks of the "way of peace" (Is 59:8; Lk 1:79; Rom 3:17).

Establishing and sustaining wholeness in all one's relationships is no easy thing. To be in right relationship with God and one's fellow creatures one must consistently do what is right, what God desires, what God requires. This is why Scripture again and again connects peace with righteousness:

> I will appoint Peace as your overseer
>> and Righteousness as your taskmaster.
> Violence shall no more be heard in your land,
>> devastation or destruction within your borders;
> you shall call your walls Salvation
>> and your gates Praise. . . .
> Your people shall all be righteous;
>> they shall possess the land forever.
> They are the shoot that I planted, the work of my hands,
>> so that I might be glorified. (Is 60:17-18, 21)

> Let me hear what God the LORD will speak,
>> for he will speak peace to his people,
>> to his faithful, to those who turn to him in their hearts.
> Surely his salvation is at hand for those who fear him,
>> that his glory may dwell in our land.

> Steadfast love and faithfulness will meet;
>> righteousness and peace will kiss each other. (Ps 85:8-10; cf. Ps 119:165)

If one of the effects of righteousness is peace (Is 32:17; cf. Is 26:2-3) and "there is no peace for the wicked" (Is 48:22; cf. Is 57:21), then it is easy to see why we are incapable of securing peace ourselves. In our fallen state we are not capable of living righteously before God and our fellow creatures. For this reason Israel came to understand that *shalom* could only be established and sustained by God. Thus the salvation and wholeness that God grants to Israel is grounded in the covenant that God establishes with his people: "For the mountains may depart and the hills be removed, but my steadfast love shall not depart from you, and my covenant of peace shall not be removed" (Is 54:10; cf. Num 25:12; Ezek 34:25; 37:26).

This theme—that peace, wholeness and salvation come only from God—reverberates throughout the New Testament. The rule or reign of God that Jesus inaugurates is a reign of peace or *wholeness*. Jesus powerfully demonstrates this through his healings and exorcisms, which bring wholeness to those whose lives are shattered and fragmented by illness and bondage. Throughout the gospels people who come in contact with Jesus experience peace, wholeness and salvation. Simeon, upon taking the child Jesus into his arms, praises God for the peace he experiences because his "eyes have seen your salvation" (Lk 2:29-30). To both the woman who washes Jesus' feet and whose sins Jesus forgives (Lk 7:50) and to the woman who reaches out in faith to touch Jesus' garment, he says, "Your faith has saved you; go in peace" (Lk 8:48; Mk 5:34). Finally, in the Gospel of John, Jesus offers his peace to his disciples as a gift: "Peace I leave with you; my peace I give you" (Jn 14:27; cf. Jn 20:19, 21, 26).

Preeminently, the New Testament teaches that our peace with God and one another has been established by God's reconciling work in Christ. This is why Paul can refer to the gospel as the "gospel of peace" (Eph 6:15), to God as "the God of peace" (Rom 15:33; 16:20; Phil 4:9; 1 Thess 5:23; cf. 2 Cor 13:11; Heb 13:20) and to Jesus as "the Lord of peace" (2 Thess 3:16). The Christian good news is that God has reconciled the world in Christ, thereby re-establishing genuine *shalom* between God and the creation. Speaking of Christ, Paul writes, "For in him all the fullness of God was pleased to dwell, and through him God was pleased to reconcile to himself all things, whether on earth or in heaven, by making peace through the blood of his cross" (Col 1:19-20; cf. Rom 5:1). Yet Paul insists that being reconciled to God brings wholeness not only to our relationship with God but also to our relationships with others. This is affirmed most powerfully in Paul's letter to the Ephesians, where he addresses the way in which the hostility between Jew and Gentile has been abolished in Christ:

> But now in Christ Jesus you who once were far off have been brought near by the blood of Christ. *For he is our peace*; in his flesh he has made both groups into one and has broken down the dividing wall, that is, the hostility between us. He has abolished the law with its commandments and ordinances, that he might create in himself one new humanity in place of the two, *thus making peace*, and might reconcile both groups to God in one body through the cross, thus putting to death that hostility through it. So he came and *proclaimed peace* to you who were far off and to those who were near, for through him both of us have access in one Spirit to the Father. So then you are no longer strangers and aliens, but you are citizens with the saints and also members of the household of God, built upon the foundation of the apostles and prophets, with Christ Jesus himself as the cornerstone. In him the whole structure is joined together and grows into a holy temple in the Lord; in whom you also are built together spiritually into a dwelling place for God. (Eph 2:13-22, emphasis added)

The imagery of the temple is striking. Because of Christ, the Gentiles could no longer be excluded from the people of God or given second-class status by being restricted to the Court of the Gentiles. Rather than being excluded from the central practices of temple worship, the Gentiles had now, because of Christ, become fellow stones with the Jews in that living and holy temple called the church. Whatever hostility had existed before was now abolished in the very body of Christ, which brought them together to form a new and culturally revolutionary dwelling place for God. Out of two peoples whose hostility toward each other was legendary, God had established one new humanity. Here we have what is perhaps the most powerful and moving example in all of Scripture of the connection between peace and wholeness. With such a radical transformation taking place in their midst, it is little wonder that the early Christians began to regard Jesus as the promised "Prince of Peace" (Is 9:6).

If God has established peace by reconciling us both to God and to one another in Christ, then we must do all we can to embody visibly the unity and harmony that are the hallmarks of our new life of peace. Not surprisingly, this peace is closely allied with love and joyful thanksgiving.

> Above all, clothe yourselves with love, which binds everything together in perfect harmony. And let the peace of Christ rule in your hearts, to which indeed you were called in the one body. And be thankful. (Col 3:14-15)

Furthermore, living peaceably requires that we pay attention to the life of Jesus, who refused to participate in the cycle of sin-violence-vengeance-death and who urged his followers to do the same. In words that echo Jesus' Sermon on the Mount, Paul offers the following admonition to the Romans:

> Bless those who persecute you; bless and do not curse them. Rejoice with those who rejoice, weep with those who weep. Live in harmony with one another, do not be haughty, but associate with the lowly; do not claim to be wiser than you are. Do not repay anyone evil for evil, but take thought for what is noble in the sight of all. If it is possible, so far as it depends on you, live peaceably with all. Beloved, never avenge yourselves, but leave room for the wrath of God. (Rom 12:14-19; cf. Mt 5:38-48)

Perhaps this is also the thrust of the passage from James quoted at the beginning of this chapter. Rather than participating in the cycle of violence, Christians participate in a different cycle made possible by God: peace-righteousness-peace. God's reconciling work brings peace, which enables us to live righteously before God and at peace with one another. So as James suggests, the fruit of righteousness grows when the seed of peace is sown, suggesting that the relationship between peace and righteousness is not strictly a one-way affair. Righteousness leads to peace, but peace also leads to righteousness.

Although peace is first of all a gift from God, it is also something to be pursued. We perhaps understand this seeming paradox best by returning to our horticultural metaphor: God brings growth, but the farmer's work remains crucial. So although Christians are right to affirm that God brings peace and wholeness as a gift, we should never take this to mean that what we do is unimportant. Indeed, Jesus insists that making peace so deeply reflects the character of God that those who do so are called "children of God"

(Mt 5:9). Similarly, Scripture admonishes us to strive for and to pursue peace (Ps 34:14; 2 Tim 2:22; 1 Pet 3:11; 2 Pet 3:14; cf. Rom 14:19).

Pursuing peace and being a peacemaker are lifelong tasks. At present we only experience in part the peace and wholeness of God made possible in Christ. Nevertheless, there is much that we can do to cultivate this peace and wholeness. Paul plainly tells the Philippians where to place their energies if they desire to be drawn ever nearer to the God of peace:

> Finally, beloved, whatever is true, whatever is honorable, whatever is just, whatever is pure, whatever is pleasing, whatever is commendable, if there is any excellence and if there is anything worthy of praise, think about these things. Keep on doing the things that you have learned and received and heard and seen in me, and the God of peace will be with you. (Phil 4:8-9)

Paul believed that there was much that Christians should "keep on doing" if they expected the God of peace to be with them. Even so, this process of sanctification—of bringing all of us to complete wholeness—is ultimately in God's hands. And we have every reason to believe that God will not be done with us until this work is finished, until we are utterly and completely whole and at peace. Thus Paul's prayer for the Thessalonians is apt:

> May the God of peace himself sanctify you entirely, and may your spirit and soul and body be kept sound and blameless at the coming of our Lord Jesus Christ. The one who calls you is faithful, and he will do it. (1 Thess 5:23-24)

Obstacles to a Life of Peace

The vision of *shalom* that emerges from the pages of Scripture stands in stark contrast to most of our lives. For most people in the United States life is marked not by peace or wholeness, but by severe and often debilitating fragmentation. The reasons for this are numerous and varied, but much of it stems from the very way in which life in societies like ours is structured. In short, fragmentation is a byproduct of our *politics*. By *politics* I do not mean that relatively narrow realm that we have come to associate with that word, a realm that involves such things as political parties and platforms, periodic elections and the exercise of power through legislation. Instead, I am speaking of *politics* in its broader and more classical sense, which refers to the myriad ways in which groups of people order their lives together. Although politics in this broader sense certainly includes politics in the narrower sense, the broader sense includes a great deal more.

It takes only a moment's reflection to consider how our daily lives are ordered and enriched by innumerable political agreements we take for granted. For example, most of us think it a good thing that there are rules about which side of the street we may drive on, how fast we may drive through a school zone and what we should do at a red light. Most of us think it a good thing that there are health regulations that pertain to the food we purchase and eat, the airplanes on which we fly, and the buildings in which we work and sleep. Most of us think it a good thing that there is an agreed upon method of determining the time of day, one's account balance at the bank and the legal boundaries of one's property. These and countless other ways in which our lives are ordered are the stuff of politics. Although such political agreements in themselves do not bring us peace or wholeness, they do at least keep some of the chaos at bay, which most of us rightly think is a good thing. But not every feature of our ordered life together is as concrete as red lights or building codes. Equally important to the political order are the unspoken convictions that govern our day-to-day lives. In this respect liberal democratic societies such as ours have their own peculiar characteristics.

This section examines some of the political convictions and their respective practices, virtues and narratives that make the United States what it peculiarly is, especially with a view toward the threats that these pose to the cultivation of Christian peace. This section focuses on convictions not only because these infuse our practices, virtues and narratives but also because these particular convictions are notoriously difficult to articulate.

Dividing the world into public and private spheres. What makes societies like ours *liberal* democratic societies is that their citizens take for granted, regardless of party affiliation, several tenets of classical liberal political philosophy. First, the primary political unit is the *individual.* For societies like ours nothing is considered more fundamental, more bedrock, than the individual person. Second, the role of government is to maximize individual *freedom and autonomy,* stepping in only when the exercise of such freedom clearly violates the recognized rights of another. In other words, in societies like ours, governments are justified in curtailing individual freedom and autonomy only when it becomes obvious that failing to intervene would cause greater harm. (This is the justification, for example, for removing children from abusive situations.) And finally, the state is obliged to remain *neutral* on substantive questions about which there is no widespread agreement—such as the purposes of human life and the shape of morality—unless these questions can be articulated in the language of *rights*. Hence, although our society seems to share no agreed upon view of the purposes of human life, we do seem to agree that we should appeal to the language of "rights" whenever we wish to make a strong public claim that harm has been done. (Witness, for example, that both "sides" of the abortion debate routinely appeal to the language of "rights," whether it be "the right to choose" or the baby's "right to life.")

These political assumptions, along with certain cultural assumptions about what counts for genuine knowledge, combine to divide the political landscape into two distinct spheres. One is the public sphere of facts, where widespread agreements in language, cultural habits and purpose make possible the identification of certain things *as* facts. For example, most people would consider it a "fact" that you are reading a book published by InterVarsity Press. However, a number of things must be in place before identifying this as a fact becomes relatively unproblematic. It assumes that you know what a book is, what it is for and the role of publishers in the process. It also assumes that you know how to distinguish a book published by InterVarsity Press from one published by someone else. What makes this fact a "fact," therefore, is not that it is self-evident to everyone, but that there are agreed upon ways to settle disagreements about it.

Distinct from this public sphere of facts is the private one of opinions, preferences and values. This sphere includes all those aspects of life that we either (1) believe it *unnecessary* to agree about, or (2) *cannot* agree about, likely because we do not have an agreed upon method for adjudicating disagreements. An example of the first type is the vast entertainment and leisure options available to many people. No method exists for determining which forms of leisure are in principle better than others since most of us think it unnecessary even to entertain the question at all. People are simply free to choose those forms of leisure that they think best for the reasons that they think count. The most relevant example of the second type is the arena we call "religion." Here liberal democratic orders are believed to have made an important contribution to modern political arrangements. Since people cannot agree on so-called "religious" matters, not least because they cannot agree on how to settle disagreements about them, this realm is routinely relegated to the private sphere, where people are free to make their own determinations. This has the obvious advantage of keeping the state from interfering with matters that many people believe are too important to be left in its hands. But there is also an obvious disadvantage: by relegating religion to the private sphere, liberal democratic societies tend to trivialize Christian convictions by encouraging their advocates to view them as little more than private preferences. As a result, abiding differences among different religions and among practitioners of the same religion are often considered on a par with one's personal preferences for certain vegetables. In other words, many people believe that the person who prefers Christianity to Theravada Buddhism is simply making a choice that is roughly akin to preferring green beans to broccoli.

In liberal democratic societies, therefore, most differences within the private realm are considered as little more than matters of personal preference and style. What are some of the consequences of such a political conviction? Perhaps most importantly, dividing our lives into public and private spheres creates an enormous fissure in both our corporate and personal lives. To see the fragmentation that results from this way of dividing up the world, we need only imagine the following scenarios:

☐ You are employed at a job that requires you to do things that are legal but which you find less than ethical. You don't like doing them, but you remind yourself frequently that this is part of the job and that you and your family have to eat. Besides, you also know that as soon as you clock out you can go home, get comfortable, plop down in front of the television and "be yourself." Your home is your castle, your haven, where you are most free to be "you."

But if the "public you" at work for forty hours each week isn't the "real (private) you," then who is it? And just as importantly, what is the connection between these different "yous"?

☐ You are at the bookstore, video-store or music store. On what basis do you determine what to purchase? How many of us read certain books, watch certain movies, or listen to certain music "in the privacy of our own homes" that we would not be entirely comfortable reading, watching or listening to in the ("public") company of our Christian friends? (I should underscore that the point of this example is *not* to level one more diatribe against certain activities, but to suggest how often we appeal, even if unconsciously, to this division between public and private spheres.)

☐ You are having a serious discussion with one of your peers about human sexuality. Once it begins to be apparent that the two of you have deep disagreements, the discussion rapidly deteriorates, with one or both of you trying to deflect criticism by exclaiming, "Well, that's just your opinion!" Both of you realize that this exclamation is not an invitation to further dialogue. The discussion is over, because everyone in our culture recognizes that "people are entitled to their own opinions." Arguing over what people consider to be opinions is as futile as arguing over one's preferred vegetables. We might not like someone else's tastes, but we usually acknowledge that nothing is to be gained by arguing about them. As the old Latin proverb states: *de gustibus non est disputandum* ("There is no disputing about tastes").

This last example illustrates the close connection between the conviction that the world can be divided into public and private spheres and the conviction that people are entitled to their own opinions. Certain public conversations are expected to get nowhere because they involve what are widely believed to be privately held opinions. This conviction is so common-place that its self-evident nature cloaks its underlying assumptions. The private world is the world of opinions, which are personal and therefore exempt from critique. Because they are exempt from critique, most people assume that one set of opinions is just as good as any other as long as they are sincerely held. This leveling of all opinions ahead of time often appears to make discussion at best frustrating and at worst pointless.

What happens when even our most deeply held convictions are relegated to the status of opinions, preferences or tastes? More often than not this strips them of their power to function *as* convictions, which is nothing less than the power to shape our daily decisions and potentially those of others as well. Moreover, if one crucial feature that makes a community possible and gives it its depth is a sense of shared convictions (and not just shared personal opinions, preferences or tastes), then perhaps the current eclipse of authentic community is partly attributable to our inability to see the important role that convictions play in nurturing and sustaining a common life. If this is true, then paradoxically this shared conviction about opinions does not necessarily draw people together but often divides them by encouraging people to think of their "opinions" as inhabiting their own private and therefore sacrosanct domain. The result is that people come to believe that their convictions, because they are private, are immune from criticism.

My hunch is that many people reading this book will have experienced the deep tension created by holding the above convictions while trying to remain a disciple of Jesus Christ. Most of us realize that being a follower of Jesus has implications for *all* aspects of our lives, not just a few "private" or "religious" ones. But trying to embody such integrity (that is, a fully integrated life) is difficult in a society that cultivates fragmentation rather than the wholeness of *shalom*.

The problem, of course, is not just "out there," that is, in the wider culture. The church itself often contributes to the privatization of our Christian faith. For example, when one speaks of one's "personal relationship with Jesus," one can easily (and often does) mean one's own private relationship. Thus we have personal pan pizzas, personal computers and personal relationships with Jesus. Many Christians seem to believe that having an individual and private relationship with Christ is the bedrock of Christian faith. The church is nice if it helps, but it certainly isn't essential to who I am as a Christian. This may account for why so many self-professed Christians believe they can be perfectly good Christians apart from the church. It may also account for why even those who are part of a congregation admit to being involved primarily as a means of supporting that which is more fundamental: their individual—

and many times private—relationship with Jesus. This also helps to explain why most Christians find the notion of church discipline so incomprehensible. When the issue *is* broached (a situation that is itself rare and therefore telling), Christians find themselves asking, What *right* does the church have to examine my personal or private relationship with Jesus? Here we see that most Christians have dragged their commitment to political liberalism—with its conviction that the individual is the primary political unit—right into the sanctuary.

Christians have also been more than willing to identify themselves as adherents of a particular religion. But in our culture "religion" defines a sphere that is fundamentally private and personal. Many Christians often reflect this way of thinking, for example, in the way in which they presume that Christianity concerns something called the "spiritual" realm (which certainly sounds like it ought to be invisible), while other, more "material" (and presumably nonspiritual) concerns such as politics and economics, remain peripheral. But we also see this in the way many Christians think about conversion. Most Christians at other times and places believed that disciples of Christ needed to make a public profession of faith. But with the privatization of the Christian faith, people are now often encouraged to pray a silent prayer to themselves (and presumably to God) in order to welcome Jesus into their hearts. No one else need know of this decision; it is strictly a matter between that individual and God.

As significant as the above convictions are in contributing to our sense of fragmentation, they are not the whole picture. We are also daily engaged in numerous political practices that cultivate and embody certain political virtues and narratives, all of which contribute to our plight. Because several of these have been alluded to or assumed in the above discussion, only brief mention is necessary.

Compartmentalizing life. The conditions of modern life have created seemingly autonomous spheres, each with its own rules, its own norms and its own expectations. For example, the rules and norms that govern the workplace are not widely accepted to be the same rules and norms that should shape our family and church life. And because each of us is forced to negotiate more than one sphere, we find ourselves constantly being pressured to conform to whatever is expected in that sphere. Moreover, in the course of a week or a month many of us find ourselves in a staggering number of different situations, and in many of those our complete anonymity is presumed if not guaranteed. These situations, coupled with our desire for novelty, often entice us to be someone else, to try on a new identity or to engage in what would normally be viewed (by us and those who know us) as uncharacteristic behavior. (It is hardly coincidence that business people who travel widely and regularly often succumb to the temptations of unfaithfulness and deceit.) Finally, rarely do we deal with the same group of people across these spheres or situations. As noted earlier, we often work, commute, live, eat, worship, shop, vacation and pursue common interests or hobbies with quite different sets of people. As a result, it's easy to be a "different" person in each of these spheres.

Within such contexts a premium is placed on cultivating the virtue of plasticity. In other words, in a cultural environment like ours the ability and willingness to adapt fluidly to one's situation appears to pay handsome dividends, especially in the short run (which is, of course, where most of us specialize). In some circles this creation and maintenance of multiple selves and identities has come to be known as "multiphrenia." And although some inhabitants of contemporary societies find this "freedom" exhilarating, others find themselves torn by these fragmented identities.

Such fragmentation does not leave our embodiments of the Christian faith unscathed. To put all of this in more conventional lingo, we might say that even though the variety of plant known as the "Sunday Christian" is not now making its first appearance in the world, the environment in which we live strongly favors such forms of Christian life. Without some attempt to cultivate a different understanding and embodiment of the Christian life, our attempts at discipleship will quite naturally be circumscribed within the arena of private religion, and the power that the Spirit might have to shape our behavior in all areas of life will be effectively dissipated.

Propagating interest-group politics. More than one commentator on contemporary life has observed that our political life is ordered by what is commonly called "interest-group" politics. Within such a scheme like-minded individuals band together to form lobbying groups that seek to advance legislation that is considered to be in that particular group's best interest. During the past few decades we have seen an enormous proliferation of interest groups like the American Association of Retired Persons, the American Medical Association, the National Rifle Association, the Sierra Club and the Christian Coalition. Such a system is often defended in the same way in which free-market economies are defended, by the so-called invisible hand. The assumption in both is that if each person looks out for his or her own interests, then everyone's interests will be secured. That most of us have been formed to think this way is why politicians often ask us such blatantly self-serving questions as, "Are you better off today than you were four years ago?" We are rarely, if ever, encouraged to consider what would be good for anyone else, especially if what would be genuinely good for them would require some sacrifice on our part. As a result, "politics" no longer involves the search for the common good, but a competition between warring factions, each bent on securing or protecting its own interests. All of this contributes to the further fragmentation of our lives, both as individuals and as a society.

Because our lives are so fragmented and because we are so accustomed to viewing issues in terms of our own interests, we commonly bring our multiple selves into the church and expect them to be serviced. This often creates strife between factions who see themselves competing for limited resources and attention. Who am I when I gather with others as the body of Christ? Am I primarily a young married man with a family whose utmost concern is to insure that my family's "spiritual" needs are met, even if this means going toe-to-toe with the college group or the retired-person's group? Or am I in some way part of a larger whole where the parts are best understood not as in competition with each other, but as engaged in mutual service for the welfare of the entire body?

Interest-group politics affect not only the way we relate to each other in the church but also the way we think of our relationship to the wider society. Too often Christians function as little more than one more interest group vying for their own interests and agenda. As a result, we find ourselves offering not an alternative vision of how God would have us live together that is rooted in God's peace or wholeness, but merely a legislative agenda we would like to see advanced that would make us feel more at home in society.

Defending our rights. As suggested above, the primary moral language of contemporary life is that of "rights." For example, we know from our country's founding documents that one of our "inalienable" rights is the pursuit of happiness and that we are free to pursue it as long as we do not violate the recognized rights of others. But such a way of thinking and acting creates a culture of fear and suspicion. In short, the assumption behind "rights" language is that we need to be protected from one another. By encouraging us to view each other as potential threats to our well-being, we inadvertently create a culture that thrives on adversarial relationships. One obvious manifestation of this is our society's current obsession with lawsuits. Such a climate of fear and suspicion cultivates habits of noninvolvement. I know of many people, for example, who will not stop to help a person with a medical emergency for fear of being sued.

The language of rights is likely essential in a society like ours, since it often serves to protect minorities from the will of the majority. Plenty of times in our country's past the language of rights has been an important touchstone in debates about how people should be treated. This has also been the case in the world arena, where disagreements are often deep and seemingly intractable. Given the prevalence of rights language and its usefulness in certain situations, Christians often have a difficult time seeing why the language of rights is not the church's first language. As a result, the language of rights often appears in odd places in our corporate life. For example, many Christians believe they have the right to interpret Scripture in whatever way they see fit. Others believe that they have the right to have their preferred style of music played during worship. Still others believe that they have a right to certain services or church programs. For example, I once heard a group of single adults complain that their rights were violated when the church planned a retreat for married couples without planning a comparable retreat for them. Given that the language of rights is rooted in the notion that people need to be protected from each other, it seems safe to say that when people in the church find themselves appealing to the language of rights, something has gone terribly wrong.

Sanctioning violence. Though the violence that characterizes our culture will be discussed more fully in a later chapter, we might pause here to consider briefly the ways in which fragmentation and suspicion foster violence. Rather than seeing violence primarily as that which occasionally interrupts our otherwise placid lives, perhaps we can see how violence is all but a natural consequence of a context that is characterized by deep-seated fragmentation and suspicion. If something like this is not the case, then how else do we explain our capacity for violence against not only those whom we admit to disliking but also—and even more disturbingly—against those we claim to love? Or asked more bluntly, how is it possible that Christians can abuse their spouses and children on Saturday night and then drive off to church the next morning in their Sunday best as if nothing had happened? It seems to me that several pertinent factors contribute to such a phenomenon. Once I see myself primarily as an individual; once I regard everyone else (including my own family members) as a potential threat to my own well-being; once I am schooled to think of my life as a conglomerate of disconnected spheres of which my Christian faith is only one among many; once I am trained to view any objections to my way of life as merely rooted in somebody else's opinion; and once I am encouraged to regard the wholeness or harmony that people seek as rooted in a view of justice that entails people getting what they deserve; then the way is cleared for me to employ and sanction violence (in any of its various forms) in whatever ways seem most likely to offer me the security and stability that my fragmented life continually denies me.

In sum, there are few voices in contemporary life that would encourage us to try to narrate our lives in any coherent way. Indeed, the most prominent voices seem to be those assuring us that such integration is no longer possible. These stories about the rise of the modern world and about the increasing fragmentation of contemporary life insist that to try to pull together all the fragments of our lives into any kind of whole is a mistake; one simply needs to learn how to dwell in the newly emerging world where the search for fixed and stable identities is understood as a form of pathology. Perhaps those who say this are right. Perhaps it is a mistake to try to pull together all the fragments of our lives into some kind of whole. But Christians, when they have been at their best, have not told that kind of story. Our story is not one of heroic action taken on our part to salvage our hopelessly fragmented lives. Rather, the good news is that God has stepped in and offered us resources to live in ways that are unthinkable apart from God. The good news is that God has intervened and made it possible for us to live lives that are a foretaste of the wholeness that is promised when God's kingdom comes in all its fullness.

Cultivating Peace

In a culture that aggressively cultivates fragmentation, strife and violence, Christians are in dire need of resources that can be used to cultivate a way of life that more adequately reflects the character of the God to whom our lives bear witness. By the grace of God such resources do exist. Here are some places where we might begin such cultivation.

Incorporating baptism. Reflecting on this central practice may offer the church a valuable resource for countering the drift toward increased fragmentation. In many Christian traditions baptism is understood as a participation in the death of Christ. In baptism we are *all* called to die. The classic passage is found in Paul's letter to the Romans:

> Do you not know that all of us who have been baptized in Christ Jesus were baptized into his death? . . . We know that our old self was crucified with him so that the body of sin might be destroyed, and we might no longer be enslaved to sin. (6:3, 6)

What Paul calls crucifying the "old self," which entails crucifying our sinful desires and ways of life, is necessary whether one has a single "self" or many fragmented selves. According to Paul, this death of our wayward desires makes possible a whole new way of being that the world does not know. As Paul writes to the Galatians, "I have been crucified with Christ, and it is no longer I who live, but it is Christ who lives in me" (Gal 2:20).

But baptism is wrongly understood if it is understood merely as the act of an isolated individual. Rather, baptism involves incorporation into the body of Christ. As such, baptism stands as a sign of a new politics, a new way of ordering our lives together (Gal 3:27-28). Paul reminds the Corinthians: "In the one Spirit we were all baptized into one body" (1 Cor 12:13). This suggests strongly that it is a mistake to drive a wedge between the body of Christ and its constituent body parts. The body parts are not more fundamental than the body as a whole any more than the body is more fundamental than its parts. You cannot have one without the other; they mutually constitute each other. This is only one important lesson that reflecting on the metaphor of the church as the body of Christ might teach us. Given the rampant individualism that pervades much congregational life, the contemporary church in this country would do well to reflect seriously on this metaphor. For example:

☐ Bodies are wrongly understood if their parts are considered to be in some way more fundamental than the body itself. The parts exist to serve the well-being of the entire body, a well-being in which each part participates and facilitates to the extent that it looks beyond its own immediate welfare.

☐ Bodies are wrongly understood if they are regarded as conglomerates of parts that have their own integrity apart from the body. No one would mistake a severed finger on the sidewalk for a body. Such a condition is not only a problem for the part but a problem for the entire body.

☐ Bodies are wrongly understood if their parts are considered to have unmediated access to the head. Each body part facilitates and participates in vital connections to the head, yet none can sustain this connection to the head alone.

I realize that such statements may make us squirm, for they are a direct challenge to the way many of us have come to view the Christian life. Although a later chapter will discuss the body metaphor at greater length, here we should note that the vision of the church as the body of Christ, with Christ as the head, offers us an extremely potent image that God might use to heal this fragmented body. Such an understanding of our corporate identity might give new urgency to Paul's admonition to make "every effort to maintain the unity of the Spirit in the bond of peace" (Eph 4:3). This leads us to one of the seeming paradoxes of the Christian faith: when we die to self and the desires of the flesh, we live at peace with God and each other. In short, death brings life. "For those who live according to the flesh set their minds on the things of the flesh, but those who live according to the Spirit set their minds on the things of the Spirit. To set the mind on the flesh is death, but to set the mind on the Spirit is life and peace" (Rom 8:5-6).

As a central and abiding practice of the church, baptism is a public and political act that announces to the world our change of allegiance and proclaims to our fellow members our interdependence as members of the one body of Christ. Once such a radically "political" view of the church is in place, several other political practices take on added urgency.

Edifying one another. As the passage from Romans 14 that opens this chapter suggests, Christians are urged to view their freedom in Christ not as a private possession, but as an opportunity to build up the body of Christ. Just as Paul admonishes the Philippians to be like Christ in looking out first of all for the interests of others (2:4-5), so Paul, in his well-known warning about causing a brother or sister to stumble, urges the Romans not to use their freedom as an opportunity for sowing discord and confusion within the church.

Paul's understanding of the church as an alternative *polis,* as an alternative way of ordering social life, also stands behind his instructions to the Corinthians about lawsuits. How is it possible, Paul asks, that Christians would allow their disputes with one another to be judged by the principles and standards of the pagan courts? Such a practice is thinkable, Paul seems to suggest, only if the Christians of Corinth hold in disdain their deep connection with their brothers and sisters in favor of defending their own personal rights and interests. "In fact, to have lawsuits at all with one another is already a defeat for you. Why not rather be wronged? Why not rather be defrauded?" (1 Cor 6:7). Of course, our knee-jerk response to Paul's questions is simple, "Because I've got my rights, that's why not." But to answer in such a fashion is merely to assert that our primary citizenship is in another *polis,* a *polis* where other people are regarded as threats and where one's first task is to safeguard one's own well-being. In contrast, this new *polis* made possible by Christ is one where the well-being of each member of the body of Christ is secured, but not by that member itself. Rather, like any well-functioning body, each member is intimately connected with other members who nurture and sustain it. Only such a body is marked by *shalom,* wholeness and salvation.

Admonishing one another. It is only within the broader political framework of the body of Christ that we dare raise the possibility (let alone the advisability) of mutual admonition. As long as we hold on to the illusion that we are primarily individuals who stand alone before God, attempts by other Christians to admonish or correct us will feel like an unwarranted imposition. "Who are you to admonish me?" we find ourselves saying. "It's none of your business. It's between me and God." Such a view makes perfectly good sense in a society where we have been trained since birth to think of ourselves primarily as individuals. But such a view won't do once we have been incorporated into the body of Christ.

Jesus did not come to bring a cheap peace, nor did Jesus come to turn a blind eye to deep-rooted problems or divisions. Although a cease-fire may be preferable to all-out war, a cease-fire is not peace. Indeed, Jesus clearly states that on one level his coming will not bring peace but division: "Do you think that I have come to bring peace to the earth? No, I tell you, but rather division. From now on five in one household will be divided, three against two and two against three" (Lk 12:51-52; cf. Mt 10:34). Jesus *doesn't* say what we would have liked for him to have said, "My coming has abolished any need for conflict and confrontation. I just want you all to live in harmony, so feel free simply to ignore each other's shortcomings and faults (and your own!) and above everything else, be nice to each other."

A friend of mine has a "lazy eye," that condition where one eye seems to stray a bit, almost as if it had a mind of its own. Although it's a bit unnerving the first time you talk to someone with such a condition, one can only imagine what a ghastly sight it would be if *every* body part had its own agenda, if *every* body part "had a mind of its own." In contrast to such a state we are called to have the mind of Christ, who directs our common activities toward a common purpose. If our common life is to serve as an embodied sign of God's present and coming reign, then the sickness of any body part is a concern of the whole body. As Paul reminds the Corinthians, "If one member suffers, all suffer together with it; if one member is honored, all rejoice together with it" (1 Cor 12:26).

We all know that the manner in which we offer and receive admonition makes all the difference in the world. If our attempts at admonition are framed by the reigning politics of our culture, such correction will be offered and received in an adversarial spirit. The one doing the correction will come across as self-righteous and the one receiving the correction will feel rejected. But if our attempts at mutual admonition are framed by the politics of the body of Christ—if we truly believe that we are in this struggle together and that at another time and place the roles of admonisher and admonishee will need to be reversed—then we have reason to hope that God will use our clumsy efforts to bring a greater measure of well-being to the entire body.

Nevertheless, we need to be honest about how difficult it will be for the church to begin engaging in such a practice again. Given the way most of us have been formed by our culture, there is no reason to believe that our experience of being admonished will be anything other than painful and awkward. We're used to going our own way and to assuming that no one will interfere with our lives. With such expectations firmly implanted within us, someone's intervening for the health of the body will inevitably feel like an imposition. At such times we would do well to remember the words of Hebrews: "Now, discipline always seems painful rather than pleasant at the time, but later it yields the peaceful fruit of righteousness to those who have been trained by it" (Heb 12:11).

Forgiving one another. The good news that Christians have to tell is this: God is in the process of restoring the created order to a state of harmony and order. This harmony and order, which we might name in many different ways—*shalom,* justice, righteousness—is rooted in God's superabundant grace, a grace we see most clearly in God's gift of forgiveness in Jesus Christ. This is truly good news! Yet as good as this is, it is only part of the story. God's intent was not that this one divine act of forgiveness would itself magically transform the creation into God's intended paradise. Rather, this supreme act of forgiveness in Christ is the very large rock dropped into the middle of a pond. The resulting ripples are not themselves the rock, but they are inexplicable apart from it. In the same way God calls us to extend his forgiveness demonstrated on the cross into all areas of our lives.

This well-known note—that we are called to be forgiving people because we ourselves have been forgiven—must continually be sounded, for too often we are like the unmerciful servant in Jesus' parable (Mt 18:23-35). Rejoicing that God in Christ has made it possible for *us* not to get what *we* deserve, we immediately rush out and insist that everyone else in the world get what *they* have coming to them. In acting thus we usually commend ourselves for upholding God's justice. But if God's justice, God's *shalom*, God's plan to restore order and harmony to all of creation, has at its very heart God's forgiveness of me, might it not also include God's forgiveness (and my forgiveness?) of those who have wronged me? And if I refuse such forgiveness in the name of justice, is it possible that my view of justice falls short of God's view, where justice, *shalom*, wholeness and salvation are not opposing goals, but different names for God's singular desire?

At the end of the book of Hosea we are offered a powerful vision of God's *shalom*, God's wholeness, God's salvation. Through the prophet Hosea, God calls Israel to turn away from trusting in foreign nations and idols and return to the true God, who alone offers healing and subsequent fruitfulness:

> I will heal their disloyalty;
>> I will love them freely,
>> for my anger has turned from them.
> I will be like the dew to Israel;
>> he shall blossom like the lily,
>> he shall strike root like the forests of Lebanon.
> His shoots shall spread out;
>> his beauty shall be like the olive tree,
>> and his fragrance like that of Lebanon.
> They shall again live beneath my shadow,
>> they shall flourish as a garden;
> they shall blossom like the vine,
>> their fragrance shall be like the wine of Lebanon. (Hos 14:4-7)

Reflection Questions and Practical Suggestions

☐ Reflect on the ways you experience the distinction between "public" and "private" in your own life. Do you find this a helpful distinction, or does it create unresolved tensions as you think and live in the world? How does the dominant culture's tendency to place "religion" firmly on the "private" side of the divide affect the way you think about and live out your Christian faith? Are you ever tempted to think that the Christian faith is primarily about "me and Jesus"? Do you see any evidence of how the cultural distinction between "public" and "private" affects your church's understanding of its identity and mission in the world?

□ Evaluate your own experience of cultural vertigo and fragmentation that are generated by functioning in a dizzying number of different contexts. Do you ever find yourself creating distinctly different personas as you move among these different settings? (When you travel, for example, or when you visit online "chat" rooms?) Do you remember being primarily troubled or exhilarated by such attempts? Do you think that the fragmentation that marks your life contributes to your willingness to respond harshly or violently in some settings while not in others? For example, do you ever find yourself being more violent in "private" settings, such as your home, than you do in more "public" ones? What do you think accounts for this?

□ Make a list of the different groups of people with whom you regularly associate. In what ways do these groups pull your loyalties and affections in different directions? Are there people in these different groups who know you in more than one setting? For example, do you work with anyone you worship with? Attempt to cultivate at least some friendships that cut across the boundaries that fragment your life. The more people who know you in more than one of these settings, the less you will be tempted to be a "different" person in each of these settings.

□ Do you think it matters whether the church urges people to make a "public" profession of faith or whether it simply encourages people to accept Jesus into their hearts? What difference do you think these different practices have on the way people conceive of the kind of commitment they are making? If your church does not already do so, consider asking those in authority to make baptisms as public and communal as possible. Rightly understood, baptism is neither a private nor an individual affair.

□ Think back on those instances in which you have you heard "rights" language crop up in the church. Do you think this language helped to resolve the matter, or do you think it made matters worse? Do you think Christians should ever use this language in their dealings with one another? In other words, if a Christian has a complaint against another Christian, does it make sense to couch that complaint in terms of rights? Can you imagine other settings or situations in which Christians might legitimately appeal to their or another's rights?

☐ Reflect on your previous experiences with admonition and correction in the church. Can you think of examples where such admonition was edifying to yourself or another? Can you think of examples when you or someone else found it harmful? What factors do you believe account for these different outcomes? Try to learn from these experiences as you seek to open yourself once again to mutual admonition and correction.

If the church in our day is to recover the practice of mutual admonition, such a recovery will take place not when certain self-appointed Christians begin correcting those around them, but when Christians who recognize the importance of mutual admonition begin giving each other permission to examine their lives. With this in mind, consider talking to a brother or sister in Christ who knows you well about the importance of mutual admonition, giving them permission to admonish you when they see something in your life that needs attention.

☐ In the same spirit and with a renewed sense of your own frailties and shortcomings, begin to make a list of people from whom you have withheld forgiveness. Our unwillingness to forgive is often rooted as much in our own pride (we don't believe *we* need to be forgiven) as much as it is in our being hurt. With the grace of God and your own sinfulness in view, resolve to offer those on your list the same forgiveness you have received from Christ. Further steps toward reconciliation might include writing these persons a letter asking them to forgive you for withholding from them the grace and forgiveness of Christ.

☐ Finally and above all else, remember that God's ultimate desire is to heal your broken and fragmented life, and to present you whole and complete. God's ultimate desire is to bring peace, reconciliation and wholeness to the entire created cosmos, of which we are but a small—but nonetheless significant—part. Pray that God will use the church not only as an instrument of that peace but also as a sign and foretaste of the reconciliation made possible in Jesus Christ.

Now may the God of peace, who brought back from the dead our Lord Jesus, the great shepherd of the sheep, by the blood of the eternal covenant, make you complete in everything good so that you may do his will, working among us that which is pleasing in his sight, through Jesus Christ, to whom be glory forever and ever. Amen. (Heb 13:20)

FIVE

Cultivating Patience in the Midst of Productivity

We know that the whole creation has been groaning in labor pains until now, and not only the creation, but we ourselves, who have the first fruits of the Spirit, groan inwardly while we wait for adoption, the redemption of our bodies. For in hope we were saved. Now hope that is seen is not hope. For who hopes for what is seen? But if we hope for what we do not see, we wait for it with patience. (Rom 8:22-25)

Be patient, therefore, beloved, until the coming of the Lord. The farmer waits for the precious crop from the earth, being patient with it until it receives the early and the late rains. You must also be patient. Strengthen your hearts, for the coming of the Lord is near. Beloved, do not grumble against one another, so that you may not be judged. See, the Judge is standing at the doors! As an example of suffering and patience, beloved, take the prophets who spoke in the name of the Lord. Indeed we call blessed those who showed endurance. You have heard of the endurance of Job, and you have seen the purpose of the Lord, how the Lord is compassionate and merciful. (Jas 5:7-11)

It's hard for me to imagine my day apart from the clock. Before we had small children, the squawking of my alarm clock normally ushered in my day. Now our children wake us early each day, yet I still instinctively glance at the clock during my first few conscious moments, responding to some deep impulse I have to know what time it is. I next stumble to the kitchen, help to fix breakfast for the children and myself, quickly peruse the newspaper, and then take up a few small household tasks, all with an eye on the clock and my schedule. I jump in the shower for seven or eight minutes, dress and leave for school. I know that it usually takes me twelve minutes to drive to work and only ten if I'm not impeded by any stop lights or school zones. I'm one of those people who prides myself on being "on time," and so I likely check my watch more than most. I hate to be late, and I'm often irritated by those who are. I know that I should give myself three-and-a-half minutes to walk (at a brisk pace) from my office to the classroom where I teach and five if I wish to stop by my campus mailbox on the way. I like to start class on time, and I am conscious throughout the class period of the passing of time, checking my watch periodically to see if we are where I think we should be in the material for the day. I eat lunch when my watch and schedule tell me that I should, whether I am particularly hungry or not. I am conscious of when Kim expects me to be home, and I try to be on time. After dinner we have playtime with the children, followed by bath time, reading time and bedtime. If either Kim or I have any energy left, whatever time remains after the children are asleep is "our" time. Is it possible that being such a slave to the clock affects the way we think about and cultivate patience?

By almost any standard, historical or cross-cultural, most people in Western societies embody a most peculiar relationship to time. To see this, it's helpful to contrast our "normal" view with the ways other people think of time. Most of us, for example, would grow impatient with some African cultures where Sunday worship lasts for most of the day, not least because it takes several hours for the congregation to gather from miles around. Because it takes such an enormous effort to gather, it makes little sense to dismiss after only a short time. Such an example suggests how closely our view of time is linked to our ability to master moving from point A to point B in a specified period of time. This sense of (or illusion of) absolute control over our own movements is perhaps accountable for why we regularly get so irritated by unexpected traffic jams and other unexpected "delays." These painfully remind us that we are not always in control. In addition to being actors, we are also being acted *upon* by others. These situations call for patience, but such patience is difficult to cultivate when our lives are constantly regimented by the clock.

The Character of Patience

Most modern English translations render the fourth fruit of the Spirit as "patience." Although such a rendering is appropriate, older versions offered a more vivid translation: "long-suffering." We often speak of people having a "short temper," but we have no contemporary equivalent for having a "long temper." If we did, such a word would be close to the meaning of the Greek word Paul uses in Galatians.

Scripture employs several different words that point to this disposition, words that are often translated as "patience," "forbearance," "endurance" and "steadfastness." The latter two, though certainly connected intimately to patience, often refer to a person's response to persecution and suffering and as such will be discussed later with the fruit of faithfulness. (This reminds us once again that these fruit do not exist in isolation from one another.)

Most of us greatly admire people who endure, who persevere, who stick it out against all odds. Our collective memory overflows with stories about people who persevered in the face of adversity. We love stories of underdogs (such as Olympic athletes) who have triumphed in the face of overwhelmingly difficult circumstances. Many of us wish we had such character, and we are not wrong to admire such people. The Bible repeatedly encourages God's people to endure hardship and persevere. But patience and forbearance are slightly different dispositions than perseverance, and they appear to be less desired and perhaps less admired by our society as a whole. To see this difference one has only to reflect on the noun form: patient. In English this noun refers not only to the character trait but also to the person under the care of a health professional. Indeed, the latter usage developed out of the notion during the Middle Ages that anyone suffering patiently was a "patient." Hence, what "being patient" and "being *a* patient" have in common is this: both require that a person come to terms with yielding control to another. That is, rather than simply viewing oneself as an *actor*, in both instances one has to come to grips with being *acted upon*.

Like all the fruit of the Spirit, patience has its roots in God's character. For example, the Old Testament speaks repeatedly of God being "slow to anger." Indeed, a refrain echoes throughout the Old Testament: "The LORD is merciful and gracious, slow to anger and abounding in steadfast love" (Ps 103:8; cf. Ex 34:6; Num 14:18; Neh 9:17; Ps 86:15; 145:8; Joel 2:13; Jon 4:2; Nahum 1:3). Scripture rarely portrays God as having a hair-trigger temper, a fact that makes the few exceptions where God seems to be so portrayed that much more puzzling. In other words, it is precisely *because* God is so consistently portrayed throughout Scripture as long-suffering that we find it difficult to understand the exceptions, such as the story of God presumably striking Uzzah dead for steadying the ark of the covenant (2 Sam 6:6-7).

The point that is easy to miss in all of this, however, is that God's patience—God's slowness to anger—represents a willingness to yield control. Although most of us may readily admit that God is patient, we may balk at the notion of God yielding control in the ways noted above. Yet Scripture speaks of God in ways that are surprisingly similar. Indeed, it seems that God's very act of creation itself manifests God's willingness to yield control. By creating that which was other than God, God created the space for the creation to go its own way. This situation is familiar to all parents who, in bringing children into the world, soon recognize that their children are not simply extensions of themselves but distinct beings capable of going their own way. Creation always necessitates a willingness to yield at least a measure of control.

Yet there is a further point that must be made about God's willingness to yield control: God doesn't seem to be in a hurry. God doesn't coerce us, doesn't force our hand, but instead waits patiently for us to respond to God's initiatives in reaching out to us. Certainly God's grace enables us to respond, but God's love is patient and does not "insist on its own way" (1 Cor 13:4-5). Thus, however it is that God exercises control over the universe, God does not appear to do it in the ways that we imagine when we glibly proclaim that God is in control. Indeed, as Christians we must come to grips with the implications of the cross of Jesus Christ for our understanding of the character of God. The cross is a startling and humbling reminder that the Lord of the universe does not reign with an iron fist; rather, this sovereign reigns from a tree. Is it possible to imagine a more stunning example of long-suffering than this: the Creator hanging on a tree on behalf of creation?

The book of James, undoubtedly echoing how Scripture speaks of God as being "slow to anger," encourages us to be the same: "You must understand this, my beloved: let everyone be quick to listen, slow to speak, slow to anger, for your anger does not produce God's righteousness" (Jas 1:19-20). A skilled listener knows that listening involves handing over control to another. I often struggle with this as a teacher. During class discussions it's tempting to believe that it's my job to jump in and correct every bit of wrong-headedness that arises. Occasionally I yield to this temptation. But in my better moments I try to be patient with students, realizing that my jumping in at every juncture is only a short-term solution. Unless I can guide students to see what I believe it's important for them to see, no "correction" of their vision will be of any long-term effect. If in the long run I want to help them see matters differently, I have to be willing to be patient, to bring them along slowly, to allow for them to continue to see things as they currently do, yielding control to them all along the way.

Perhaps this willingness to forgo short-term control in service of long-term purposes is similar to what God does. For example, Peter notes the intimate connection between God's patience and our repentance, using the apparent delay of Christ's return as an example of God's different way of reckoning time:

> But do not ignore this one fact, beloved, that with the Lord one day is like a thousand years, and a thousand years are like one day. The Lord is not slow about his promise, as some think of slowness, but is patient with you, not wanting any to perish, but all to come to repentance . . . . Therefore, beloved, while you are waiting for these things, strive to be found by him at peace, without spot or blemish; and regard the patience of our Lord as salvation. (2 Pet 3:8-9, 14)

God's patience does have a purpose; it is not simply restraint for the sake of restraint. God is *slow* to anger, but God does get angry. God bears with people for a time, but a time of judgment is coming. Paul reminds the Jews that being God's chosen people does not exempt them from judgment: "Do you despise the riches of his kindness and forbearance and patience? Do you not realize that God's kindness is meant to lead you to repentance?" (Rom 2:4). Paul even points to his own life as an example of God's patience. After acknowledging that he is foremost among sinners, Paul writes, "But for that very reason I received mercy, so that in me, as the foremost, Jesus Christ might display the utmost patience, making me an example to those who come to believe in him for eternal life" (1 Tim 1:16).

God's patience has not only a purpose but also a clear object. In the New Testament patience typically has a *personal* object: we are called to be patient, not for the sake of patience, but for the sake of another. This other-directedness of patience distinguishes it from stoic resignation, which is an attempt to keep one's life from being disturbed by one's own or another's misfortunes. In contrast, Christians are called to be patient with others *for the sake of* others. Paul notes that God's active love, the kind of love that seeks the good of another, is patient and endures all things (1 Cor 13:4,7). Paul sounds a similar note in his letter to the Romans:

> We who are strong ought to put up with the failings of the weak, and not to please ourselves. Each of us must please our neighbor for the good purpose of building up the neighbor. For Christ did not please himself, but as it is written, "The insults of those who insult you have fallen on me." For whatever was written in former days was written for our instruction, so that by steadfastness and by the encouragement of the scriptures we might have hope. May the God of steadfastness and encouragement grant you to live in harmony with one another, in accordance with Christ Jesus, so that together you may with one voice glorify the God and Father of our Lord Jesus Christ. (Rom 15:1-6)

The connection between peace and patience should now be evident. Patience is a necessary prerequisite for establishing peace. One's willingness to be wronged, to absorb evil patiently without retaliating, helps to break the cycle of vengeance and opens up the possibility for healing and peace. Hence, though forgiveness is a constitutive practice of peace (the act of forgiveness itself helps to constitute peace), forgiveness is unimaginable apart from patience. We see this perhaps most clearly, along with the intimate connection between divine and human patience, in Jesus' parable of the unmerciful servant. The immediate context for this parable—which could just as aptly be called the parable of the impatient (or unforgiving) servant—is Peter's question to Jesus about how many times Peter was obligated to forgive the person who continued to sin against him. Jesus rejects Peter's suggested answer (seven times) and, in suggesting his own (seventy-seven times), hints that Peter's question itself was inappropriate. Jesus then tells the following parable:

> For this reason the kingdom of heaven may be compared to a king who wished to settle accounts with his slaves. When he began the reckoning, one who owed him ten thousand talents was brought to him; and, as he could not pay, his lord ordered him to be sold, together with his wife and children and all his possessions, and payment to be made. So the slave fell on his knees before him, saying, "Have patience with me, and I will pay you everything." And out of pity for him, the lord of that slave released him and forgave him the debt. But that same slave, as he went out, came upon one of his fellow slaves who owed him a hundred denarii; and seizing him by the throat, he said, "Pay what you owe." Then his fellow slave fell down and pleaded with him, "Have patience with me, and I will pay you." But he refused; then he went and threw him into prison until he would pay the debt. When his fellow slaves saw what had happened, they were greatly distressed, and they went and reported to their lord all that had taken place. Then his lord summoned him and said to him, "You wicked slave! I forgave you all that debt because you pleaded with me. Should you not have had mercy on your fellow slave, as I had mercy on you?" And in anger his lord handed him over to be tortured until he would pay his entire debt. So my heavenly Father will also do to every one of you, if you do not forgive your brother or sister from your heart. (Mt 18:23-35)

The echoes of Jesus' petition in the Lord's Prayer—"and forgive us our debts, as we also have forgiven our debtors"—are clear (Mt 6:12). In both cases we are taught that God forgives with the expectation that we will do likewise; to presume otherwise is to assume wrongly that God has forgiven us merely for our own benefit. God has broken the cycle of vengeance and expects us to do the same. Only by patiently forgiving one another do we have any hope of being that community which God has called us to be. Hence, the New Testament connects the virtue of patience with the practice of "bearing with" others in two powerful passages. Paul begs the Ephesians to "lead a life worthy of the calling to which you have been called, with all humility and gentleness, with patience, bearing with one another in love, making every effort to maintain the unity of the Spirit in the bond of peace" (Eph 4:1-3).

The Colossians are given a similar admonition:

> As God's chosen ones, holy and beloved, clothe yourselves with compassion, kindness, humility, meekness, and patience. Bear with one another and, if anyone has a complaint against another, forgive each other; just as the Lord has forgiven you, so you also must forgive. (Col 3:12-13)

Obstacles to a Life of Patience

As noted earlier, at the heart of any culture, of any way of life, is an understanding of time. Usually this understanding is not so much articulated as it is embodied in countless day-to-day activities. Trying to articulate a particular culture's view of time is notoriously difficult, not least because of the mystery that time itself is. Most people who have stopped to consider what time *is* find themselves as perplexed as the fourth century theologian Augustine: "I know well enough what it is, provided that no one asks me; but if I am asked what it is and try to explain, I am baffled."[1] If we could see more clearly the way in which our culture's temporal habits shape our lives, perhaps we would be in a better position to see why patience is so difficult to cultivate in this soil.

Segmenting and regulating time. How we experience time is inseparable from how we measure it. One of the most fascinating topics in cultural anthropology is how different cultures think about, experience and live in time. For example, throughout history most people's view of time has been intimately linked to the rhythms of the created order: the rising and setting of the sun, the phases of the moon, the seasons of the year. For the most part people's days were ordered by the ebb and flow of night and day and by their own mundane activities. We do, however, see examples of other ways of telling time that functioned alongside of these more "natural" ways. For example, in sixteenth-century rural France, time was regularly measured in Aves (the amount of time it takes to recite one Hail Mary).[2] Such a practice of telling time is instructive for at least two reasons. First, it reminds us that precision and uniformity have not always been the most critical issues when it came to telling time. Second, it suggests that there is nothing about *time itself* that requires us to segment it in such "inhumane" ways. That is, this antiquated way of telling time helps us see that the unit of time has not always been something abstract, artificial and lacking any inherent relationship to human life (as is the case with the hour, minute or second), but that it has sometimes been intimately connected to the concrete and vital practices of people's lives, such as prayer. This more fluid and flexible way of conceiving time was changed dramatically with the invention of the mechanical clock, a device developed in the West by Benedictine monks as an aid to their rigorous schedule of prayer and work. Ironically, this invention paved the way for viewing time as something other than a seamless, endless flow. Now time was a resource, something to be segmented, scheduled and managed.

We are so accustomed to thinking of time in this manner, so accustomed to assuming that our way of viewing time is "normal," that we can scarcely get ourselves to realize that this way of thinking about time was invented relatively recently. Those of us who glance at our clocks and wristwatches countless times a day likely find it difficult to imagine that our modern concept of an hour was completely foreign to most people in the Middle Ages. Nor is it easy for us to comprehend that our concept of the second did not appear until the early 1700s. Such historical reminders are important, for they create the critical distance necessary to imagine other ways of understanding time.

There are, of course, obvious advantages to regulating our lives by the clock. Particular kinds of cooperative endeavors are more productive when people are assembled together at the same time. Teaching would in many ways be more frustrating were we to begin class "sometime after breakfast." Who can imagine running a business that employed scores of "hourlies" (a telling category) without having a clock to punch? And how could we possibly organize our evenings around our favorite television shows if we didn't know what time they were being aired? (It is interesting to note, however, that many students admit that it works the other way around: they know what day it is and what time it is by noting what program is on the television. For some people, therefore, the television is itself an instrument for segmenting and organizing time. That people often regulate their daily activities in order to be able to see their favorite shows only underscores the way in which the television is capable of imposing a discipline every bit as rigorous as the clock.)

Yet for all of its advantages the precise segmentation and regulation of time has led to a kind of bondage to the clock. Like so much of culture, that which came into being as our tool is now in danger of becoming our master. Or as Thoreau once remarked, we are in danger of becoming the "tools of our tools." So much of life is regulated by the precision of the clock that it becomes all but impossible to see time as a gift; instead the clock becomes the great taskmaster that cracks the whip to make sure we are where we are supposed to be, when we are supposed to be there.

This bondage to the clock is so much a part of our lives that we usually remain oblivious to it. The times I have been most aware of it were those times when I was suddenly thrust into an environment where clock time meant nothing. Before we had children, Kim and I used to spend several days a year at a cabin tucked away in the mountains of western North Carolina. The cabin had no clocks, no radio and no television. In fact, we always made it a habit of taking off our watches as soon as we arrived. We were always amazed at the difference this made in the way we experienced our days together. And it was a painful reminder of how our days were normally ordered. The words on a small wooden plaque that hung on the cabin wall captured well our own experience: "Time is slow here; a friend, rather than a master."

Hoarding time. As noted above, our increased consciousness of time encourages us to think of it as simply one more resource. Or more likely, it now becomes the most important resource in our possession. I naturally think of "my time" as my own. It is mine to control. It is a possession, a commodity. This conviction is so deeply rooted in our culture that we regard it as a maxim that "time is money." If one doubts the hold that such a commodified view has over us, consider the ways in which we routinely speak about time: we spend time, buy time, save time, waste time, manage time and invest time. Within such an environment how can we learn to experience time as a gift? Ours is not the only culture that is finding this increasingly difficult. Reflecting on life in Southeast Asia, Kosuke Koyama writes:

Time was traditionally experienced as being unlimited as a loving mother's milk is unlimited to her baby. Time was generously given. It was not sold as pork chops are sold. There was no business engagement about time. Time was cyclical, that is to say, calm and levelheaded. . . . It was communal. Indeed, the essence of our experience of time can be said to be a sense of continuity of communal fellowship. We never experienced time in isolation. Apart from community no time existed. . . . Now this has been changed without any consultation with us! Time is now to be understood in terms of business achievement. Time is now located in the export-import companies, motorcycle manufacturers, stores and shops, instead of being in the paddy field, under the coconut trees and in the temple yards. Time is now violently grasped. It was once public community property. It is now private business property. Once it was shared, now it is monopolized. Time does not heal us now. Time wounds us.[3]

Because we routinely view time as our own resource to "spend" as we see fit, interruptions in our daily agenda are inevitably viewed as intrusions. For instance, if I have grasped a two-hour block as my own in order to do some writing, a student who drops by unannounced to discuss a problem is no longer a person but an interruption. And even if I know I shouldn't feel this way, I still often do. Unfortunately, people now expect us to be stingy with our time, which is likely why they find it necessary to always apologize for "taking" so much of our time. Isn't that how we feel? That people have taken (stolen?) from us something that wasn't theirs? Can we really hope to be patient with people as long as we believe that our time is our own? Can we really hope to be patient with people when all too often our assumption (even if unarticulated) is that people are unwelcome intrusions into our preplanned schedules?

Exalting productivity. By precisely segmenting time and transforming it into a scarce resource, the West has created the conditions for the appearance of a new virtue: productivity. Productivity is simply this: a quantifiable amount of work achieved during a specified length of time. The more work per unit of time, the greater the productivity. Few virtues are more exalted in Western societies, a situation that exerts subtle and not-so-subtle pressures on most every citizen. For example, once productivity is regarded as the key benchmark by which we assess our worth, the question that naturally follows is this: What do you have to show for your time? We usually expect the answer to this question to take some tangible form—a paycheck, a grade on a test, a nice meal. But what happens when demands are placed on our time and there is seemingly nothing to show for it? How do we feel? I can still vividly remember the frustration I felt during the three years I worked on my dissertation. Often weeks would go by with little measurable progress. Although I knew Kim understood the frustration I felt, I still found it difficult not to take her well-meaning inquiries as indictments of my lack of productivity. Otherwise, why would her simple question: "How did things go today?" so unnerve me?

As noted in an earlier chapter, many stay-at-home parents (who are in most cases women) experience enormous frustration functioning within a system that validates only that work that is visibly productive and tangibly compensated. What messages does our culture send such a parent about the value of her time and hence even of herself? Are such people "wasting" their time by "spending" it on such things as stacking blocks with their children, reading them books or changing their diapers? What, after all, do they have to show for it at the end of the day? The fact that most of us, myself included, suspect that devoting ourselves fully to such "unproductive" work would have devastating effects on our sense of self-worth, says something profound about how thoroughly most of us have internalized our culture's views about time and productivity.

Kim and I have had a long-running joke in our marriage about "being productive." Neither one of us finds it easy to sit still. Even before we had children, our time was filled with completing tasks that when finished we would dutifully check off of our "to do" lists. This is so much a part of our lives that it has become common for each of us, when asked by the other what we're going to do during the next period of time, to respond mockingly, "Be productive." Simply recognizing our own participation in our culture's "cult of productivity" has not by itself freed us from the grip that cult has on our lives. Nearly every day we fight off feelings of anxiety about devoting ourselves to matters that do not lend themselves to being checked off or that do not yield quantifiable results. For instance, I desire to be a more devoted father and husband, but how do I check that off my "to do" list? I also desire to continue to mature as a Christian for the rest of my life, and I know that growth will likely come slowly and imperceptibly, but how do I think about that in a culture that only counts tangible, measurable results?

One final comment about the connection between time and productivity. Economists and social scientists have long observed that the value of time rises with increased opportunities. In other words, the more options I have for ways to "spend" my time, the more valuable that time becomes. For people with "nothing to do," time is cheap; it is the one commodity of which they have an ample supply. But for those of us whose lives are constantly "busy," time suddenly appears scarce and therefore more valuable. This partly accounts for why we have become the culture of the "disposable": we believe that the time "saved" is more valuable than both the products thrown away and the landfills needed to hold them.

Surely being immersed in this way of life has an impact on whether—or to what extent—our lives bear the fruit of patience. We pride ourselves on being "people of action" who are constantly productive and incessantly busy. With such a mindset firmly implanted, being patient, being willing to be acted upon, understandably looks and feels like passivity. Being patient often feels like weakness, if not death. What could be worse, we wonder, than "doing nothing," which is often what being patient seems to entail?

Or to take a specific example and return to a previous discussion: How many of us feel enormously time-conscious when it comes to our corporate worship? Is it possible that there is a connection between our time-consciousness and our sense that we are engaged in an activity whose productivity is suspect? Does the way we find ourselves talking about worship ("I didn't get anything out of the service today") betray a conviction that worship ought to be productive? (Translation: "Given the time I spent at church today, I'm disappointed that I've nothing more to show for it.") Perhaps our fixation with productivity instills in us a deep sense of impatience, an impatience that might partly be responsible for our lack of joy in worship. How can we joyfully engage in worship if we are continually mindful of all the other more productive things we could be doing with our time (and will be doing once this service is over)?

Perhaps the impatience that characterizes so much of our lives spills over into other areas of our corporate life as well. Do we really have time for each other? And even more specifically, do we have time for those among us who may be an incredible drain on our time and energies? I've been disturbed lately to read in several church newsletters "positive thinking" advice that encourages church members not to let themselves get "bogged down" with depressed and otherwise "negative" people. Is it possible that we've been given the freedom to devote ourselves to one another even if what comes of it cannot be measured in any tangible way? In short, have we been given the freedom to be involved with others in ways that may appear unproductive?

Going faster. If what is said above accurately characterizes our culture, then we can perhaps understand more clearly why our culture places such an enormous premium on speed. Because we have more and more things that we *want* to do with our time, we have less and less time to do the things we *have* to do. Once we regard time as a scarce resource, we then feel the pressure to do whatever needs to be done as quickly as possible. As a result, we have become a society characterized by its love affair with "time-saving" devices. Every year hundreds of products flood the market that promise to save us precious minutes. But what happens to all the time we ostensibly save with all these wonderful gadgets? Don't these devices merely enable us to cram those few extra moments with further attempts to justify our existence by being even *more* productive? In strange and subtle ways, therefore, many of these devices that were supposed to liberate us have instead contributed to our further enslavement. Rather than having more time, we feel as if we actually have less.

How many times have we found ourselves saying or thinking, "If I only had more time, I'd do . . ."? We incessantly complain that we never have enough time. When anyone asks us, our lives are always too busy and too hectic. (When was the last time you heard somebody say, "My life is wonderful. Just the right balance of things to do and time in which to do them"?) If we as a society share a common story, one of its story lines is surely how the pace of life keeps increasing, almost exponentially. Yet I often wonder if we notice how we contribute to this increasingly frenetic pace. We get up in the morning and eat our instant oatmeal and drink our instant coffee. If we're not feeling too rushed, we quickly scan the headlines of the newspaper and read our *One-Minute Bible*. On our way to work we fill up our car with gasoline at the pay-at-the-pump service station, drop off our film for one-hour photo development and our clothes for one-hour cleaning. After what is inevitably a "busy" and "hectic" day, we rush home to a meal of instant rice, microwaved vegetables and instant pudding. Whatever conversation we manage with our families is likely rushed and superficial as we hurry off to our evening activities. Finally, we climb into bed mindful of all the things we failed to get done and even more mindful of all the things to be accomplished the following day when the proverbial rat race begins all over again. Why do we allow ourselves to get caught up in this vicious cycle? Why is it that almost all of us long to slow down, and yet we seem so incapable of doing so?

There seem to be very few places left in our society where we are encouraged to wait. When combined with self-interest the fixation on speed accelerates the drive toward immediate gratification. We want *what* we want, *when* we want it, and that is almost always *now*.

In contrast, waiting involves slowing down. Waiting inevitably involves "wasting" time. Perhaps this is why the few situations that routinely require us to wait often bring out the worst in us. Why do I get so frustrated waiting in line in a grocery store? Or why do I get irritated if the person in front of me at a stoplight doesn't accelerate the instant the light turns green? Or why do I find myself resenting the person driving in front of me on the way to work who putts along at ten miles an hour below the speed limit, even though I know perfectly well (because I've calculated it!) that I am being "delayed" no more than a few seconds?

Relying as we do on newer and ever-faster technologies of speed, we have acquired (and continue to acquire) whole new sets of expectations that encourage impatience. Is it possible that our fixation with speed, nurtured as it is by a culture characterized by its jet airplanes, microwave dinners and Pentium chips, spills over into other areas of our lives, including our so-called spiritual lives?

For example, we have become a culture of quick fixes. We have no patience for the long haul. If something is wrong, it ought to be able to be fixed immediately. This way of thinking has become so ingrained in us that it shapes the ways we think about the Christian life. As a result, many of us find ourselves exceedingly impatient about Christian growth. Yet maturity takes time; fruit does not grow overnight. Cultivating a life in the Spirit is slow, painstaking work. But most of us (myself included) secretly long for the day when we will wake up and find that we have been instantly transformed. (Perhaps you have even found yourself growing impatient with the analysis sections of these chapters, wishing that I would get to the "application" section more quickly so you would know what you are supposed to do to be a more "productive" Christian!)

We have come to believe that arriving at the desired result or final destination is all that matters. Because we consider the journey or process as wasted time, we routinely seek to speed up the process as much as possible. If a machine can make a chair faster than a person can, then why not let the machine do it? The point is to produce a chair with the least expenditure of resources (including time), right? Or what if I am a parent who hopes to instill certain virtues in my children. Does it matter what I have to do to get the desired result, or is the desired result all that matters? Or what if I am a student hoping to be accepted someday into medical school. Should I take what appears to be the quickest and surest route to this goal, even if it means snubbing personal relationships while I bury my head in the books? Or should I also be concerned about the kind of person—and doctor—I am becoming along the way?

Much about our culture seems to preclude us from even asking such questions. The deck is stacked. The answers are obvious. Yet there are other experiences that we have from time to time that call our culture's goal-oriented obsession into question. For example, Kim and I have found over the years that some of our best talks have come during long car trips to see family (or at least this was the case before we had a van load of children!). Indeed, these talks became such a central feature of our marriage that we missed them whenever we flew to our destination. So although much in our culture insists that the most important thing is to arrive at the destination, many of us have had experiences that remind us how important the journey can be.

Not surprisingly, this tendency to focus on the goal to the exclusion of the process is often reflected in our churches as well. For example, I suspect that our view of time and productivity affects the ways decision-making is carried out in many churches. There is a clear difference between operating by consensus and by majority vote: although the latter promises more productivity, choosing to operate in this manner only makes sense if one has already determined that the final outcome of a decision is more important than the process. Furthermore, there seems to be little incentive for the majority to listen patiently to the concerns and objections of the minority if the former is certain that they have the necessary votes to impose their will. But what if God cares about not only the decision (and what results from it) but also the kind of people we become in the process? Operating by majority rule in the name of productivity and efficiency also assumes (wrongly I suspect) that God normally votes with the majority. It seems hard to account for why Israel needed the prophets, or for the lack of democracy displayed when the twelve spies returned from their trip to Canaan (Num 13—14), if one assumes that the best way to determine God's desires is simply to take a vote.

Cultivating Patience
Cultivating the fruit of patience in the midst of a culture obsessed with productivity and speed is no easy matter. Yet God has provided us with abundant resources for cultivating this important fruit. Here is just a sampling of these manifold resources.

Remembering our story. When we gather together each week, we need to remember that at the heart of the Christian story is a God who is patient, a God who works slowly and diligently over many generations to create a people who will, by their very life together, bear witness to that God. A God who takes these people into the wilderness for forty years to teach them about dependence and trust. A God who becomes incarnate in Jesus of Nazareth, who in turn devotes thirty years of his life preparing for his ministry. A slow, patient God, rather than a God-in-a-hurry God. Or as Kosuke Koyama remarks, a God who moves at walking pace, a "three-mile-an-hour God." But even this is not the whole story.

> Jesus Christ came. He walked towards the 'full stop'. He lost his mobility. He was nailed down! He is not even at three miles an hour as we walk. He is not moving. 'Full stop'! What can be slower than 'full stop'—'nailed down'? At this point of 'full stop', the apostolic church proclaims that the love of God to man is ultimately and fully revealed. God walks 'slowly' because he is love. If he is not love he would have gone much faster. Love has its speed. It is an inner speed. It is a spiritual speed. It is a different kind of speed from the technological speed to which we are accustomed. It is 'slow' yet it is lord over all other speeds since it is the speed of love.[4]

There's something liberating about remembering that our God isn't in a hurry. There's something liberating about remembering that our God entered our world, moved among us at a walk and demonstrated the love of God most preeminently by being "nailed down" for us. And there's something liberating about remembering that in so doing, God acted to justify us (even if we're not sure how), thereby freeing us from the need to justify ourselves by hurrying here or there, or accomplishing this or that. Once we are mindful of these simple yet profound truths, we are free to embody different relationships with one another, relationships rooted in a different understanding of time.

Reckoning time differently. The church is called to embody a different posture toward time. For Christians the past is not a deterministic series of cause and effect relationships whose trajectories inevitably lead to the present. Rather, the past—like the present and the future—is the arena of God's creative activity. The story of God that the church rehearses in its weekly liturgy is the story of a God who continually acts to do a "new thing" in the midst of creation, a "new thing" that could not have been anticipated and that cannot be explained by merely tracing its preceding causes. For example, Christians do not believe that the cosmos was created because it *had* to be, or because it was a necessary effect of a prior cause. Christians believe that God acted freely to create the cosmos, to call Abraham, to liberate the Hebrew slaves from Egypt, to reveal the Torah and to create countless other new and unforeseen possibilities, including the unfathomable possibility of becoming incarnate in our very midst. Rehearsing such stories reminds us that despite the powerful impact that the past does exert on the present and the future, neither God nor God's creatures are destined to live in bondage to that past. As Christians, our relationship to the past can never be marked only or primarily by regret and despair; rather, God's past creative action on the world's behalf serves as a wellspring of hope in the present and the future.

Christians are also called to embody a different relationship to the future. Contrary to most contemporary clichés, we do not believe that the future is ours, nor do we believe that "our children are our future." Instead, Christians are called to embody an eschatological posture. To view time eschatologically is to have one's view of time informed by God's ultimate purposes for the cosmos. What shape will the reconciled cosmos have when God's cosmic work of reconciliation is completed at the *eschaton* or end? Obviously we have not been given a comprehensive blueprint. Yet the witness of the church across the centuries has been that in Israel, in Christ, in the church, we are offered an important window into God's desires for all of creation. Moreover, part of God's past and present desire was to call out a peculiar people who by their very lives together might bear witness to God's intention for all of creation. God's people stand as an imperfect yet useable witness to God's ultimate desires. As such, we have been given a very high calling: to offer to the world in the present a foretaste of the ultimate glory that God is bringing definitively in the future.

Such a view of the future has dramatic and far-reaching implications. The future is no longer that arena in which we strive to work out our own agendas. Nor is it that arena we need constantly fear because it invariably threatens to arrive and snatch away our hard-earned achievements. The future—like the past and the present—remains the arena of God's sovereign activity, and as such the future always remains an open future. We can never say with absolute certainly what will happen in the future. The future belongs to God. Yet as Christians we do believe that the future has a definite shape. Our conviction is that the future will be profoundly marked by the death and resurrection of Jesus Christ. The exact shape of that cruciform future we do not know, yet we are called as God's people to remain constantly open to God's Spirit as we seek in the present to embody in the midst of the world a foretaste of that future.

With such a view of the past and the future, Christians are free to embody a quite different posture toward the present. Time is not to be understood as a scarce commodity, the shortage of which hangs over our heads like a cloud and threatens our feverish attempts to make something of ourselves and our lives. Instead, by the grace of God and with a view to what God has done in the past and desires to do in the future, Christians are freed to view time as a gift and to dwell graciously in the present, knowing that God has liberated us from the necessity of justifying ourselves. In short, God has created a "timeful people" whose existence offers the world a foretaste of the kingdom. These people have been freed from the tyranny of believing that their ultimate destiny or joy is tied to how they "spend" their time. This freedom makes possible the appearance of a "new" time: a time for caring for those—like the elderly, children and the mentally handicapped—whose productivity is suspect; a time for being with those—like the poor, the downtrodden and the discouraged—who do not promise to contribute to our status or to guarantee that we will leave feeling upbeat; and a time for entering into the gratuitous and joyful worship of a God who promises *not* that things will always work out the way we believe they should, but of a God who promises *never* to leave us or forsake us.

Embodying a different rhythm. The age of the church is an age of waiting and working in this time between Christ's initial and final advent. This means that central to our story is the activity of waiting. This posture of waiting is powerfully embodied in those traditions that follow the liturgical year. For example, the season of Advent is dedicated to cultivating this spirit of anticipation and patience. Indeed, the entire cycle of the church year—though unfamiliar to many Christian traditions—has the potential for cultivating within our communities of faith a quite different rhythm, a quite different experience and understanding of time.

Another potentially effectual resource for the church would be the age-old practice of observing the sabbath. Christians through the ages have certainly not been of one mind about how, when (or even whether) to observe this ancient practice of setting aside one day each week for rest. For the Jews such a practice reminded them continually of how their own lives were expected to be patterned after the ways of God. Just as God rested from work on the seventh day, so were Jews to rest from all their labors. Such a practice must have seemed strange to Israel's neighbors. How can one ever hope to get ahead in the world (or even get a little less further behind!) if one sets aside an entire day each week to "do nothing" while the rest of the world continues its mad rush toward "more" and "better"?

For all its potential to call into question our incessant strivings, observing the Christian sabbath is only one possible option and resource for Christians. Another long-standing and potentially fruitful tradition of the church is to view Sunday not simply as the Christian sabbath nor even as the first day of the week, but as the "eighth day of creation." This tradition, particularly vibrant in Eastern Orthodoxy, encourages us to view our weekly gatherings as bearing witness to the new act of creation that God initiated in the resurrection of Jesus Christ. In the light of Easter we see clearly that God's new creation has begun. Indeed, the power and impact of this Easter event are so far-reaching that our normal ways of telling time cannot circumscribe it. The new creation has broken into the old, the future has broken into the present, and it has not left things as they were. When we gather for worship, therefore, we are not simply marking the beginning of another week; we are gathering to celebrate God's new and definitive act of re-creation begun in the resurrection of Jesus Christ and in conformity to which God is drawing all creation. We gather, therefore, to celebrate this new day of creation, this "eighth day of creation." Here, it seems to me, is an enormously rich resource that might aid our attempts to embody a genuinely eschatological posture toward time.

Reflection Questions and Practical Suggestions

With the new millennium upon us, many people are more keenly aware than ever of the grip that human ways of marking time have upon their lives. Yet despite all the millennial fever and all the expectations created by such a seemingly momentous event, my conviction is that the everyday lives of most of us are shaped more by the way we mark our hours, days and weeks than by the ways we mark our years, centuries and millennia. This seems especially to be the case when we pause to reflect on the obstacles to cultivating lives that would bear the fruit of patience. It is with this conviction in mind that I offer the following questions and reflections.

☐ Reflect on your own life during the past few days, considering those times when you have found yourself growing impatient. How do you think your understanding of time contributed to your impatience? Can you, for example, think of times when your impatience and frustration was rooted in your conviction that your time was your own? More specifically, can you recall times when you have grown impatient because people were not meeting *your* expectations or were not conforming to *your* timetable?

☐ In learning to think of time differently, we might begin by reforming our ways of speaking about time. We might, for example, begin by trying to avoid talking about time as if it were one more commodity to be saved, spent or wasted. In a similar way, we might try to avoid thinking and talking about "investing" our time in one another and start thinking and talking about "devoting" our time to people. I admit that such changes may seem small and incidental, but I would not want to underestimate the power that certain ways of thinking and speaking have over our imaginations and affections. If I "invest" my time in something (or someone), by definition I do so with an expectation of a return on my investment. In contrast, to "devote" my time to someone is already to acknowledge his or her worth; the act itself is one of devotion.

☐ This raises the troublesome (and guilt-inducing) issue of daily devotions. Although I will take up the practice of prayer more fully in a later chapter, a brief mention is called for here. Many of us insist that we cannot find the time to engage in such activities, while others of us do so on a regular basis, but do so primarily to be able to check off one more thing from our "to do " lists. Both groups of people seem to be driven by an overriding preoccupation with productivity. If we are honest, many of us do not take the time to engage in daily prayer because we do not see the point; that is, it seems like a waste of time. Some Christians might see it as their responsibility to try to convince such people that they are mistaken about this. I am not persuaded, however, that such convincing is necessary or even desirable. On the contrary, I am increasingly persuaded that each of us needs to come to see the importance of what Henri Nouwen aptly termed "strange periods of uselessness."[5] If prayer so understood has any benefit, it will not be because prayer will come to be seen as a wise investment of time, but because prayer so understood will free us from the need to be constantly productive.

□ In a similar way, those among us whose lives are increasingly dictated by their appointment books would do well to find creative ways of building in "slack" time. If time is not my personal possession to be grasped, but a gift to be freely given and received, then it would seem incredibly wrong-headed to begin each day by constructing elaborate strategies for hoarding what does not belong to me. Furthermore, if I begin "*my* day" (itself an interesting locution) knowing that I have planned nearly every minute, it is difficult to imagine that I will be patient when unexpected situations and people pop up. (It is probably appropriate that my computer crashed during the initial writing of this paragraph, a crash that resulted in my losing about a day's worth of writing. I hadn't realized at the time that I needed another opportunity to experience what I was writing about, but I suppose that I did.) Of course, planning our days so that people can be treated as people rather than as interruptions in our agendas entails a refusal to bow down to the gods of efficiency and productivity. Admittedly we can always plan to get one more task accomplished in any given day, but such planning almost always comes at a cost, and too often that cost entails sacrificing this person in front of me here and now.

□ Perhaps we might also cultivate some places in our lives where we would resist the notion that we must always do things the quickest way possible. Could there be times where we deliberately choose to do things a slower, seemingly-less-efficient way? I am always deeply touched, for example, by people who give our family a gift of home-baked bread, for I know such things take time. The message is never merely "Here is some bread for your empty stomachs," but "I care enough about you to devote time to you." I also suspect we might benefit from learning to walk places to which we could easily drive. The point, of course, would not simply be to save gasoline (though that might be a consideration), but to be reminded of what it is like to move at a much slower, more humane pace, a pace that allows you to be mindful of so much more. Such practices might serve as powerful reminders of all those things (and people) we often miss in our all-out race against the clock.

☐ We might also make some modest attempts to liberate ourselves from our bondage to the clock. I have a friend who, rather than wearing a wristwatch, carries a pocket watch. The reason he does so is to resist, even if only minimally, the hold that clock time has over his life. How many times do we find ourselves taking a quick glance at our watch to see what time it is, even though it doesn't really matter? My friend finds that with a pocket watch he only looks when he really needs to know. Another friend of mine doesn't carry a watch at all, because he finds that there are nearly always plenty of clocks around when he really needs one, and when there isn't one handy, he welcomes the human interaction necessitated in asking someone else. These are small gestures, to be sure, yet such gestures might open up the space in our lives for the Spirit to cultivate the fruit of patience.

☐ And what about our corporate life? How might we work together to cultivate a different relationship to time? Those congregations unfamiliar with the Christian liturgical year might commit to studying the matter and discerning whether it offers a fruitful alternative for structuring their community's experience of time. In a similar way, congregations could consider what it might mean for their corporate life to begin thinking and talking about the day they gather as "the eighth day of creation." What kind of activities, for example, should we be engaged in on such a day if we hope genuinely to embody this new thing that God is doing in our midst?

☐ A related issue that affects our life together concerns the "time consciousness" that often places severe restrictions on our gatherings. Is it really conceivable that we will ever learn to be patient with each other when many of us gather to worship with one eye on the hymnal and the other on our watches? I find it telling and sad that so many congregations now pride themselves on the precision with which they can manage a worship service, guaranteeing that it will conclude precisely at an appointed time. Such pride suggests that we have not yet come to see ourselves as the family of God, for what self-respecting family, in gathering to engage in vital family matters, would do so only if each family member were assured that such matters could be concluded within an hour? Being part of a family involves a willingness to have one's schedule "interrupted" by another family member's needs. Perhaps many congregations might learn something vital from those traditions (such as many African-American and Pentecostal ones) that routinely conclude their services not when the clock strikes the hour, but when family business has been completed.

☐ Those congregations and pastoral staffs that customarily operate by majority vote might commit themselves, at least for a trial period, to making decisions by consensus, knowing ahead of time that such an approach will be slower, less efficient, and require them to be much more patient with each other than they have any need to be currently. Such a commitment to forging consensus might help us to see that what we learn along the way about each other, ourselves and what God desires of us might be more important than always striving to be quantifiably productive.

☐ We might also consider seriously whether the contemporary church needs a renewed sense of seriousness about preparation for initiation into the body of Christ. The fact that many of the early Christians spent several years in adult catechesis before becoming candidates for baptism stands as a sobering reminder of the seriousness of becoming a Christian. Transferring one's allegiance from the kingdom of darkness to the kingdom of light was not considered an easy or speedy process. Whether such preparation comes before or after baptism, we need a way of communicating clearly to new members of the body that patience is both a prerequisite for and consequence of growth in the Spirit.

☐ Finally, let me encourage you to be patient with yourself as well as others as you and they seek to grow in the Spirit and bear fruit. This book is not intended to make you an "instant" anything. If it serves any use at all, it may be as a reminder of how difficult and slow the journey will likely be and how necessary it will be for us to extend to ourselves the same kind of patience we are learning to extend to others. I say this with the full realization that there are many voices in our culture that would encourage us to "be patient with ourselves" and to "give ourselves a break." In urging you to be patient with yourself I do not mean to encourage an irresponsible indulgence that turns a blind eye toward your own faults and shortcomings or those of others. Rather, I am encouraging you to embody a wide-eyed patience and long-suffering. No farmer expects the seedlings to produce ripe and robust fruit in only a few days. This patience embodied by the farmer does not, however, keep that very same farmer from diligently uprooting the weeds that threaten and inhibit good growth. Pray, therefore, for the wisdom to recognize the difference between patience and indulgence.

Lead lives worthy of the Lord, fully pleasing to him, as you bear fruit in every good work and as you grow in the knowledge of God. May you be strong with all the strength that comes from his glorious power, and may you be prepared to endure everything with patience, while joyfully giving thanks to the Father, who has enabled you to share in the inheritance of the saints in the light. (Col 1:10-12)

SIX

Cultivating Kindness in the Midst of Self-Sufficiency

Yet it was I who taught Ephraim to walk,
I took them up in my arms;
but they did not know that I healed them.
I led them with cords of human kindness,
with bands of love.
I was to them like those
who lift infants to their cheeks.
I bent down to them and fed them. (Hos 11:3–4)

If you do good to those who do good to you, what credit is that to you? For even sinners do
the same. If you lend to those from whom you hope to receive, what credit is that to you?
Even sinners lend to sinners, to receive as much again. But love your enemies, do good,
and lend, expecting nothing in return. Your reward will be great, and you will be chil-
dren of the Most High; for he is kind to the ungrateful and the wicked. Be merciful, just as
your Father is merciful. (Lk 6:33–36)

Billboards with the slogan began appearing sometime in the early 1990s. *Since* then there have been books written about it, talk shows devoted to it and thousands of bumper stickers promoting it. And although I don't remember when or where I first saw a billboard with the slogan, I *do* remember having no idea what was being advocated. The plain black-and-white billboard simply urged: "Practice Random Acts of Kindness."

Some time later I read a newspaper account about this movement. According to Gavin Whitsett, the author of a little purple handbook entitled *Guerrilla Kindness*, the movement is a response to the "random acts of violence" that fill the news each day. Whitsett and others like him encourage people to do such things as pay bridge tolls for cars behind them, buy a pack of mints for a friend with bad breath, wave to kids in school buses, send flowers to a convalescent home or sow nickels in a playground sandbox. Admittedly their objectives in doing all of this remain modest: "My aim is only to remind people of the kind impulses that all of us have, remind people of something they already know, which is that it feels good to act on those impulses." With this in mind, Whitsett's book offers "some fun, neat things you can do to surprise people and feel good at the same time. That's all."[1]

What a powerful commentary on our society. Our lives are so filled with the pursuit of self-interest, so disconnected from one another, so void of the sense that we actually *need* each other, that we must create momentary connections and goodwill by practicing "random acts of kindness." I have to confess that I remain a bit suspicious of a movement whose aim is largely to provide opportunities for us to feel good about our random beneficence. Although I certainly don't think it's a terrible thing to walk into a donut shop and pay for the next twenty coffees, I wonder in what sense this act is "kind." Is it possible that this way of practicing kindness—where both the benefactor and the beneficiary remain ignorant of each other's most profound needs—reflects some of our culture's deepest (and most problematic) impulses? Are such acts what Paul had in mind when he wrote that the fifth fruit of the Spirit is kindness? Or are "random acts of kindness" a kind of dwarf species that grows in a culture like ours?

My seeming nit-picking will undoubtedly perturb some readers. "Shouldn't we be glad," some will surely remark, "that people are engaging in random acts of kindness rather than random acts of violence or indifference?" I am sympathetic to such rejoinders and realize that in raising questions about such a movement I am likely to be accused of focusing on the "half-empty glass." My reason for raising the example, however, is not to try to get people to quit doing so-called random acts of kindness. Rather, my probing concerns how Christians should understand the relationship between these efforts and the fruit of kindness that the Spirit nurtures in our lives. To gain more clarity about that matter, we must turn to Scripture to examine the ways in which the concept of kindness functions there.

The Character of Kindness

Virtues or dispositions are often profoundly displayed through stories. The Old Testament, for example, tells of the deep and abiding friendship between David and King Saul's son, Jonathan. When the king becomes jealous of David's military prowess and threatens to have David executed, Jonathan intervenes and warns David, making it possible for him to escape. But before he flees, David and Jonathan make a covenant with each other, promising that they will care for the descendants of the other should one of them be killed (1 Sam 20). Some time later both King Saul and Jonathan are killed in battle. David, who is now king, remembers his covenant with Jonathan and inquires about Jonathan's living descendants, "Is there anyone remaining of the house of Saul to whom I may show the kindness of God?" (2 Sam 9:3). Upon learning that Jonathan left a crippled son named Mephibosheth, David sends for him and informs him that he will eat at David's table like one of his own sons. This act of covenant love David calls "the kindness of God."

The Hebrew word that David uses is one that we have already encountered: *hesed*. And although modern versions often translate it as "love" or "steadfast love," they also use "kindness," "lovingkindness," "mercy," "goodness" and "devotion." It is what Job claims his friends have withheld from him (Job 6:14) and what the writer of Proverbs says that we should pursue along with righteousness in order to find life and honor (Prov 21:21). It is one of three things that Micah tells his audience the Lord requires of them: "to do justice, and to love kindness *[hesed]*, and to walk humbly with your God" (Mic 6:8). And when the word of the Lord comes to Zechariah, the Lord says, "Render true judgments, show kindness *[hesed]* and mercy to one another; do not oppress the widow, the orphan, the alien, or the poor, and do not devise evil in your hearts against one another" (Zech 7:9-10).

The Greek word most often translated as "kindness" is *chrēstotēs*, a word that appears in the New Testament only ten times. We get an idea of the range of its meaning when we note that the King James Version most often translates this as "goodness" or "kindness," though in the fifth chapter of Galatians the King James Version renders it as "gentleness." (This creates some confusion, because most recent translations render the *eighth* fruit of the Spirit as "gentleness.")

But the picture is even more complicated because the Greek version of the Old Testament (the Septuagint) occasionally uses the word *chrēstos* to translate the Hebrew word *tôb*, which is often translated as "good" or "goodness." Thus at the close of Psalm 23, David writes, "Surely goodness *(tôb/chrēstos)* and mercy *(ḥesed/eleos)* shall follow me all the days of my life." Indeed, so closely connected are God's kindness and God's steadfast love that they are often treated as synonymous. For example, the most common refrain that echoed throughout Israel's worship was, "O give thanks to the LORD, for he is good *[tôb]*; for his steadfast love *[ḥesed]* endures forever" (1 Chron 16:34; 2 Chron 5:13; 7:3; 20:21; Ezra 3:11; Ps 100:5; 107:1; 118:1, 29; 136:1-26; Jer 33:11).

The upshot of this brief foray into lexical details is simple: we are confronted again with the overlapping character of the Spirit's fruit. Just as there is no precise point on the rainbow where red ends and orange begins, so there is often no tidy way to distinguish between one fruit of the Spirit and another. What we call God's steadfast love cannot be neatly distinguished from God's goodness, nor can either one be easily distinguished from God's mercy and kindness. Just as Paul wrote to the Corinthians that love is patient, so he acknowledges that love itself is kind (1 Cor 13:4).

Kindness is a particular manifestation of love's other-directedness. Kindness seems to manifest itself as a certain way of being helpful to those who need help. Such helpfulness stems first of all from God's helpfulness, of which the Christian is imminently mindful. That is, Christians are moved by the Spirit to reach out and help others because their own identity is intimately tied to the help they have received at God's hand. To paraphrase 1 John 4:19: "We help because God first helped us."

This fruit by its very character, therefore, is one of the most outwardly *visible* fruit of the Christian life. Kindness is neither a state of mind nor an invisible attitude or emotion. Neither do we think people kind simply because they refrain from doing unkind things. Rather, we regard people as kind because they go out of their way, often quietly and without fanfare, to engage in kind actions. Nitty-gritty, concrete, everyday kinds of actions. We know from the early church fathers that many people during the first century were confused about what these strange followers of Jesus were called. Because the Greek word for Christ (*christos*) was so similar to the word for "kind" *(chrēstos),* apparently many people mistakenly (though perhaps fittingly) called Jesus' early followers not "Christians" but "the kind ones."

Are Christians today likely to be identified by those around them as "the kind ones?" Because much about our society inhibits the cultivation of kindness, those who desire to bear the fruit of kindness would do well to reflect on those common stories, practices and convictions that regularly thwart the Spirit's work.

Obstacles to a Life of Kindness

Perhaps we can position ourselves to name some of the obstacles that inhibit the cultivation of kindness if we begin with the assumption that kindness, at its most basic level, involves the giving and receiving of help. Is there anything about our society that inhibits the giving and the receiving of help?

Promoting self-sufficiency. Even the casual observer is likely to answer with a resounding yes. From an early age we hear extolled the virtues of self-reliance, independence and autonomy. In a similar way, we figure out quite early that to ask for help is not only potentially burdensome to someone else but also tantamount to failure. To seek help is to admit weakness and inadequacy. To accept help is to admit that you cannot do it on your own. Parents routinely acknowledge that one of their goals for their children is to help them be "independent" as soon as possible. Young people growing up in our culture know that they are being readied for the day when they will be "on their own," part of which requires them to be economically self-sufficient. Our society admires those who have "made it," by which is usually meant the attainment of economic self-sufficiency; moreover, we particularly sing the praises of those who have made it "on their own." In the past we have paid such people the ultimate compliment by identifying them as self-made men.

Perhaps one of the reasons we find it difficult to be kind, therefore, is that from an early age our society instills in us a certain subtle prejudice against the giving and receiving of help. In a society like ours, to offer help is always to run the risk of offending the persons being helped by implying that they are weak and inadequate. For the same reasons, most of us likely find it difficult to *receive* help, preferring instead to handle matters "on our own," lest we be perceived as weak. I believe that it is telling that most of us are quite willing to admit our dependence on certain kinds of technologies and conveniences ("I simply couldn't live without my microwave or my cell phone"), while we have become increasingly reluctant to admit that we need one another.

In calling attention to the one-sided and unhealthy emphasis our society places on self-sufficiency, I do not mean to suggest that we should prefer relationships of utter dependency. The dehumanizing character of dependency has been widely reported during the recent national debate over welfare reform. Many people seem to agree that placing people in situations where they are completely dependent upon others for their survival can have insidious long-term consequences. These discussions may oversimplify the matter, however, when they identify the culprit in such situations as simply "dependency." This suggests that all forms of dependency are illegitimate and harmful. I would argue to the contrary that what is dehumanizing is not dependency per se, but dependency without opportunity for reciprocity. By denying people an opportunity to give something back, such situations often create an unbearable burden of indebtedness.

Let me elaborate by returning to the practice of gift giving. Most societies have sophisticated (even though often unarticulated) ways of deepening, extending and cementing human relationships through networks of obligation and reciprocity. For example, friendships are often established and sustained through rituals of gift giving. Offering another person a gift creates a sense of indebtedness and obligation, whether the gift is a tangible item, an act of hospitality, or some other act of kindness. To accept that gift is to accept the "burden" of indebtedness that goes along with it, realizing that in due time, if the relationship continues, you are expected to seek out an opportunity to reciprocate. Therefore, any healthy friendship requires the willingness to give and to receive, to place another in one's debt and in turn to be placed in theirs. In short, giving and receiving one another's acts of kindness binds us to one another.

Most of us have internalized these assumptions and expectations long ago, even if we have rarely reflected upon them. We assume that people who choose not to reciprocate are not necessarily rude but are likely sending a signal (whether conscious or not) that they are unwilling to extend or deepen the relationship beyond its current level. Similarly, most of us also have internalized certain assumptions about reciprocity and timing. If you give your friend a gift today and she in turn shows up on your doorstep tomorrow with a gift for you, you are apt to wonder about the health and status of the relationship. Such an action betrays an unwillingness to be indebted to you. Because nearly all relationships involve webs of indebtedness, your friend's action suggests an unwillingness to be in an ongoing relationship with you. By attempting to settle the score so quickly, your friend has sent a signal (albeit not a very subtle one) that she prefers not to be obligated to you any longer and therefore not to be bound to you in any way. Such expectations about the timing of acts of reciprocity even seem to hold for something as seemingly mundane as offering another person a compliment. We have all probably had the experience of complimenting another person only to have them turn around and immediately offer *us* a compliment. The irritation that we likely feel is primarily the result of having our act of kindness rebuffed by someone who cannot accept a gift without immediately reciprocating. Such a response undercuts our gift *as* a gift and transforms it into little more than a clumsy exchange.

As I noted in the earlier chapter on love, one of the striking features of our society is how much of our lives are structured around market exchanges. Such exchanges, if allowed to dominate all areas of our lives, undercut attempts to offer and receive love and kindness by turning all such acts into mutually beneficial and ultimately self-interested exchanges. The widely acknowledged advantage of market exchanges is that they are remarkably efficient; the less-often-recognized disadvantage is that these exchanges are also remarkably impersonal. As a result, these exchanges feed my illusion of self-sufficiency. I come to believe that because I work hard at my job, bring home a decent paycheck and pay my bills with my own hard-earned dollars that I myself have secured my (and my family's) well-being.

We need only to reflect a moment, however, to see how such thinking is deeply deceptive. Market exchanges give the illusion of self-sufficiency because they create so little conscious sense of attachment, so little sense of indebtedness. When I go through the checkout line at the grocery store, I am largely oblivious to the thousands upon thousands of people who have made it possible for these items to be readily available. Consider, for example, how many people are involved in bringing to your grocery shelf a single box of breakfast cereal. In addition to the obvious participants—farmers, people who process the grain, people who work in production plants, transport personnel at various stages and people who stock shelves—think as well about all the support personnel who make it possible for *these* people to do *their* jobs. Here we have such people as fuel suppliers and utility company workers, manufacturers of machinery and administrative personnel. Yet the chain doesn't stop there, for countless other people make it possible for *these* people to do *their* jobs, who are in turn supported by countless others. Where could one plausibly stop this seemingly endless chain of mutual support and *inter*-dependence?

Once we recognize this rather obvious fact—that all of us are profoundly indebted to millions of people we have never met and will never meet—we are faced with an even more obvious frustration. It is seemingly impossible to feel indebted to these countless people because every person who works hard to produce a box of cereal or a jar of peanut butter remains largely invisible and anonymous to me. What does it mean to be indebted to hundreds or thousands of faceless people? How can I possibly thank them? How do I reciprocate?

Yet the crucial point is that most of us feel no need either to thank anyone or to reciprocate. Why is this? Because all of us, whether consciously or not, well understand that this relationship is of a different kind, one that we identify as a market exchange. In short, I do not have to feel obligated to anyone because I have *already* reciprocated: I paid for my groceries. I need not feel obligated because I got what I wanted and they (whoever they are) got what they wanted. No ongoing indebtedness. No need for reciprocity. We're even.

What does all this mean for our life together as a society? We live in a society (and a world) that is creating ever-more complex and intricate webs of interdependence. But because so many of these relational webs are structured around self-interested market exchanges and are mediated by impersonal means (such as money and electronic technology), we are offered the illusion of self-sufficiency. For Christians such an illusion often inhibits the work of the Spirit in our lives as we seek to cultivate the fruit of kindness. How do we learn to be kind to those around us and freely offer our help when their (and our) stated goal in life is to become ever more self-sufficient? Equally vexing is learning to *receive* acts of kindness from others without seeing this as an indictment of our weakness. How do we learn to admit that we need help and, subsequently, to receive that help graciously, when we live in a society that teaches us that all requests for help are signs of weakness and incompetence?

Christians who desire to nurture the fruit of kindness need to recognize that at the center of our society stands a fundamental contradiction. We live in a society where people's day-to-day existence has never before been so dependent on the service rendered by other people, yet more and more people (including many Christians) have as their stated goals in life independence and self-sufficiency. What could such goals possibly mean in an age like ours? Why are such goals even desirable?

Nurturing autonomy. This last question leads us to consider briefly another "plant," in addition to self-sufficiency, that our society nurtures and highly prizes. Although this plant looks very similar to that of self-sufficiency, it bears its own kind of fruit and poses its own threat to the cultivation of kindness. This plant is what we call "autonomy."

To be autonomous is to be self-directed and self-governed. Historically autonomy has been especially valued in the West since the European Enlightenment of the seventeenth and eighteenth centuries. The elevation of autonomy to a place of privilege was usually paired with the rejection of other forms of authority. The center of authority was no longer located in the prince, the church or the traditions and teachings of the past, but in the individual person. Rather than having one's life directed by external authorities of one kind or another, the new goal was to be an autonomous individual, one whose life was directed by the dictates of one's own reason and one's own moral compass. To such understandings of autonomy all forms of dependence (including interdependence) pose a serious threat. To be anything other than self-directed is to remain in servitude and bondage.

Before we turn to the problems that such a one-sided emphasis has spawned, we should acknowledge that many people believe that Enlightenment advocates of autonomy had a legitimate point. What Immanuel Kant and others objected to was the servile and unthinking ways in which people accepted the pronouncements of those occupying traditional positions of authority. Although it might be acceptable to expect a five-year-old to do something simply because "Mommy said so," Kant and many others since his time have insisted that such reasons are insufficient and must give way to more "substantive" reasons. Indeed, on one level the history of moral argument and reasoning in the West since that time can be read fairly as a debate about what kinds of reasons would count as being more substantive.

Some parties to this debate have insisted that any reasons rooted in tradition are likely insufficient. The watchword for Kant and others was "Dare to think for yourself." Yet we are far enough down the road since Kant's day to see that such advice by itself undercuts attempts at forging agreements about how we as a society should conduct ourselves. Hence, although our society takes it as axiomatic that encouraging dependence amounts to encouraging irresponsibility, we are now better positioned to see that fostering independence and autonomy can do so as well. As a society we seem loath to admit that we are now in a large part reaping the harvest from the seeds of autonomy we have for so long planted and nurtured. For example, we smugly identify fathers who "shirk their family obligations" as irresponsible or as deadbeat dads. But on what basis do we as a society make this judgment? Where did these obligations come from and who is authorized to say that we must keep them? Is it possible that many of these fathers are simply living out the dream of being an autonomous individual? "Why should I be tied down by a family," they might ask, "when doing so infringes on my autonomy, my right to be self-directed and self-governing? How can I do *what* I want to do *when* I want to do it, when I have to keep answering to my wife and children? I don't want my life to be directed by their needs and desires; I want to do my own thing." How can a society praise unconditionally the value of autonomy and then condemn people when they exercise it?

Underwriting self-sufficiency and autonomy. As I hope the above makes clear, self-sufficiency and autonomy are not simply disembodied ideas. Rather, as deeply held convictions about the aim of human life, they offer direction to human enterprises. If we look at a few examples, we can see how deeply these convictions are woven into the fabric of everyday life.

Most of us will spend a huge portion of our lives working. Many of us began working in high school to earn money for gasoline and clothes, continued to work through college to help with expenses and gain valuable experience and then pursued a career after college that would be both personally satisfying and financially rewarding. Over the years it became second nature to believe that our talents and abilities belonged to us, that they were *our* resources to exploit for our own gain. Within such a framework, work is not first of all mutual service but the way in which we secure our own wants and desires by our own hands. Moreover, fellow workers are often viewed as competitors who are vying for the same scarce resources: a compliment from the boss, a raise, a promotion.

Much of our education system underwrites a similar perspective. Regardless of the subject or the setting (public, private, parochial), we come to learn that what most counts is what *I* learn, what *I* know, what *my* grades are. As a result, we routinely view our peers primarily as competitors. We learn at an early age that whatever intellectual abilities we have are ours and should be exploited for our own benefit. Why should I use my gifts and abilities to help anyone else learn?

So widespread is this perspective that it spills out into many areas of our lives. Many high school coaches, for example, find it next to impossible to get players focused on working together rather than for individual honors. "Why should I work together if doing so means someone other than me might be named MVP?" Similarly, many marriage partners find it difficult to view their spouses as *partners*, so accustomed are they to viewing other people as

144 ■   Life on the Vine

competitors. If one spouse receives an honor or a promotion, does the other feel a sense of satisfaction knowing that he or she helped to make this possible? Or does the other spouse feel slighted, believing that the honor or promotion was earned at his or her "expense"?

We might be inclined to view all this self-seeking as just another example of human selfishness. Although such a view has merit, I believe there is more going on, for the issue is not simply whether we are selfish, but whether certain societies encourage us to see things primarily through self-serving lenses. By encouraging us to view ourselves as self-sufficient and autonomous, cultures like ours encourage us to evaluate our present well-being almost exclusively in terms of our own contributions. At least this seems to be so when things are going well. In other words, when we are pleased with the state and direction of our lives, we are inclined to take the credit, noting those ways in which we have secured our current success. When things go poorly, we often look for someone else to blame, a situation that has created what some people have termed a "culture of victims."

Yet those who critique this "culture of victims" often fail to recognize that most of us do not complain when things go well. When something happens in our life that we take to be good, no one cries out, "I've been victimized!" This suggests that the problem is not, as some have suggested, that people no longer want to take any responsibility for their lives. The problem, rather, is that we are highly selective, taking *more* credit than we ought to when things go well and taking *less* than we ought to when things go poorly. The great challenge in a culture such as ours, a culture that so values autonomy and self-sufficiency, is to recognize the intricate ways in which our lives are woven together. Our actions *do* have an impact on other people, and their actions *do* impact us. We are not self-sufficient and autonomous, nor would it be a good thing if we were. As a result, the sooner we recognize that our well-being is always bound up with that of others, the better off we'll all be.

Although such a posture of interdependence would seem to resonate with much about the Christian story, it appears that many Christians and churches find it difficult to challenge their cultural indoctrination into the virtues of self-sufficiency and autonomy. Most of us do not see ourselves as dependent on or responsible for our fellow brothers and sisters. Rather, most of us regard ourselves as autonomous individuals and as members of one another only in some derived sense. If you are honored, I may try to muster a congratulation, but I do not feel honored myself. Similarly, if a tragedy strikes your life, I may feel sorry for you and may even offer to do what I can to help, but I likely feel none of your pain. Your life is your life and mine is mine. Moreover, my bank accounts, my insurance policies, my accumulated stuff are my ways of insuring, whether consciously or not, that I won't need to depend on you or anyone else in the future. There is no need for you to believe that I will ever need your help; I can take care of myself quite nicely, thank you.

Seen in this light, is it possible that Jesus' warning about laying up for ourselves treasures on earth (Mt 6:21-23) was a warning about the posture of independence (from God and others) that such hoarding creates, a posture that undercuts Christian community and all gestures of kindness? Is it possible that there is a profound connection between the absence of God that we often experience and the fact that we have so arranged our lives as to make God (and even each other) all but superfluous?

Cultivating Kindness

As the discussion above suggests, the dominant culture does not necessarily mount a frontal attack on the virtue of kindness. It is not as if our society is set on uprooting kindness and replacing it with hard-hearted and mean-spirited plants. But as indicated early on, the absence of hard-heartedness and mean-spiritedness hardly makes one kind. The problem seems to be that by nurturing self-sufficiency and autonomy, our society unwittingly inhibits the growth of kindness. Fortunately God has given us much needed resources for nurturing the fruit of kindness in our lives.

Remembering our story. Once again we begin with worship and with an obvious observation: we gather regularly to acknowledge God as creator and sustainer, a fact that should serve as a constant reminder that we did not get here on our own. However easy it may be in our culture to continue the charade that we have secured whatever we have by our own hands, such notions should not find fertile ground among God's people. Surely people who gather regularly with other believers to give thanks and praise for God's unbounded grace should find it difficult to think of themselves as in any sense self-sufficient.

Not only is our gathering for worship itself a gesture of dependency, but the story we rehearse each time we gather also has as one of its central themes our utter dependence upon God. From the opening chapters of Genesis, where we are told that we are *creatures,* to the closing chapters of Revelation, where we behold something of the future that *God* is bringing, Scripture reminds us again and again that we are not "self-made men." Furthermore, that God's people need constant *reminding* of this simple but profound truth is *also* part of our story. For example, when the children of Israel are poised to enter Canaan after their many years of wandering, God warns them that their future prosperity will tempt them to forget their past, tempt them to forget how they have come to be where they are and tempt them to believe that it was by their own power and might that they have prospered (Deut 8; cf. Ps 44).

In the New Testament, Paul echoes this warning about trusting in our own strength and power by suggesting that at the heart of the gospel is a corollary truth: God glories in working through human weakness. When we act out of our own strength, we are often tempted to glory in our own abilities, our own prowess in making things happen. But when God works through our weaknesses, we are reminded that God's grace, not our abilities, is sufficient. Hence, when Paul appeals to God three times to remove his "thorn in the flesh," God replies, "My grace is sufficient for you, for [my] power is made perfect in weakness" (2 Cor 12:9).

In sum, when we as Christians remember our story, we remember a story of matchless and inexhaustible grace. As Paul insists, God has shown us "the immeasurable riches of his grace in kindness toward us in Christ Jesus" (Eph 2:7). Our story is not one of impressive accomplishments achieved by our own talents, our own abilities, our own hard work; rather, ours is a story about receiving what we did not deserve, what we in no way earned, what we could not secure for ourselves. We are and will always remain recipients of God's good gifts. What sets us apart from others is not that we've received these gifts and they haven't, but that we know whom to thank and they may not. As a result, we are free both to offer and to receive acts of kindness without having this threaten our identity or self-understanding.

Nurturing connections. One of the most precious gifts that God has given us is each other. That we regularly fail to appreciate this suggests how deeply we have assimilated our society's teachings about self-sufficiency and autonomy. Rather than see each other as gifts from God, we are often inclined to view each other as potential threats or competitors. How could it be otherwise in a society so steeped in individualism and so bent on cultivating self-sufficiency and autonomy?

Even if we were disposed to temper our culture's emphasis on the individual, most of us would view with suspicion any emphasis on "the community." Even if many of us recognized that an overemphasis on the individual could be unhealthy, the stories that continue to underwrite individualism in this society warn us of the manifold dangers of communities. These dangers include such things as totalitarianism, groupthink and homogeneity. In sum, whatever worries we may have about the acids of individualism, most of us worry *more* about the dangers seemingly inherent in emphasizing group identity.

These worries are partly rooted in the very ways we have come to understand the relationship between individuals and groups. We tend to think of individuals and groups as discreet entities; the only debating point concerns which entity is given pride of place. According to this view, some people believe that the group exists to serve the needs of the individual, while the rest believe the opposite—that the individual exists to serve the needs of the group. In the former view the individual is all-important, while in the latter view, the group is. The problem with both views, however, is that they understand these as discreet entities and then pit them against each other, insisting that we determine which one is more important.

To understand the shortcomings of such a perspective, we need only reflect on what is arguably the most profound image employed in the New Testament to describe the church: the body of Christ (Rom 12:3-8; 1 Cor 12; Eph 4:1-16). As noted in an earlier chapter, this beautiful and powerful image radically challenges most of our common understandings. For example, when one thinks of a healthy, functioning body, it makes little sense to ask whether the body parts exist for the body or whether the body exists for the body parts. It makes no sense to think of the body and the body parts as discreet entities and then to ask which one of them has priority over the other. The mistake is to assume you can have one apart from the other. But this is not possible: you cannot have a body without already having body *parts*, and you cannot have functioning body parts unless they already belong to a *body*. So rather than pitting the body and its parts against each other, we need to think of them as *constitutive* notions; that is, they are notions that come together, constituting each other as coherent notions.

Once we get clear about this matter, we can stop asking such questions as: Which is more important, the individual Christian or the church? According to Scripture, Christians *have* no separate identity apart from the body of Christ. Becoming a Christian and becoming engrafted into the body of Christ are the same thing. This is why Paul can insist that we belong to each other, that we are "members of one another" (Rom 12:5; Eph 4:25). Belonging to each other is not so much a question of possession as it is a question of connection. We belong to each other because God has brought us together, connecting us to one another through and in Christ. Without such vital, life-giving connections, there is no body. None of us would regard as a body a collection of body parts warehoused in proximity to each other yet lacking vital, life-giving connections.

If we are in no sense the body of Christ apart from these connections, then perhaps we should reflect on the *character* of these connections. How does Scripture talk about them? How are they created and sustained? Paul argues in several places that these connections are created by God, not least by God's complementary gifting of the body of Christ. In other words, God has given each member of the body distinct but vital gifts that the rest of the body requires for its health. In short, God has so created the body that each member needs the others. This means that the very character of the body as ordained by God is rooted in mutual service. I need what the other body parts contribute to the health and well-being of the body, just as they need what I offer. God has so arranged the life of the body that none of us can secure our own well-being, just as no foot (or other body part) can establish or sustain itself. We need each other.

If we remember that politics is the practice of ordering a people's life together, then contained within Paul's understanding of the giftedness of the body of Christ is a profoundly different politics. This people's life is not ordered around the belief that their gifts are their own. On the contrary, Paul insists that the gifts given to the church have been given "to equip the saints for the work of ministry, for building up the body of Christ, until all of us come to the unity of the faith and the knowledge of the Son of God, to maturity, to the measure of the full stature of Christ" (Eph 4:12-13).

The New Testament image of the body of Christ radically challenges our contemporary notions of self-sufficiency and autonomy. By being grafted into the body of Christ, Christians have been freed from the burdensome requirement of securing our own well-being and from the isolation that inevitably accompanies an overemphasis on autonomy. As a result, Christians have been empowered for mutual service, which includes the giving and receiving of acts of kindness.

Listening to one another. If Christians truly are to function as the body of Christ, we will need to foster stronger and more intimate connections with each other. To do this, we will need to learn to listen. Listening to each other will be greatly facilitated by our no longer viewing each other as threats to our well-being. Within the dominant culture that emphasizes self-sufficiency and autonomy, there is little reason for us to listen to each other. Why should I listen to you? I don't want to hear about the good things that have happened in your life; they just make me more depressed about my own lack of accomplishment. I don't want to listen to your problems; I have my own. Nor do I care to listen to your advice or admonition; I can take care of my own problems by myself.

But once we are given eyes to see each other as gifts rather than as threats, listening to each other becomes vitally important for our life together. I need to learn to take appropriate pride in your accomplishments, and you in mine, because we realize that neither of us have done this on our own. I need to listen carefully to your problems, for as a fellow member of the body of Christ your problems are my problems. Similarly, I need to be willing to share my problems as well, since learning to receive acts of kindness graciously is also central to our identity as the body of Christ. Finally, I need to learn to receive your advice or admonishment not as a threat to my self-sufficiency and autonomy but as a gift of God for my own well-being and thus for the well-being of the entire body. Do I really believe that I can learn to hear the voice of God when I cannot even bring myself to listen to the voice of my brother or sister? Even more to the point, is there not plenty of scriptural precedent for a word of God coming through the voice of another person?

Carefully listening to another is itself an act of kindness, and it may sometimes lead to further action on another's behalf. But how will I know what you actually need, or you me, if we do not take the time and effort to really listen to each other? In many ways genuine listening is a little like death, for it requires us to set aside our agendas for the moment in order to be fully present to and for another human being. In so doing we offer ourselves to others as vehicles for God's presence and grace. Like each of the fruit of the Spirit, it is this other-directedness that makes kindness part of the spectrum of God's love that we are called to reflect to the world.

In the final analysis this lack of genuine other-directedness may be the primary limitation of "random acts of kindness." Too often such acts encourage me to do little more than create opportunities for me to feel good about having done something "kind" for somebody else, regardless of what they really needed. Such acts usually demand little of me—no listening, no discerning what is needed and no time-consuming involvement with another person's life. Similarly, such acts neither create nor sustain any long-term relationship; the anonymity of my action coupled with its randomness guarantees that. Instead, I enjoy a certain "buzz" from having done something unusual and unexpected. To the degree to which such acts draw me out of my everyday preoccupation with myself in order to attend to the lives of other people, we might identify such acts as either precursors to acts of kindness or as a kind of dwarf species of kindness. However, to the degree to which such acts continue to place my own ego and its desire for attention and "strokes" at the center, we would be more honest to identify such fruit as stemming from some other spirit than that which animated the life and ministry of Jesus Christ.

Reflection Questions and Practical Suggestions

☐ Reflect on your own life and the way you narrate your own life story. How important are others to that story? To see this more clearly, conduct the following exercise: try to imagine what it would be like to narrate your life story without reference to anyone else other than yourself. How much of your story could you tell? How interesting would it be? What does such an exercise tell us about our alleged self-sufficiency and autonomy?

☐ Do a New Testament word study of the Greek reciprocal pronoun *allelon*, which is translated into English most commonly as "one another." Note how frequently the New Testament writers exhort believers to do something (admonish, comfort, do good, be kind and so forth) to or for "one another." You may be surprised how many New Testament exhortations are couched in such language, a language that makes no sense unless people understand themselves to be in relationships of *inter*dependence.

☐ Take some time to reflect on the New Testament metaphor of the body of Christ. How does this image illuminate your own experience as a Christian? In what ways do you believe you are vitally connected to other members of the body? Have there been times when you have sensed more of a connection with the body than others? What do you think accounted for this sense of connection?

☐ Carefully consider the gifts and abilities you believe you have been given. Did you discover these gifts completely on your own, or did you come to see them by interacting with other people who identified and affirmed your abilities? In what ways have you been led to believe that these are your own, that they are yours to exploit for your own benefit and gain? What would it mean for you to begin to think of these gifts as existing both for the edification of the body of Christ and for the benefit of the reign of God?

☐ Reflect on the relationships that you most cherish and admire. In what ways are they characterized by *inter*dependence? If Christians are to nurture such relationships in a society that works hard to deny their importance, we might begin by noting the ways in which our lives are already woven together. As noted earlier in this chapter our lives are already intricately woven into the lives of many other people, even if we rarely notice. Granted, few of these relationships touch us at our core, because most of them are sustained at superficial levels that operate independently of who we are. That is, my life may be connected in some complex way to all those who produce my breakfast cereal, but most of them care little whether I purchase it or my neighbor does. Nevertheless, we do well to notice these connections, even if they are superficial, because they remind us of how little of our lives can be described as in any way self-sufficient or autonomous.

Beyond that we need areas of our lives where we nurture cooperation and where such cooperation brings us into closer relationship with one another. What would it mean, for example, for Christians to think of their work (whatever shape that takes) as service to others rather than as simply a means to secure their own (or their family's) livelihood? What would it mean for us to consider *other* people's work as service to us? Most of us are surrounded everyday by people who perform acts of service for us. We could (and largely do) ignore them as simply doing what they have to do in order to survive. But why not rather express our gratitude to them in some small way that acknowledges that our lives are richer because of them?

□ Finally, we come to the matter of listening. Many of us would do well to admit that one of the biggest impediments to our listening to other people is our incessant busyness. We are so wrapped up in our own lives, going here and there, doing this and that, that we find it difficult even to hear other people, let alone truly listen to them. To address this matter, we might try implementing something like the centuries-old Benedictine practice of *statio*. *Statio* involves stopping one thing before beginning another, with the hope of being more fully present to those with whom one is engaged. This might involve, for example, my turning off the radio five or ten minutes from home in an attempt to focus my thoughts and attention on the needs of my spouse and children, so that when I walk through the door I am not preoccupied with my own agenda but am more fully present to and for them. It might mean focusing my thoughts on my students as I walk from my office to my class—rather than mulling over the last article or book that I have read—so that I am prepared to be truly present for them when I walk into the classroom. In short, most of us will find it difficult to be kind if we have not learned to listen, and yet we will not learn to be good listeners as long as our minds and hearts are focused exclusively on ourselves. The practice of *statio* encourages us to create a space in our lives so that we may welcome in another.

As the quotation at the beginning of the chapter suggests, God does not parcel out kindness by using some kind of formula that offers blessings in proportion to our worthiness. God is "kind to the ungrateful and the wicked," and Jesus urges *us* to offer this same kind of mercy-filled kindness. As Jesus noted, most of us find it easier to be kind to those who are kind to us, yet such "kindness" reflects little of the light from God's kingdom. As people empowered by God's Spirit, we are called to reach out in kindness to our neighbors—those who are easy to love and those who are not—as a channel for God's grace and presence. Toward that end we might do well to reflect on the following quotation from Martin Luther, who urged his fellow Christians in the sixteenth century to view their freedom in Christ as an opportunity to benevolently serve their neighbors:

> We should devote all our works to the welfare of others, since each has such abundant riches in his faith that all his other works and his whole life are a surplus with which he can by voluntary benevolence serve and do good to his neighbor. . . . He ought to think: "Although I am an unworthy and condemned man, my God has given me in Christ all the riches of righteousness and salvation without any merit on my part, out of pure, free mercy, so that from now on I need nothing except faith which believes that this is true. Why should I not therefore freely, joyfully, with all my heart, and with an eager will do all things which I know are pleasing and acceptable to such a Father who has overwhelmed me with his inestimable riches? I will therefore give myself as a Christ to my neighbor, just as Christ offered himself to me; I will do nothing in this life except what I see is necessary, profitable, and salutary to my neighbor, since through faith I have an abundance of all good things in Christ." . . . Who then can comprehend the riches and the glory of the Christian life? It can do

all things and has all things and lacks nothing. It is lord over sin, death, and hell, and yet at the same time it serves, ministers to, and benefits all men. But alas in our day this life is unknown throughout the world; it is neither preached about nor sought after; we are altogether ignorant of our own name and do not know why we are Christians or bear the name of Christians. Surely we are named after Christ, not because he is absent from us, but because he dwells in us, that is, because we believe in him and are Christs one to another and do to our neighbors as Christ does to us.[2]

Do not grieve the Holy Spirit of God, with which you were marked with a seal for the day of redemption. Put away from you all bitterness and wrath and anger and wrangling and slander, together with all malice, and be kind to one another, tenderhearted, forgiving one another, as God in Christ has forgiven you. (Eph 4:30-32)

SEVEN

Cultivating Goodness in the Midst of Self-Help

For you were once darkness, but now you are light in the Lord. Live as children of light (for the fruit of the light consists in all goodness, righteousness and truth) and find out what pleases the Lord. Have nothing to do with the fruitless deeds of darkness, but rather expose them. (Eph 5: 8-11 NIV)

Either make the tree good, and its fruit good; or make the tree bad, and its fruit bad; for the tree is known by its fruit . . . . The good person brings good things out of a good treasure, and the evil person brings evil things out of an evil treasure. (Mt 12:33, 35)

Those who have been to their local bookstore in the last several years know that one of the fastest growing sections is the area marked "self-help." Here one can find a wide range of titles that offer readers advice on how to live more satisfying lives. Many focus on unlocking hidden resources or uncovering debilitating fears, while others offer some technique for getting more out of life. While browsing through two local bookstores, I compiled the following list of representative titles from their "self-help" sections:

Finding Joy: 101 Ways to Free Your Spirit and Dance with Life
The Family: A Revolutionary Way of Self-Discovery
Unlimited Human Potential . . . A New Definition
Unlocking the Secrets of Your Childhood Memories

Beyond Negative Thinking: Reclaiming Your Life Through Optimism
You Can Heal Your Life
Love 101: To Love Oneself Is the Beginning of a Lifelong Romance
Love Yourself, Heal Your Life Workbook
Help Yourself to Happiness
Beyond Fear: The Quantum Leap to Courageous Living
The Doctor's Guide to Instant Stress Relief
How to Handle Trouble: A Guide to Peace of Mind

If you wonder who reads such books, the answer is that lots of people do. Many of these books are bestsellers, having sold hundreds of thousands of copies. What does the popularity of such books tell us about what people are looking for and where they are looking for it? First, I couldn't help but notice that several titles explicitly state that they deal with such things as love, joy and peace. Second, it is also hard to miss the characteristic North American virtues that find their way into these titles: freedom, optimism, happiness, individualism, immediacy ("instant stress relief!"). Finally, although these authors may not agree with each other on what "the good life" entails, there appears to be a remarkable consensus that people have within themselves what is necessary to attain it.

On one level, one hears in all of this a clear echo of many of the themes from the previous chapter, especially with regards to the premium placed on self-sufficiency and autonomy. But there is also a subtle difference. Whereas the value our society places on self-sufficiency shapes us to think that receiving help is a sign of weakness or incompetence, the cult of self-help encourages us to think that we are not only competent to take care of our own problems but also morally equipped to do so as well. I admit that this subtle difference may be less than obvious, but I hope that after we have examined the notion of "goodness" we will be able to see why cultivating this fruit in our contemporary situation presents a slightly different, if no less formidable, set of challenges.

The Character of Goodness

Trying to grasp the character of the sixth fruit of the Spirit poses several difficulties. First, the word that Paul employs in his letter to the Galatians *(agathōsynē)* does not appear at all in secular Greek, only appears three additional times in the New Testament and only occurs about a dozen times in the Greek Old Testament. In other words, there are not a lot of places to go to see how the word was commonly used. Second, examining the related words does not necessarily help. As in English the Greek word translated "goodness" is closely linked to the concept of "good" *(agathos)*. But this term has such a wide range of meaning and is so common in both the Greek Old Testament (over five hundred occurrences) and the New Testament (over one hundred occurrences) that we may still find it difficult to determine what goodness entails.

The word *good* usually points to some excellence (what the Greeks called *aretē*) that is befitting the object described. As such, the notion of "good" cannot usually be separated from some idea of that object's purpose. For example, if I remark that I have a good watch, most will understand me to be commenting on the watch's worth as an instrument for keeping time. That there is little room for misunderstanding here says less about my watch and more about the agreements our culture has about the purpose of watches. But we do not share such agreements about a lot of other things. If a young man says that he has a good car, what we think he is talking about will likely be connected to what we think he believes about the purpose of cars. If he is interested primarily in transportation, his comment will mean one thing; if he is concerned more about his status with a certain group of friends, his comment will likely mean something else. And if he is an antique collector, his comment will most certainly mean something else again.

What do we mean when we say that someone is a good person? As with kindness, we usually mean more than the purely negative judgment—that this person abstains from engaging in evil and malicious acts. We are usually also making an affirmation—that this person does what is "right" or "good." But as with the good watch, making such a judgment about a good person entails believing something about the purposes of human existence. Where do we get our notions of the purpose of human existence and of what counts for goodness? Three important points must be made at this juncture.

First, the consistent witness of Scripture and the church is that God alone is unequivocally good. As noted in the previous chapter, the common refrain of Israel's worship life was, "O give thanks to the Lord, for he is good *[tôb];* for his steadfast love *[hesed]* endures forever." Normally the Septuagint translates *tôb* with the Greek word *agathos* (although, we also noted in the last chapter, it occasionally translates it as *chrēstos*—"kind"). One of the most powerful echoes of this witness in the New Testament are Jesus' words to the rich young man, who addresses Jesus as "Good Teacher." Jesus responds, "Why do you call me good? No one is good but God alone" (Mk 10:18; cf. Mt 19:16-17, Lk 18:19). Paul is likewise adamant that "goodness" does not characterize our sinful human condition. He writes:

> For I know that nothing good dwells within me, that is, in my flesh. I can will what is right, but I cannot do it. For I do not do the good I want, but the evil I do not want is what I do. Now if I do what I do not want, it is no longer I that do it, but sin that dwells within me. . . . Wretched man that I am! Who will rescue me from this body of death? Thanks be to God through Jesus Christ our Lord! (Rom 7:18-20, 24-25)

Second, if human bondage to sin makes us incapable of goodness apart from God, we are nevertheless created with the capacity and potential for goodness. This capacity for goodness stems from our being created in the image of a God who is perfect goodness. Although our bondage to sin weakens our capacity for goodness, this capacity is capable of being renewed by the work of the Holy Spirit within us. A new way of life is made possible by Christ and the work of the Spirit. Paul has such confidence in the work of the Spirit that he can assert, later in his letter to the Romans, that they are "full of goodness *[agathōsynē]*, filled with all knowledge, and able to instruct one another" (Rom 15:14). Or as Paul tells the Ephesians, we are "created in Christ Jesus for good works" (Eph 2:10). Finally, in one of Scripture's most arresting passages, the Second Epistle of Peter strikingly asserts that God's divine power has provided us what we need in order that we may participate in the divine nature, in the very life of God:

His divine power has given us everything needed for life and godliness, through the knowledge of him who called us by his own glory and goodness *[aretē]*. Thus he has given us, through these things, his precious and very great promises, so that through them you may escape from the corruption that is in the world because of lust, and may become participants of the divine nature. For this very reason, you must make every effort to support your faith with goodness *[aretē]*, and goodness with knowledge, and knowledge with self-control, and self-control with endurance, and endurance with godliness, and godliness with mutual affection, and mutual affection with love. For if these things are yours and are increasing among you, they keep you from being ineffective and unfruitful in the knowledge of our Lord Jesus Christ. (2 Pet 1:3-8)

Third, if God alone is good and humans are capable of good only by the work of God's Spirit, then knowing what counts for good can also only be determined under the guidance of God's Spirit. In other words, humans should not necessarily trust their notions of goodness, because there is reason to believe that our notions of goodness are themselves corrupt. Paul certainly suggests as much when he urges the Romans to be transformed in order that they will be able to discern what is good: "Do not be conformed to this world, but be transformed by the renewing of your minds, so that you may discern what is the will of God—what is good and acceptable and perfect" (Rom 12:2). In a similar way, prayers were being offered on behalf of the Colossians that "you may be filled with the knowledge of God's will in all spiritual wisdom and understanding, so that you may lead lives worthy of the Lord, fully pleasing to him, as you bear fruit in every good work and as you grow in the knowledge of God" (Col 1:9-10).

Understanding the connection between the work of the Spirit and goodness may explain why Barnabas is described as "a good man, full of the Holy Spirit and of faith" (Acts 11:24). Moreover, it may also suggest why leaders in the church are required to be "lovers of goodness" (Tit 1:8) and why Christians are warned that in the last days people will be "haters of good" (2 Tim 3:3).

Paul brings to a close his first letter to the Thessalonians with what might at first glance appear to be a hodgepodge of disconnected admonitions. (That this passage has traditionally been broken into eleven separate verses no doubt contributes to this impression.) But given the ways in which we have seen that the fruit of the Spirit are interconnected, perhaps we can see some connections that are at first glance difficult to see:

> But we appeal to you, brothers and sisters, to respect those who labor among you, and have charge of you in the Lord and admonish you; esteem them very highly in love because of their work. Be at peace among yourselves. And we urge you, beloved, to admonish the idlers, encourage the faint hearted, help the weak, be patient with all of them. See that none of you repays evil for evil, but always seek to do good to one another and to all. Rejoice always, pray without ceasing, give thanks in all circumstances; for this is the will of God in Christ Jesus for you. Do not quench the Spirit. Do not despise the words of prophets, but test everything; hold fast to what is good; abstain from every form of evil. (1 Thess 5:12-22)

These various admonitions, like the fruit of the Spirit themselves, share a common feature: their other-directedness. As a result, such practices as "doing good to one another" cannot easily be divorced from the practices of admonishing, encouraging, helping, rejoicing, praying and giving thanks. We must remember that being transformed into the image of Christ requires our being transformed into people who are capable of deep communion with God and one another. Thus the other-directedness that characterizes the life of goodness is nothing less than the posture that is required if we are to live out the purpose for which God has created us all.

Obstacles to a Life of Goodness

If discussions about "goodness" and "good" are inseparable from understandings of the purposes of human existence, then it should come as no surprise that many of us are deeply confused about both. Or more precisely, because most people believe that views about the purpose of human existence are part of the private realm (as discussed in an earlier chapter), they regard their views about goodness and the good to be likewise private and personal.

As a result, people in our society not only disagree about the purposes of human existence, but they have no way to adjudicate these disagreements. Indeed, because these disagreements are in the private realm, there is little reason to try to adjudicate them.

Democratizing goodness. For some people, of course, it is a mistake even to inquire about the purposes of human existence. For them, as for Shakespeare's Macbeth, life is little more than a "tale told by an idiot, full of sound and fury, signifying nothing." But for the vast majority, it appears that the purposes of human existence are not so much absent or illusory as they are derived and sustained purely at the personal level. This suggests why we find it increasingly difficult to discuss what used to be called "the common good." In its place we have substituted the notion that individuals should be free to determine for themselves what is "good" and "right" in any particular situation. Although there are some legal boundaries that would restrain us from doing what we agree is wrong to do, there is little that would help us know what is right or good to do. As a result, the "good" and the "right" are increasingly being reduced to what is legal; in short, if one has not broken any laws, one is a "good" or "moral" person. Or even more to the point, if one is merely decent, one is increasingly considered good. For example, note that we routinely call one of our favorite Bible stories the "parable of the good Samaritan," even though Jesus nowhere identifies him as such. Jesus simply identified him as a "certain Samaritan," presumably because he did no more (and certainly no less) than any decent Samaritan would have done. In contrast, we tend to think of him as the *really good* Samaritan, as if what he did was exceptional or even heroic.

We also see this tendency toward "democratizing goodness" in that widespread cultural conviction that all non-law-breaking people are on a moral par with one another. People who suggest or act otherwise by embodying convictions that they believe are more than simply their own personal preferences are routinely derided as being "self-righteous goody-goodies." Indeed, most children learn from an early age that you do not want to be distinguished from your peers by being too good, for doing so will often as not earn you their scorn.

It is perhaps telling that we often see such tendencies in the church as well. Most Christians rightly acknowledge that they are called to live differently than their non-Christian neighbors, and many believe (perhaps justifiably) that they really are better people. Most of us are not murderers, rapists or terrorists (though neither are most of our non-Christian neighbors), and so we easily fall into the trap of thinking that all in all, we are pretty good people. When we gather together as the people of God, we often act as if everything is okay, that we've got our lives under control and that whatever small or petty sin we may or may not be wrestling with is a matter between each of us and God. But we often forget that the story we've been called to embody before the world is not one where we get to be the "good guys." Jesus was crucified on account of my sins and your sins—past, present and future—and so when we gather there is little reason for pretense. We are the company of the forgiven, and yet when we gather together we often work very hard to give the impression that we are the company of those who "have it together."

But this is only half of the story. Although we work hard, at least on Sunday mornings, to give the impression that our lives are "together" and that we are generally good people, most of us don't really want to be too good the rest of the week, to live in such a way that our lives are distinctive. Indeed, we often find ourselves justifying our lack of goodness by resorting to the ever-popular slogan, "I'm only human." For Christians, democratizing goodness in this way is not an option. For us, God's desires for human life are defined by reflecting on the life of Jesus. Thus the Christian affirmation that Jesus was fully human should serve as a welcome reminder that "human" is not simply synonymous with "prone to error or sin." Rather, in the light of Jesus' life we come to realize that our problem is not that we are "only human" but that we are not human *enough.* Blaming our shortcomings on our humanity, therefore, makes a mockery not only of the life of Jesus but also of the lives of those saints throughout the ages who have sought to be human in the ways that he was human.

Sitting in the dark. One of the consequences of democratizing goodness is that we tend, as a result, to pay far too little attention to moral formation. If most people are for the most part already good, why bother to worry about moral formation? In contrast, most cultures of the past have devoted considerable time and energy to the task of moral formation. In most of those cultures this moral formation was facilitated largely by identifying exemplars to be imitated and through the telling of stories. Both practices mutually reinforced each other, because stories of virtuous people made it possible to recognize them in your midst, while flesh and blood exemplars served to remind us that the most powerful stories are embodied ones. The matter of imitation will be taken up more explicitly later in this chapter; at this juncture we focus on the cultural practice of storytelling and its place in the cultivation of goodness.

In most contemporary Western cultures the important task of telling stories has largely been handed over to popular media such as television and film. The question that arises, therefore, is whether these popular media are capable of telling the kinds of stories that can contribute to our moral formation in positive ways. Or asked another way, can television and film offer us convincing portrayals of characters whose lives are marked by goodness in such a way that they can serve as exemplars of goodness? I believe the answer to this question is theoretically yes; however, I also believe that there are several powerful reasons why we should not, at least in the short run, expect this to happen very often.

First, television and film are commercial enterprises, and as such they seek to hold our attention, either in order to entertain us (which is something for which we are willing to pay) or in order to provide a ready audience for advertisers (which is something for which they are willing to pay). This means that those who are involved in this enterprise are not usually first concerned about issues of moral formation. This is not to suggest that the stories these media portray have no impact on our moral formation, but only that this is likely not their creator's first concern. Their task is to hold our attention. As it turns out, one of the easiest ways to hold our attention is to present us with portraits of darkness and evil. Although in real life goodness is often attractive and evil repulsive, these poles seem to be reversed in these worlds of unreality. What often fascinates us about the evil portrayed in television and film (and in a good deal of literature as well) is that we are allowed to brush up against it without fear of harm. For example, though most of us would be terrified if not repulsed to be alone in the same room with "Hannibal the Cannibal" (a central character in the blockbuster film *The Silence of the Lambs*), many people find themselves strangely attracted to him when he enters our living rooms via the VCR. If popular commercial media are saturated with evil and sinister characters, this is partly because such characters more easily hold our attention.

But there is another and perhaps more interesting reason why television and film are largely populated with characters few of us want to hold up as moral exemplars. Stated bluntly: goodness is much more difficult to portray compellingly by means of a medium dominated by the visual. Audiences know firsthand that goodness is terribly difficult to live out, and so it is only interesting if people actually are embodying it, rather than simply pretending to in the realms of unreality known as television or film. Or more precisely, embodying goodness always involves a deep, internal struggle, yet television and film are poor media for exploring such struggles, not least because they offer so few engaging ways to explore human consciousness (an ability, in contrast, that literature routinely exploits to good effect). In short, most of us sense, even if unconsciously, that "being good" on television or in film is often too easy and therefore uninteresting. This, I believe, accounts for why so many "good" characters come across as flat and one-dimensional. Only if we become acquainted with them over time (either through a television series or full-length film) and are allowed to see their struggle does their goodness begin to become believable. It is worth noting that television and film are also ill-equipped to explore the genuine depths of human evil (for the same reasons listed above), but this does not handicap such portrayals nearly so much, because not understanding the motivations or intentions behind such evil often has the effect of making such evil characters more sinister and menacing and thus more capable of holding our attention.

Another reason that television and film are often populated with less-than-exemplary characters is that we seem to require ever-greater doses of evil to get the same effect, to continue to hold our interest. Therefore it should come as no surprise that television and film create darker and darker characters; indeed, actors like Dennis Hopper have made a career out of depicting warped and twisted characters. Another way to up the ante of evil and violence is to strip the story of anyone remotely good or virtuous. For example, films like *Batman* or *Speed* demonstrate that the line between heroes and villains no longer has anything to do with a person's character or his actions: everyone uses violence and deceit. Or perhaps more accurately, the "bad guys" use violence and deceit indiscriminately while the "good guys" only use it against the "bad guys."

I suppose some Christians might argue that such depictions of deep and abiding human sinfulness are quite in line with the view of human nature I have been sketching in this chapter. At one level, this is certainly true. One could reasonably argue that the unambiguous morality plays of yesteryear, with their clearly identifiable heroes and villains, did not do justice to the moral ambiguities of our lives. Yet perhaps their purpose was less to mirror our lives and more to train us to think and feel certain ways about good and evil. For example, not long ago one could recognize heroes because they would not stoop to the level of their adversaries; in contrast, the clear message of our contemporary morality plays seems to be that the only way to overcome indiscriminate evil is with clever, shrewd, discriminate evil. Within this way of thinking about the world, being "good" translates into little more than being less evil than the cinema's latest antihero. In short, "goodness" means little more than the absence of "badness."

Let me be clear: my point is not to blame television or film producers for our declining sensibilities about good and evil. Rather, Christians need to realize that if the limitations of the medium and our own fascination with evil make it easier to hold our attention with portrayals of evil, then a culture whose pervasive media are television and film will likely be surrounded with many more exemplars of evil than of good. Although television and film might provide welcome distractions, a culture that takes many of its cues about good and evil from these worlds of unreality certainly cannot contribute much to the formation of "good people." The shared cultural stories that these media offer us simply do not lend themselves to such formation. But if we cannot learn to be good by attending to the stories that circulate most widely in our culture, what other options are there? For many people the answer is simple: if goodness is not found in the world around us, we need only look within.

Helping ourselves. Ironically, such a strategy is deeply rooted in our cultural heritage, grounded as it is in our culture's stories. Our society's characteristic emphasis on the individual, combined with its characteristic optimism about human persons, has created a popular movement whose effects have been far-reaching both inside and outside the church. Often referred to as the "Self-Help Movement," this movement encourages us to believe that the resolutions to our problems are only the next technique or how-to book away. Of course, this tradition of self-help is not new in this country. As far back as the mid-1800s Ralph Waldo Emerson was extolling the virtues of "self-reliance," calling people to free themselves from the limitations of tradition and to rely on their own inner resources. The human spirit, according to Emerson, has the capacity for unlimited possibilities.

This confidence in the self runs from Emerson right through to the positive thinking movement of Norman Vincent Peale and others. Such confidence in the individual—especially when combined with psychotherapy's insistence that any authority outside the self is likely a source of bondage and pathology—has produced more than one generation whose view of self is inseparable from notions of inwardness and self-realization. For these generations goodness is to be found by turning inward, and the good life (or at least a "better" life) is to be found by cultivating one's own potentialities. To look outside one's self for direction or meaning is to court frustration if not disaster; only by looking within can one hope to unlock the secrets of human existence.

If self-help ways of thinking are as pervasive as they seem to be, then we might wonder whether and to what extent they have influenced how people think about the Christian faith. Predictably, increasing numbers of people consider the Christian faith as a form of self-help, as a technique for self-improvement. Indicators of this include not only the number of "secular" self-help books being read by Christians but also the number being written by and for Christians. In fact, one might argue that there is little or no substantive difference between self-help books written by and for Christians and those written for the general population. For example, I mentioned at the beginning of the chapter that my list of self-help titles came from two bookstores. What I did not disclose is that half of these titles were found in the self-help section of a Christian bookstore. My hunch is that most people would be unable to identify which titles were found in which bookstore. Now I admit that titles rarely tell the whole story, and we can certainly hope that Christian self-help books differ from their "secular" counterparts in significant ways, but my cursory reading in both groups suggests that they are remarkably similar.

Indeed, the more of these books I read the more I sense that the whole notion of "Christian self-help" is fundamentally misguided. Isn't "Christian self-actualization" a contradiction in terms, an oxymoron? Can we really tell the "good news" and still hold on to notions like "self-help"? A pivotal part of this gospel is the good news that we need no longer strive to help ourselves (because we cannot help ourselves enough to make any difference in God's eyes) and so are called to accept the only help that is real help—the help that God has freely offered. For this reason those Christians whose central creedal affirmation is that "God helps those who help themselves" need to reconsider their convictions in light of God's abundant grace.

If the self-help movement has likely influenced the way we think of the Christian faith, it has also likely impacted the way we think of ourselves. I suspect, for example, that the pervasiveness of this movement has made it increasingly difficult for our churches to talk about sin. Much of popular psychology, as well as the self-help movement, insists that talking about sin leads to debilitating guilt and other destructive pathologies. What people need is not to be told that they are sinners, but to be affirmed and accepted, to be encouraged to reach their potential. Thus in place of sermons that would help us name our sins we have positive-thinking sermons, and in place of sermons that would remind us of our need for Christ, we have "feel good" sermons that invite us to develop and rely on our own potentialities. This temptation—to substitute what people want to hear for what God wants to tell us—is hardly new. For example, Timothy is admonished about the necessity of proclaiming God's message regardless of whether his listeners desire to hear it or not:

> In the presence of God and of Jesus Christ, who is to judge the living and the dead, and in view of his appearing and his kingdom, I solemnly urge you: proclaim the message; be persistent whether the time is favorable or unfavorable; convince, rebuke, and encourage, with the utmost patience in teaching. For the time is coming when people will not put up with sound doctrine, but having itching ears, they will accumulate for themselves teachers to suit their own desires, and will turn away from listening to the truth and wander away to myths. (2 Tim 4:1-4)

Cultivating Goodness

The New Testament suggests that the people of God are called to be a light in the midst of a dark world—a "city on a hill" to their non-Christian neighbors. Although the New Testament is clear that such relative goodness in no way puts us in better stead with God, it does suggest that such goodness might serve to point our neighbors to something beyond ourselves. Thus goodness is other-directed in two ways. First, because we are not ourselves the standard of goodness, we take our cues about goodness from that Other who alone is truly good. And second, our capacity to reflect God's goodness both comes from God and is designed to draw others to God. This ability of God's reflected goodness to draw others to God is testified to in Scripture several times. For example, in the Sermon on the Mount Jesus admonishes his followers to "let your light shine before others, so that they may see your good works and give glory to your Father in heaven" (Mt 5:16). Paul urges the Philippians to "do all things without murmuring and arguing so that you may be blameless and innocent, children of God without blemish in the midst of a crooked and perverse generation, in which you shine like stars in the world" (Phil 2:14-15). In a similar way Peter admonishes his fellow Christians to live honorable lives, even though some of their practices will likely be misunderstood: "Beloved, I urge you as aliens and exiles to abstain from the desires of the flesh that wage war against the soul. Conduct yourselves honorably among the Gentiles, so that, though they malign you as evildoers, they may see your honorable deeds and glorify God when he comes to judge" (1 Pet 2:11-12).

Learning to name our sin. Even though God calls us to live lives of goodness, part of our ongoing story is that we repeatedly fail to do so. This is why it is imperative for Christian churches to incorporate into their weekly worship a period of confession. This has been an important practice of the church for centuries, and yet it is becoming less popular in the age of self-help and feel-good religion. We are not the ones who have it all together, and our worship should testify to this. Coming into the presence of our holy and perfect God should make us more mindful than ever of our rebelliousness and hard-heartedness. Each of us should be encouraged to confess not merely our generic sinfulness, but our specific sins. Healing requires accurate diagnosis; a doctor who told us we were generically sick would impress none of us. Yet many of us shy away from naming (or having named for us) the sins that so easily and frequently entangle us.

As important as personal confession is, the church desperately needs to encourage confession beyond the individual level. The people of God need to be able to confess together that they have not been the kind of community that they have been called to be in their specific time and place. Confessing as a church will no doubt be more difficult, not least because such confession presumes the existence of a corporate identity, something that many churches lack. Or said another way, we will not be able to confess as a church the ways in which we have failed as a church until we understand what it means to be the church. Here again we bump up against the centrality of purpose for understanding identity. Until we better understand God's purposes for the church, we will not be able to confess specifically the ways in which we have failed to embody those purposes.

Attending to God's voice. Fortunately God has not left us bereft of resources to understand those purposes. One of the most important of those resources throughout the history of the church has been the preaching of the word of God. Certainly this is not the only way that the word of God can come to God's people, but God's people gathered together to hear and discern a word from God remains a central and defining practice of the church. Here, God addresses us not simply individually, but corporately as well.

There is, of course, a proper place for personal reflection on Scripture, but the abuses to which such study is open within a culture that fosters hyper-individualism are many. For example, it is easy in a culture obsessed with individualism to believe that the most determinative way to read Scripture is by oneself. But we are never truly alone when we are reading; rather, we are always reading in the company of other voices that are shaping our readings in crucial ways. Thus one of the central questions that Christians must always ask themselves is this: With whom are we reading Scripture? Which of the myriad voices around us are influencing our reading of Scripture? Unfortunately, we are never urged to ask such questions when we are under the illusion that we are reading Scripture "alone."

In a culture that teaches us that what we take to be our own personal interpretations are just as legitimate as anyone else's, the church needs a time and a place where we discern together what God has to say. We need a time and place where we can inquire together concerning which voices have truly captured our attention. Obviously there is no guarantee that a clear word from God will be either preached or heard during any gathering. Nevertheless, I suspect that whether such a word is preached or heard at any given gathering has less to do with whether God has anything to tell us and more to do with whether the parties involved (preacher and congregants) come with the expectation that God's presence will be manifested and God's voice heard.

Christians throughout history have firmly believed that preaching and teaching had to involve more than simply offering personal advice or wisdom. The word of God proclaimed must have some connection to the word of God written. That we expect those who proclaim the Word to do more than simply read from Scripture suggests that we believe God's message to us will involve more than the words of Scripture; most Christians, however, do not think that it can involve less than that. And although there is no doubt that the word of God frequently brings a word of encouragement, it often brings a word of judgment and admonition. This is not because God is not a God of encouragement, but because God understands what we most need and given our inclination to sin, what we often need is correction. Hear again one of the passages of Scripture that is frequently quoted by conservative and evangelical Christians:

> All scripture is inspired by God and is useful for teaching, for reproof, for correction, and for training in righteousness, so that everyone who belongs to God may be proficient, equipped for every good work. (2 Tim 3:16-17)

Sometimes debates about these verses have so focused on the character of inspiration that we have forgotten what these verses claim is the function of Scripture: to teach, reprove, correct and train in righteousness. Presumably, the object of such reproof and correction is not simply our neighbors—who we routinely assume to be in error—but also us. I suppose that if we found it easy or natural to desire what God desires, then we would have much less reason to need God's word, either in its embodied, written or proclaimed forms. But given our penchant for wanting things our own way, we need to be reminded constantly of God's ways. Gathering each week with the expectation that God has something important to tell us as a congregation is crucial to our being able to cultivate God's goodness in our lives.

Imitating the saints. Simply hearing repeatedly what God wants of us is not enough. As important as hearing the word of God is, knowing how to respond is equally important. Indeed, it may be that many of us know in our heads quite well what God expects of us; what we lack is the ability to translate this knowledge into daily action. This is why God has not only given us Scripture to guide us but also other Christians to imitate. In fact, there may be a much closer connection between these two resources than we have often realized. The verses that precede the famous Timothy passage quoted above, though less-often cited, are no less important:

> Now you have observed my teaching, my conduct, my aim in life, my faith, my patience, my love, my steadfastness, my persecutions and suffering the things that happened to me in Antioch, Iconium, and Lystra. What persecutions I endured! Yet the Lord rescued me from all of them. Indeed, all who want to live a godly life in Christ Jesus will be persecuted. But wicked people and imposters will go from bad to worse, deceiving others and being deceived. But as for you, continue in what you have learned and firmly believed, knowing

from whom you learned it, and how from childhood you have known the sacred writings that are able to instruct you for salvation through faith in Christ Jesus. (2 Tim 3:10-15)

Timothy is encouraged not only to ponder what he has learned but also to remember from whom he has learned it. At first glance, this may appear to be a simple power play: "Ponder what you learned and take it to heart, because I taught you and I'm in charge." But Timothy is not simply urged to obey those in authority; rather, he is reminded of the authority of embodied witness. In short, Timothy is asked to remember what gives the writer authority: Timothy has observed his teaching, conduct, aim in life, faith, patience, love, steadfastness, persecutions and sufferings. In other words, Timothy was not simply taught what to believe, but was also clearly shown what difference any of it makes for how one lives. This was why the *what* that he learned and the *from whom* he learned it could not be easily separated.

Thus, learning to live a Christian life requires not simply learning the right words, but learning how to embody a way of life. As the letter to the Hebrews urges, "Remember your leaders, those who spoke the word of God to you; consider the outcome of their way of life, and imitate their faith" (Heb 13:7). John writes, "Beloved, do not imitate what is evil but imitate what is good. Whoever does good is from God; whoever does evil has not seen God" (3 Jn 11). Or as Paul reminds the Thessalonians, the persuasive power of the gospel message was inseparable from the way Paul and other Christians lived before them, a way of life that the Thessalonians took to heart and imitated:

> For we know, brothers and sisters beloved by God, that he has chosen you, because our message of the gospel came to you not in word only, but also in power and in the Holy Spirit and with full conviction; just as you know what kind of persons we proved to be among you for your sake. And you became imitators of us and of the Lord, for in spite of persecution you received the world with joy inspired by the Holy Spirit, so that you became an example to all the believers in Macedonia and in Achaia. (1 Thess 1:4-7)

Many of us would like to keep the Christian faith out of the imitation business, for we rightly sense the dangers of imitating other people. Or more precisely, while many of us are comfortable with the idea of imitating Christ, few of us feel at ease with imitating our fellow pilgrims, and even fewer of us are comfortable with people imitating us. But there is no way around it, for we only know what it means to imitate Christ as we see other people following Christ in this way rather than that way. Moreover, the issue is not *whether* people will imitate us—they already do whether we like it or not—but whether they will be led to imitate *Christ* by imitating us. In other words, it is not an either/or decision, a matter of following Christ or following fallible people; it is a matter of following fallible people who are empowered by the Holy Spirit to follow Christ.

This is why Paul writes, "I appeal to you, then, be imitators of me. For this reason I sent to you Timothy, who is my beloved and faithful child in the Lord, to remind you of my ways in Christ Jesus, as I teach them everywhere in every church" (1 Cor 4:16-17). Later on in the same letter he writes, "Be imitators of me, as I am of Christ" (1 Cor 11:1). Prior to the selection from Ephesians with which I began this chapter, Paul urges his hearers to be "imitators of God" (Eph 5:1). Given the quite specific exhortations that Paul offers before and after this admonition, Paul in no way considers being "imitators of God" to be an abstract exercise. Imitating God or Christ or Paul may be difficult, but it is hardly abstract. What are needed are concrete embodied examples of what such imitating looks like.

The problem is that many contemporary Christians mistakenly believe that learning to follow Christ is analogous to learning how to use a new computer program. What is required is little more than the patience to decipher the manual and the ability to follow written directions. However, learning how to follow Christ is less like learning how to use a new computer program and more like learning how to swing a baseball bat. The latter is a kind of skill that you learn primarily by imitation. You can certainly learn something about swinging a bat by reading books about it and by watching others do it, but most people don't learn to swing a bat this way. Most learn by having someone who is willing to stand behind them, to place their hands on the bat along with their own and to go through the awkward yet necessary movement of swinging the bat. The reason they can have confidence that they are doing it right, even though it doesn't feel right, is that someone who knows how to do it better than they do is doing with them and guiding their movements.

Many of us could learn a great deal about how to live the Christian life more faithfully from those saints around us if we were but willing to acknowledge that they know how to do some things better than we do. Granted, they still have their flaws and they will continue to falter, just as we will. But perhaps we can also learn something important about the Christian life from their response to their failures, as well as to their victories. Paul knew better than anyone that he was far from perfect; nevertheless, this foremost of sinners repeatedly instructed his fellow Christians to imitate him. Dangerous advice, most assuredly, but perhaps no more dangerous than leaving each of us to decide for ourselves what following Christ should look like. Perhaps once again we are in a position to hear an oft-quoted passage with fresh ears:

> Finally, beloved, whatever is true, whatever is honorable, whatever is just, whatever is pure, whatever is pleasing, whatever is commendable, if there is any excellence *[aretē]* and if there is anything worthy of praise, think about these things. Keep on doing the things that you have learned and received and heard and seen in me, and the God of peace will be with you. (Phil 4:8-9)

Reflection Questions and Practical Suggestions

Confession, preaching, imitation. These are three important activities we need to recover if God is going to cultivate goodness in the life of the church. Each of these three requires frank admissions for which the self-help movement in no way prepares us. First, we are sinners before God who need to name those sins. Second, because we do not have what is necessary to help ourselves, we need a vision of the good beyond ourselves. Finally, we need not only a vision of the good, but concrete exemplars to imitate. Given that the recovery of these three crucial practices will not come overnight, where might we begin?

☐ Reflect on these practices in light of your own fears. Why are we afraid to confess our sins to one another? Are we afraid that people would not love us if they really knew what we were like? Is this why we expend such enormous energy constructing and maintaining façades that we hope will lead people to believe that we have our lives together? But if the gospel is about God reaching out to us because our lives were (and are) such a mess, shouldn't we—of all people—be able to gather together without the pretense of being something we are not?

Why do we devote so little time during our corporate gatherings to discerning whether or not we have heard a clear word of God? Is it because such discernment would be difficult, messy and time-consuming? Or are we also afraid that if we were to risk such discernments, and we were to acknowledge that we had heard such a word, then we would have little excuse for not responding? In other words, is our refusal to discern whether we have heard a word from God really a thinly veiled strategy for endlessly deferring the necessity of responding in obedience?

Why are we afraid to make a concerted effort to imitate other Christians or have them imitate us? Is it simply because we recognize the potential danger of such imitating, recognizing that other people are as capable of leading us astray as we are of them? Or is it also because we would rather not take responsibility for the way other Christians are already imitating us, even if we've never given them permission to do so? It seems that by refusing to acknowledge the ways in which imitation is already taking place, even if haphazardly, we continue to underwrite the charade that our Christian life is a strictly private affair. Moreover, by sidestepping the matter of imitation, we are allowed the luxury of simply admiring other Christians without pondering whether we are being called to live more like them and hence more like Christ. Perhaps this helps explain why exemplars like Mother Teresa are more often admired than imitated.

These are likely only some of the debilitating fears that plague us. As you strive to be honest about these and others you may have, try to focus less on these fears and more on the potential for confession, preaching and imitation to be avenues of God's grace. As you do so, consider taking one of the following baby steps, or another that seems more appropriate given your own circumstances.

☐ If it is not already present, encourage those in leadership to include during worship a period of confession, both individual and corporate. This will likely be most difficult at the corporate level, but stumbling to articulate our joint failings as a congregation or parish will likely go some way toward instilling a necessary sense of corporate identity.

For too long, Protestants have abandoned the importance of Christian confession because of abuses in the past. But contrary to the privatistic way most of us have come to think of our sin, James encourages his hearers to "confess your sins to one another, and pray for one another, so that you may be healed" (Jas 5:16). As long as we continue to think of our sin as simply a private matter between each of us and God, we continue to cut ourselves off from one of the resources God has given to the church for our healing. With this in mind consider asking a close Christian friend if you may confess your sins in his or her presence. Pray together about those sins and be willing to be held accountable for your repentance.

☐ Determine that you will seek more diligently to hear God's voice. This might take several different forms, but I often wonder what would happen if the people of God began to take preaching more seriously. What if we really expected God to speak to us? Perhaps we should begin by doing a better job of preparing our hearts and minds each week to receive God's word. What do we do to prepare to hear God? Perhaps our own lack of expectation and preparation is closely tied to our lack of reception: we have not heard God because we did not come expecting to hear God. In addition, we can probably do a better job of letting those charged with proclaiming the word of God know that we expect nothing less. Those so charged are often hesitant to proclaim the full counsel of God because they sense that those gathered do not want to hear it. We need to remind them that we have come not to hear what *we* want to hear but what *God* wants us to hear. How many times have we dropped our pastors a line thanking them for speaking a word of God to us? I suspect that if we did this more often, many ministers—reminded that we are listening attentively to their words for the voice of God—would take the task of preaching even more seriously than they currently do.

☐ Consider seeking out more public ways of responding to God's word.

When I was a child and my mother or father spoke to me, they expected a response, for it was in such a response that they could discern whether or not I had really heard them. They did not speak merely because they liked the sound of their voices; they spoke because they thought I needed to hear them and to respond appropriately. Likewise, if we come expecting to hear God's word and we do hear it, might not God rightly expect us to respond in some way? And shouldn't this response take a form that goes beyond each of us responding in our own way, oblivious to how others are responding? Or asked another way, if God's word to us really is a word to *us* (and not just a word to each of us individually who just happen to be in the same place), then shouldn't at least part of our response take a corporate form? Why is it that the "application" portion of the sermon almost always gives suggestions for how this message might affect *me*, but rarely for how it should affect *us*? If nothing else, aren't we as a congregation responsible for discerning whether the message we have heard is from God or not? What kind of forum do we need to test these spirits, to discern if they are of God? I fear that congregations all over the country have been unwittingly trained not to respond to the word of God because no opportunity for corporate response is offered. For most of us, we simply hear (or don't hear) the word of God, go home for the week and then come back to hear (or not hear) the following week. What is the point of this? Perhaps we should begin by devoting time each week to asking some questions of each other. Have we heard the word of God or not? What was that word specifically? And what should our response as a congregation be to that word? I could be wrong, but my sense is that such a practice would radically transform not only the way we listen to the word of God, but also the way we embody our life together.

☐ With regard to imitation, ask God to give you the courage to ask a person in your congregation whom you respect if you can "hang out" with them occasionally. We need opportunities to see what such people's lives look like day to day. What challenges do they face and how do they meet them? Similarly, consider encouraging a younger person in the faith to look over your shoulder, not because you have the Christian life down pat, but because you rightly sense there is no other way of learning how to embody a life marked by goodness.

□ In addition to the practice of imitating a fellow flesh-and-blood pilgrim—or as a temporary alternative for those not yet ready to take up such a practice—we would do well to immerse ourselves in the stories of the saints across the centuries. If Christians are to resist having their imaginations stunted by the relatively narrow repertoire of stories circulated by the dominant culture, we will need to recover and begin circulating among ourselves a much wider set of stories. The stories of the people of God across time and space are capable not only of inspiring us by reminding us of God's goodness and faithfulness, but they are also capable of enriching our parochial notions of God's goodness and God's desires of and for us. Hence, those who seek to have the fruit of goodness cultivated in their lives would do well to immerse themselves in the stories of those Christian saints across time and space whose lives have already borne this fruit. By allowing such "good seed" to be sown in our hearts and imaginations, we take an important and necessary first step toward allowing the fruit of goodness to be cultivated in our own lives.

> *Do not be deceived; God is not mocked, for you reap whatever you sow. If you sow to your own flesh, you will reap corruption from the flesh; but if you sow to the Spirit, you will reap eternal life from the Spirit. So let us not grow weary in doing what is right, for we will reap at harvest time, if we do not give up. So then, whenever we have an opportunity, let us work for the good of all, and especially for those of the family of faith. (Gal 6:7-10)*

EIGHT
Cultivating
Faithfulness
in the Midst of
Impermanence

But as for that [seed] in the good soil, these are the ones who, when they hear the word, hold it fast in an honest and good heart, and bear fruit with patient endurance. (Lk 8:15)

Let us hold fast to the confession of our hope without wavering, for he who has promised is faithful. (Heb 10:23)

The story has been repeated so many times that we know it almost by heart. The group began in 1990 with seventy men and a football coach. The following year 4,200 men attended the first official rally. In 1992 over five times that many came, and the next year 50,000 men packed into a single stadium in Denver, Colorado. In 1994 the rallies spread to seven stadiums around the country, with attendance topping 275,000. This phenomenal growth continued during the next three years, with attendance at twenty-four stadium rallies in 1997 reaching 1.25 million.

Whatever one thinks of the Promise Keepers movement, their growth during the early 1990s was nothing short of phenomenal. The movement also worked hard to get racial reconciliation on the agenda of many churches that had long ignored the implications of the gospel for that area of their lives.

Moreover, their very name—Promise Keepers—drew national attention to a practice that is vital to any society but rarely discussed: the making and keeping of promises. One might assume, given the chord that the Promise Keepers movement has struck, that plenty of people find such activities difficult within the dominant culture. Why might this be so? At their root, promise making and promise keeping presume a willingness to bind oneself to another person or group of people. Are there features of the dominant culture that inhibit our willingness to so bind ourselves? Before attempting to answer that question, we need to examine more carefully what this fruit of the Spirit entails.

The Character of Faithfulness

Like each of the fruit, the Spirit's fruit of faithfulness has its roots in the very character of God. When we allow the Spirit to do its work in our lives, we do not simply become more human; we also become more like God, in whose image we were created. That image is slowly but most assuredly being restored by the work of Christ through his Spirit.

The Greek word that Paul uses in his list in Galatians is *pistis,* the same word that in other contexts is translated as "faith." Although some of the older translations render this fruit as "faith," given the clear ethical character of the fruit previously listed, a better rendering may be "faithfulness." It would be a mistake, however, to drive a wedge between these two meanings, since there is an obvious connection between faith as trust and faithfulness as trustworthiness. Or said another way, if we stop thinking of faith in purely cognitive terms and accentuate instead faith's character as trust, then faith itself will be seen to have ethical implications. Surely one's life is profoundly shaped by whether, whom, what, when and how one trusts. Once we recover this richer sense of faith, we are in a better position to see God's double claim on our lives: God calls us both to trust God (who is trustworthy) and to emulate God's trustworthiness. Trust requires steadfastness. Trust cannot be fickle, but must be constant and firm. Thus Paul tells the Colossians that he rejoices to see the "firmness" of their faith and encourages them to continue to live their lives in Christ Jesus, "rooted and built up in him and established in the faith, just as you were taught, abounding in thanksgiving" (Col 2:5-7).

In the Old Testament the Hebrew words that modern versions routinely translate as "faithfulness" are *ᵓmet* and *ᵓmûnâ*. In older translations these words were often rendered as "truth." For example, when Abraham's servant travels to find a wife for Isaac and is led to Rebekah, he announces, "Blessed be the LORD God of my master Abraham, who hath not left destitute my master of his mercy [*ḥesed*] and his truth [*ᵓmeth*]" (Gen 24:27 KJV). Or, as the well-known translation of Psalm 100 states, "For the LORD is good; his mercy [*ḥesed*] is everlasting; and his truth [*ᵓmûnâ*] endureth to all generations" (Ps 100:5 KJV). Given that our contemporary understandings of mercy and truth are relatively narrow, simply substituting our contemporary understandings for these words is inadequate and perhaps even misleading. Contemporary translations have done a better job of capturing both the richness of these Hebrew concepts and the intimate connections between them:

> Blessed be the LORD, the God of my master Abraham, who has not forsaken his steadfast love and his faithfulness toward my master. (Gen 24:27)

> For the LORD is good; his steadfast love endures forever, and his faithfulness to all generations. (Ps 100:5)

Reliability, steadfastness, constancy, fidelity, dependability, trustworthiness. Few would doubt that these characterize God, for God truly is "a faithful God, without deceit" (Deut 32:4). When Moses receives his epiphany of God, the Lord passes before him and proclaims, "The LORD, the LORD, a God merciful and gracious, slow to anger, and abounding in steadfast love and faithfulness" (Ex 34:6). Here again we see the intimate connection between God's steadfast covenant love [*ḥesed*] and God's faithfulness. Indeed, this close connection echoes throughout the Old Testament (Gen 32:9; 2 Sam 2:6; 15:20; 1 Kings 3:6; Ps 25:10; 26:3; 36:5; 40:10-11; 57:10; 61:7; 85:10; 86:15; 88:11; 89; 92:2; 98:3; 100:5; 108:4; 115:1; 117:2; 138:2; Lam 3:22-23; Hos 2:19-20). This is hardly surprising, since even translations of *ḥesed* themselves—either as "steadfast love" or as "covenant love"—contain within them the notion of an abiding faithfulness.

Anyone who has read Scripture knows that the God depicted there is a God who keeps promises made. Whether it is God's dealings with Noah and his family, with Abraham and Sarah or with Moses and the children of Israel in the wilderness, throughout the pages of Scripture God is depicted again and again as a covenant-making and covenant-keeping God. In fact, many of us are so familiar with these stories that they no longer strike us as extraordinary. The God revealed in these stories is not a start-the-world-spinning-and-leave-it-to-its-own-devices sort of God; rather, this God is a God who chooses both to enter into a covenant relationship with a particular people in a specific time and place, and to be bound by that covenant forever. This is extraordinarily revealing. This God is not an aloof, abstract God. This God desires to be known through these concrete relationships: God created these people (the children of Israel) as a people, and God continues to sustain them as a people. Indeed, apart from this God, these people have no identity. Yet even more remarkably, apart from this people, this God would not have the identity that this God desires to have. This God chooses to be bound to this people and by being so bound, to reveal the mysterious depths of this God's love.

Here we glimpse another facet of God's other-directedness. Even in God's choosing of a specific people, God remains other-directed. The people of Israel are reminded that they were not chosen because they were special (Deut 7:7-9), but that they were chosen for a purpose, a mission—to be a light to the nations (Is 42:6; cf. 60:3). God does not choose to be bound to this people because it serves some need God has; on the contrary, God enters into covenant relationship with Israel as a strategy for reconciling all of creation to its creator. It is precisely through this covenant people that the nations will come to see something of the character and nature of this God that desires to be in intimate relationship with all creation.

Once we see how central this practice of being bound to others is to the very identity of this God, we need no longer draw a sharp distinction between God's love and God's faithfulness. God's faithfulness is not something added to God's love, but stands as one of the very hallmarks of God's love: God loves with a faithful, steadfast love. As noted earlier, this suggests that God's faithfulness is not rooted in anything about us, but in God's very character. God loves this way because this is who God is. God's inability to deny God's own character is the basis for the following affirmation, words that have likely been incorporated into this pastoral letter from an early Christian hymn:

> The saying is sure *[pistos]:*
> If we have died with him, we will also live with him;
> if we endure, we will also reign with him;
> if we deny him, he will also deny us;
> if we are faithless, he remains faithful *[pistos]*—
> for he cannot deny himself. (2 Tim 2:11-13)

In the pages of the New Testament this affirmation that God is faithful becomes almost formulaic. For example, Paul affirms that our calling in Christ is a direct result of God's faithfulness to us. He writes, "God is faithful; by him you were called into the fellowship *[koinōnia]* of his Son, Jesus Christ our Lord" (1 Cor 1:9). Likewise, John insists that our confidence in God's forgiveness is rooted in God's faithfulness: "If we confess our sins, he who is faithful and just will forgive us our sins and cleanse us from all unrighteousness" (1 Jn 1:9).

Because hardship often tempts us to doubt God's providential care, the New Testament addresses specifically God's faithfulness in the midst of suffering and trials. In a passage already referred to in an earlier chapter, James encourages his fellow believers to see the connection between testing and maturity:

> My brothers and sisters, whenever you face trials of any kind, consider it nothing but joy, because you know that the testing of your faith *[pistis;* "trust" or "faithfulness"]* produces endurance; and let endurance have its full effect, so that you may be mature and complete, lacking in nothing (Jas 1:2-4; cf. 1 Cor 10:13; 1 Pet 4:19).

Our God is a faithful God, and even though those who are emissaries of this God are likewise called to be faithful, Scripture consistently testifies to our habitual unfaithfulness. Our ancestors in the faith are identified as a "stubborn and rebellious generation, a generation whose heart was not steadfast, whose spirit was not faithful to God" (Ps 78:8). Like Israel, our unfaithfulness often stems from our lack of faith or trust in God. The wilderness experience of Israel is a stark reminder of how easily we doubt God's providential care, even in the face of powerful testimony to God's faithfulness. The entire third chapter of the book of Hebrews contrasts the unfaithfulness of those who were disobedient to God in the wilderness with the faithfulness of Christ. Scripture is replete with stories of people who, rather than trust in God's ways, determined to take matters into their own hands, often with disastrous consequences. Too often we follow directly in their footsteps, reaping similar results.

Over and over again God's prophets ring out stinging rebukes of Israel's unfaithfulness (cf. Jer 5). Indeed, these rebukes can be read as a reminder that God refuses to give up on those to whom God is bound. We see this most poignantly in what is perhaps the most moving prophetic enactment in all of Scripture: God's command to Hosea to marry the prostitute Gomer. God instructs Hosea to bind himself to Gomer as a visual, embodied reminder of the way God has chosen to be bound to God's people despite their unfaithfulness. Despite Gomer's past and despite her future unfaithfulness, Hosea is called to bear with her just as God bears with Israel. As Paul reminds the Romans, our unfaithfulness cannot provoke God to unfaithfulness:

> What if some were unfaithful? Will their faithlessness nullify the faithfulness of God? By no means! Although everyone is a liar, let God be proved true. (Rom 3:3-4)

Even God's judgment of Israel is an example of God's other-directed love, a point not lost on Paul in his discussion of Israel's future (Rom 9—11). Rather than understanding God's judgment as a vengeful act of an impatient God, Paul insists that God's treatment of Israel is other-directed in two important ways. First, Israel's rejection of Jesus has led Israel to stumble, but this stumbling has provided a providential opportunity for God's other-directed love to reach the Gentiles, who are to be grafted into Israel. Second, this spurning of Israel is intended for its ultimate good, as a way of provoking

Israel to jealousy and thus drawing Israel back to God. Hence, even in Israel's "rejection," God's other-directed love is working for Israel's ultimate good and thus is no final rejection at all.

As disciples and servants of the Faithful One, we are called to be faithful. Several times in the New Testament we are reminded that stewards are called to be faithful or trustworthy with that which they have been entrusted. In Jesus' parable of the talents the first two servants are commended for being good *(agathē)* and faithful *(pistos)* slaves (Mt 25:21-23; cf. Lk 19:17). It is perhaps with this parable in mind that Paul tells the Corinthians, "Think of us in this way, as servants of Christ and stewards of God's mysteries. Moreover, it is required of stewards that they be found trustworthy *(pistos)*" (1 Cor 4:1-2). Indeed, faithfulness is so central to the character of the Christian that when Paul commends to his hearers a fellow Christian, he routinely describes them simply as "faithful" (1 Cor 4:17; Eph 6:21; Col 1:7; 4:9).

Obstacles to a Life of Faithfulness

In stark contrast to the faithfulness and reliability of God, we live and move within a dominant culture increasingly characterized by rapid change and instability. Although every age must grapple with the challenges evoked by change, the sheer scope and pace of change in most Western cultures over the last one hundred years has been unprecedented. Hence, if we desire to cooperate with God's desire to cultivate faithfulness in our lives, we will have to do so in the midst of a culture that traffics in the impermanent and the fleeting.

Nurturing ephemerality and disposability. In an earlier chapter I argued that contemporary practices of advertising, aligned as they are with the drive toward novelty, cultivate within us a paradoxical "loyalty" to the transitory and fleeting. We are, in short, encouraged to be deeply committed to being uncommitted. Although most of us learned at an early age that, contrary to popular belief, the grass is *not* always greener on the other side, our lives continue to embody this sentiment in countless ways. Rather than sticking with anything for any length of time—whether it be spouses, jobs, friends, churches or hobbies—we tend to flit from one thing to the next in search of that missing "something." As a result, convictions and practices of faithfulness and commitment rarely get the chance to sprout, let alone thrive.

One of the telling features of the dominant culture and one that tends to choke out convictions regarding commitment and faithfulness is the value placed on disposability. We have disposable plates, napkins, eating utensils, packaging, razors, diapers, contact lenses and cameras. Indeed, almost every week a new product comes on the market whose primary "virtue" (read "selling point") is its disposability. For a throwaway culture the obvious advantage of disposables is that such products require no upkeep. Rather than service those things that serve us, we create products that we can simply discard. We euphemistically tell ourselves that we buy and use these products for their convenience; what we mean is that these products require nothing of us. They do not need to be washed, sterilized, cleaned or repaired. They are designed so that their usefulness will be so short-lived that it will be easier to throw them away than to service them. What, after all, would be the point of washing paper plates or diapers, since the whole point of using them is to avoid doing this in the first place?

But the disposable mentality is not limited to merely those items that are created and marketed as disposable; it also extends to countless other items whose obsolescence (planned or otherwise) encourages us to dispose of them rather than service them. For example, Kim and I were once shopping for an inexpensive cassette tape player for one of our children's birthdays. Much to our surprise we found one for around ten dollars. When this tape player stops functioning in two or three years, as it most certainly will, are we really going to take it somewhere to have it fixed, knowing that parts are likely not available and that a technician's fees are around $35 per hour? Why not just trash this one and get another? I hate throwing things into the local landfill, but what choice do I have? Or take another common example. Even as I write, our family is trying to decide what to do with a computer for which we paid $3,000 several years ago, but which now needs over $500 worth of repairs to it, even though the computer is now only worth about $200 on the open market. How often do we find ourselves making this kind of choice, a choice between the old, out-dated and now expensive-to-keep-up item and the new, up-to-date and seemingly more cost-effective product? Don't most of us feel like fools when we find ourselves explaining that we are currently putting more into something than it is ostensibly worth?

Within such a culture should we really be surprised if we find it easier and easier to "dispose" of relationships once they too have outlived their usefulness? Employers now speak of "disposable workforces" that consist of part-time employees with low wages and no benefits. Such workforces command no loyalty from their employers; employees are simply dismissed when they are no longer needed. Couples decide to live with each other and "keep their options open" rather than make what they consider to be unrealistic promises. Each mistakenly assumes that they have the best of both worlds: all the benefits of an intimate relationship without any of the risks and liabilities of long-term entanglements.

How does functioning within a "disposable" culture affect the church? Not a few Christians have a tendency to jump ship when the going gets tough at a particular congregation. If they try to change things, try to move the church along, and it doesn't happen, they're tempted to pack their bags and go elsewhere. Such a practice seems to reflect a level of commitment no deeper than the average consumer's commitment to a given product; once dissatisfied, the search is on for something better, where what is "better" is typically determined by what will best meet one's perceived needs. This easy willingness to "move on" also rests on the assumption that congregations and their constitutive relationships are fully interchangeable. Although there is something positive about knowing that we belong to a worldwide community of brothers and sisters in Christ, we perhaps do more damage than we know to the body of Christ by appealing to the catholicity of the church in order to avoid committing ourselves to any specific group of Christians.

Shunning commitments. This last example suggests that a "disposable" culture might dispose us to avoid making commitments in the first place. That is, in a culture marked by evanescence, where everything appears to be changing rapidly, it makes no sense to limit your options by committing yourself to any one person, group of persons, or even course of action. Surely everyone knows that making commitments, promises and covenants in an environment of constant change and mobility is a sure recipe for heartache and disappointment. Why bother?

Such sentiments, although understandable, remind us of how reverently our culture continues to worship at the altar of the individual. Within the cult of the individual there simply are no satisfactory answers to questions such as: Why should I keep my promises? Or (more to the point) why should I even *make* promises? If what is most important is the individual and the individual's desire to remain as unconstrained as possible, then making—let alone keeping—promises appears to be an ill-advised, if not ridiculous, practice. And in a culture as mobile as ours, such practices make even less sense. Why bind yourself to other people when neither you nor they know whether six months from now you will even be around to follow through?

In an odd kind of way this reticence to make commitments may reflect a lingering sense of their importance. Even people who haven't thought about it very hard realize that promises bind us to other people. Hence, one strategy for avoiding being so bound (and therefore, so limited) is to shun commitments altogether. Why promise Kim that I will be home from work this afternoon at four o'clock, knowing full well that in so doing I both create certain expectations for her and limit my own options? Why tell the children that we will play baseball after dinner this evening, when doing so will raise expectations on their part and thereby discourage me from changing my mind and doing what I want to do after dinner? Why tell my Sunday-school class that I am available to help with a service project next weekend when in so doing I limit my options for next weekend? Why not simply tell Kim that I will be there when I get there, put the children off by telling them "we'll see," and keep my options open for next weekend by saying that "You'd better not count on me because I think we already have other plans"?

"You'd better not count on me." This serves as the unofficial motto of many people in our society. Although on the surface these words appear to be a safeguard against disappointing other people, in truth they are more often employed to safeguard our own independence and autonomy. The consequences for the cultivation of faithfulness are profound: many of us don't have to learn what is involved in remaining faithful because we have insured that no one is counting on us. Predictably many of these same people experience profound loneliness, cut off as they are from the intimacy created by being bound to other people through webs of promises and commitments. Such intimacy remains impossible as long as the only person I am committed to is myself.

Learning the proper objects of our loyalty. So far, the discussion has been limited to those ways in which the dominant culture discourages faithfulness. But it would be misleading to stop there, for this is only part of the problem. The balance concerns how the dominant culture disciplines us to be faithful or loyal to certain things in certain ways. Thus we need to inquire briefly about the objects of our faithfulness.

As suggested above, strong currents in our culture would encourage us to be faithful or true to ourselves. Typically, however, such faithfulness extends no further than loyalty to our own admittedly fickle feelings and moods. We see this best, perhaps, in the ways we have cultivated a deep aversion to doing anything out of obligation, telling ourselves in the process that it is more "authentic" or "honest" to do nothing at all than to do something "merely" from obligation. So if one doesn't feel like visiting one's grandparent in the nursing home this weekend, better to stay home and keep one's integrity and authenticity intact than visit out of obligation.

If the dominant culture teaches us to be true to ourselves, it also encourages us to be loyal to a few other people, as long as such loyalty is understood (and expressed) in specific ways. Employees are often expected to prove their loyalty to the company by doing things they might prefer not to do. Most of us know people, for example, who are routinely expected to lie for their bosses ("Oh, he's out of the office right now"), manipulate data for the benefit of their company, or tell their superiors only what they want to hear. Such, we are told, is what it means to be a loyal employee. In similar ways, friends (and spouses) often make unspoken agreements to tell each other less than the truth, believing that in doing so they are demonstrating their loyalty. As a result, being a person's friend often entails little more than tacitly agreeing to affirm them in whatever they determine to do. In contrast, admonishing one's friends, or calling their attention to possible self-deceptions, or encouraging them to be more than they currently are, are widely regarded as actions unbecoming of a true friend.

Finally, there are also ways in which we are encouraged to be "true to *us*," meaning, to our country. Most citizens of this nation would readily acknowledge that they owe a significant measure of allegiance and loyalty to the United States. But is this faithfulness to one's country total and unconditional, in the same way in which we are called to be faithful to God? What happens when this loyalty calls us (or those acting on our behalf) to die or to kill in the name of the nation-state and that for which it stands ("freedom")? Surely Christians, who are called to love their enemies, should at least be willing to discuss such difficult questions with each other, even if they must admit that easy answers to these questions are unavailable.

Cultivating Faithfulness

If God is to cultivate faithfulness in our lives, Christians will need to focus on those resources God has provided us for so doing. What kind of resources can the people of God draw on as they seek to reflect more fully God's abiding faithfulness in the midst of cultures like ours?

Celebrating God's abiding presence. If we begin again by reflecting on worship, we are quickly reminded that one of the church's deepest convictions is that God is present when we gather. We rightly spend little or no time wondering whether God is present when we worship because we have been promised that God would be so present. It would be easy to miss this obvious point because we so easily take for granted God's faithful presence. Yet the simple act of gathering itself is both an opportunity for God to make good on that promise to meet us in the gathered community and an opportunity for us to celebrate God's faithful presence.

Yet we do not simply gather. We gather to immerse ourselves again, by various means, in the stories of God and God's people, a major theme of which is God's remarkable faithfulness. As noted earlier in this chapter, Scripture testifies abundantly to God's faithfulness, so when we gather to hear this story again we will inevitably be reminded that we serve a God who is faithful and who calls us to be faithful as well. We are called to be disciples of the one whom the book of Revelation calls "the faithful witness" (Rev 1:5). It is worth noting that the Greek word translated here as "witness" *(martys)* is the same word from which we derive our English word *martyr*. The history of the church is filled with stories of people who, by God's grace, were such faithful witnesses, often to the point of death (cf. Rev 2:10). Although most of us will never be called to physical martyrdom, the witness of those who have been called stands as a powerful reminder that faithful discipleship is always costly discipleship.

Yet the church must not only tell the stories of those who have remained faithful; it must also tell the stories of those who have not. The church has nothing to gain by papering over its checkered past and present; indeed, the promise that God remains faithful even in our unfaithfulness would be unnecessary if we could assure God of our faithfulness. But God's grace triumphs in our failures as well, and though we in no way desire or court failure in order that God's grace may abound (Rom 6:1), we realize that we will never be found completely faithful until God's work has been completed in us. Short of that, we continue to stand in awe of God's unrelenting faithfulness, a faithfulness that refuses to let us go until God's perfect work has been brought to completion.

Making and keeping promises. Christians have reasons for making and keeping promises that other people may not have. We make such promises because we worship a promise-making and promise-keeping God who has called us to do the same as a witness, even if an imperfect one, to God's own faithfulness. Thus like God, we choose not to be known apart from the relationships we have entered by means of covenants and promises.

Marriage is one of the few practices left in our culture where we make public promises, and perhaps the recent decline in people getting married says as much about our unwillingness to make promises as it does our confusion about marriage. In the midst of this confusion about the purpose of marriage, Christian marriage stands as one of the central practices of the church and one of its most important resources when it comes to embodying faithfulness. Although Christian marriage is many things, when rightly understood it functions as a vital and visible embodiment and reminder of God's faithfulness. By making lifelong vows to each other the couple entering Christian marriage makes public promises that they themselves lack the resources to keep. This is certainly part of the risk of Christian marriage: only if God is faithful do they have any hope of having their union serve as a reflection of God's faithfulness. I can still remember being deeply moved during our wedding ceremony when the entire congregation bellowed out all the verses to "Great Is Thy Faithfulness." Kim and I were rightly convinced that our relationship to that point had been nurtured and sustained by God's faithfulness; we also knew we could only expect to fulfill our marriage vows, "till death do us part," by the continual and faithful outpouring of God's grace.

The longer I am married, the more clearly I see the ways I remain unfaithful to Kim. For too long my unfaithfulness remained cloaked by our culture's tendency to equate "being unfaithful" with "having an affair." In ways reminiscent of the last chapter, we too easily define faithfulness negatively; that is, I am considered a faithful husband if I am not sexually active with anyone other than my wife. But for Christians who have been called to embody in their own relationships a reflection of God's other-directedness, faithfulness and unfaithfulness cannot be reduced to matters of sexuality. When I stood before God and the church and made my vows, I promised to do a good deal more than not sleep around. For starters, I pledged to love and cherish her. Like most lifelong commitments, we grow into them, and I must admit that after many years of marriage, I am only now beginning to understand what loving and cherishing Kim entails. One matter is clear, however: loving and cherishing Kim entails being much less self-absorbed and much more other-directed than I am generally inclined to be. Being married to Kim calls me to transformation. Contrary to much popular opinion, making promises does not simply limit one's options: it also opens up new possibilities. By agreeing to have my life inextricably bound to Kim's, I opened myself up to the transforming power of God's grace that is at work in and through that intimate relationship called marriage.

Of course, marriage is not the only way in which we bind ourselves to other people, nor is marriage the only kind of intimate relationship through which we might be transformed. Whether we are married or unmarried—and both are fully legitimate options for Christians—all of us know how impoverished our lives would be without those whom we call friends. Though our society offers a rather anemic and pitiful notion of friendship, a more robust practice of friendship both assumes and underscores the importance of faithfulness. This is perhaps seen most clearly in the close relationship between friendship, faithfulness and truth-telling.

Telling the truth. Faithful friendships and marriages have at least one thing in common: they are sustained and nourished by a vision that encompasses more than simply maintaining that relationship. Never satisfied simply to maintain the status quo, our faithful friends and partners always call us to be more than we currently are. Their love, of course, is not contingent on our being or becoming more; on the contrary, their longing for us to be more is itself a mark of the abiding love they already have for us.

For Christians the vision of "more" that compels us is the person of Jesus Christ, into whose image we are being daily transformed. Christians believe that they are called to be conformed to the image of Christ, and yet they also know that they are not yet so conformed. This double recognition serves as a constant reminder of a profound and life-ordering truth: we are not yet what we will be.

Because this truth stands at the heart of the Christian faith, we are granted a remarkable measure of freedom to speak the truth in love to one another. Such truth-telling, when engaged in out of love, stands as a profound act of faithfulness. If each of us knows that we are not yet what we will be, yet we continue to desire to be what we will be (and desire this for others as well), then we are free to help each other recognize those areas of our lives where we continue to fall short. Obviously, such discernments must be made with great sensitivity and humility, because none of us can presume to speak definitively for God. Nevertheless, part of what the crucible of Christian friendship requires is the courage to help each other discern where and how we continue to fall short of God's desires for us. To do this, we need to be able to tell each other the truth.

If learning to tell the truth to one another can be understood as a way of cultivating and embodying faithfulness, we should also realize that faithfulness helps to make truth-telling possible. Friends are free to tell each other the truth because they don't have to worry whether such truth-telling will shatter a fragile and unstable relationship. All of us have probably been in relationships where we felt as if we were walking on the proverbial eggshells, always fearful that if we spoke too truthfully the relationship would be over. Friends or partners who have not pledged lifelong fidelity to one another often find it more difficult to tell each other the truth. It often seems much safer to perpetuate a lie than to try to tell the other person the truth and risk sending them packing. In contrast, I would like to think that Kim has the freedom to tell me the truth about myself—regardless of how painful it may be or how much I may want to deny it—because she doesn't have to wonder whether I'll still be there in the morning. By pledging to remain faithful to one another, regardless of the circumstances, we help create and sustain conditions conducive to truth-telling.

God in Christ has told us the truth about ourselves: we are not yet what we will be. Because Christians take this as a given, we are free to bind ourselves to each other in Christian friendship and marriage for our mutual good, as crucibles in which our transformation might be aided. By so binding ourselves to each other, we make possible further acts of faithfulness, not least of which is telling each other the truth.

Reflection Questions and Practical Suggestions

☐ Reflect on the ways in which the impermanence fostered by the dominant culture impacts you most directly. Where in your life, for example, do you most experience the impact of rapid change and mobility? Where do you sense that the culture in which you are immersed most threatens the cultivation of faithfulness? Are there ways in which that culture encourages the cultivation of faithfulness? If so, how is such faithfulness understood, and to what or to whom is such faithfulness directed?

☐ List specific examples from your own experience of how the dominant culture has encouraged you to view other people and your relationships with them as disposable. Can you think of times in your life when you were led to feel as if *you* were disposable? Can you think of times when you likely led others to feel this way?

A "disposable" culture encourages us to view most everything (and perhaps most everyone) from the point of view of our own convenience. If I am not even willing to wash a plate or a napkin for you because it's "too much trouble," what reason would you have for thinking that I would ever be willing to be "troubled" or "inconvenienced" by you? Although there are good creation-care arguments that would rightly urge us to avoid using disposable products whenever possible, we might also choose to avoid them because of the subtle ways in which a "use-without-servicing" mentality may have on other areas of our lives.

☐ Make a list of all the people to whom you have made promises or commitments in the last few months. Make another list of those people on whom you believe you could rely to be there for you regardless of the circumstances. In light of these lists consider your own willingness to have your life bound to the lives of other people. Have you ever found yourself hesitant to commit yourself to other people lest your life become entangled with theirs? Have you ever urged others not to count on you as a way of "keeping your own options open"? Consider what your life would be like and who you would be if the people on your two lists were not involved in your life or you in theirs.

It is important to acknowledge that people have lots of different reasons for avoiding commitments. Some people, for example, have suffered horrible abuse in the past and find it difficult even to imagine a future, let alone commit to it. Such persons cannot simply be cajoled into being committed; instead, they need people who are willing to draw near to them, developing relationships of trust with them in order to make it possible for them, over time, to begin imagining a future that would include trusting other people.

☐ Devote some time to reflecting on your relationships, both past and present, that you believe were and are marked by faithfulness. To what extent are those relationships also marked by the willingness to tell each other the truth? Can you think of specific examples from your own life of the connection between faithfulness and truth-telling?

☐ If you have not done so already, seriously consider committing yourself to a congregation of believers for the long haul. As long as you believe the Spirit is still present there, covenant to stay and remain faithful, speaking (and receiving) the truth in love. There will, of course, be tremendous pressure to view your choice of congregation as little more than a consumer choice. Do your best to leave open the possibility that God might be able to use you—and transform you—in a particular place despite your being less than satisfied with your experience there. It may be that many of us are modern-day Jonahs who, in the name of our own needs and desires, run away from the very challenges God has placed before us. If we find ourselves frustrated with the lack of reform or vision of our local congregations, why should we think that leaving would help that congregation? Or is it only that leaving will likely help us? It seems conceivable that God might use us to help bring the very reform we rightly desire and in the process transform us as well.

☐ This raises another issue that warrants further exploration: the matter of mobility. Our society continues to be one of the most mobile in the entire world, and although we did not directly address in this chapter the threat mobility poses to faithfulness, it requires little imagination to see how this might be the case. For example, have you ever found yourself pulling back from developing deeper friendships with those in your parish or congregation because you were unsure, given the mobility of people in our culture, about the future of such relationships? Because many people don't know whether they will be around six months from now, there seems to be a certain disincentive to devoting time and energy to developing relationships whose termination will bring heartache and loss. Yet surely our fellowships should not be marked by such self-protective strategies. Christians who have placed their lives in the hands of a faithful God can risk becoming involved in other people's lives without calculating whether the potential benefits of those relationships outweigh their potential for heartache.

☐ Christians in this society are in desperate need of fresh ways of thinking about conflicting loyalties and allegiances. Often we are taught to think of the problem of conflicting loyalties as a problem of something called "priorities." If we just get our priorities straight, we are told, everything else will fall into place. On the purely formal or abstract level I have no disagreements with such advice. My worry, however, comes when people assume that such advice offers us useful guidance in discerning how we should order our lives and make decisions. Such advice too easily implies that simply knowing how to order one's priorities on a piece of paper is equivalent to knowing how to order one's life. Put bluntly, what most Christians need is not to be convinced that God needs to be "Number One" but to be helped to see what "seeking first God's kingdom" might actually look like in terms of how we live day to day. What does my commitment to remain faithful to God and God's kingdom mean for my commitments to my family, friends, neighbors, fellow workers and country? Obviously there is no way to answer that question in the abstract, for the way it is answered will have everything to do with the specific conflict that arises in a particular context. Yet the reality of such particularity also suggests that these conflicts cannot be made to disappear by simply asserting that all we need to do is get our priorities straight. Just as Kim would not likely be impressed if I simply told her, day after day, that she was "the most important person in my life," while little or nothing in my life gave any credence to such a claim, so God is not likely impressed by simply occupying the first position on our master list of priorities. Being faithful to God entails more than that, yet seeing precisely what it might entail in this or that situation will require a willingness on our part to be drawn into difficult and sometimes agonizing discussions with one another about how best to sort through these conflicting commitments that make us who we are.

☐ Toward that end our imaginations might be fruitfully enriched were we to immerse ourselves, as well as our children, in the stories of faithful Christians across the ages. This is particularly important because discerning what faithfulness requires in a given situation often demands seeing options that are not immediately evident. Retelling stories about the lives of faithful Christians can often open up our limited imaginations to see new possibilities as we come to see what faithfulness has demanded in other times and places. Equally important, the stories of these faithful Christians remind us of God's faithfulness, something we can all too easily lose sight of in the midst of our everyday worries and struggles.

☐ Finally, we should also seek to be attentive to the exemplars of faithfulness that God has placed in our immediate context. Because faithfulness is usually quiet rather than ostentatious, exemplars of faithfulness may be right in front of our eyes, yet remain largely invisible to us. This has, I fear, been one of the unfortunate (and undoubtedly unwitting) consequences of the Promise Keepers movement. By calling men away from their homes and family obligations for weekend gatherings where the virtues of promise keeping could be trumpeted, this movement may have blinded some men to the quiet, less self-congratulatory exemplars of faithfulness in their own homes. What some men most need is not another man who can help them keep their promises but to learn that the best exemplar of faithfulness may be their own wives. Can we imagine a million women heading off for the weekend to declare their commitment to promise keeping while their husbands stayed home with the children? If not, does this tell us anything important about faithfulness? Is it possible that many women are too busy *being* faithful in innumerable and gentle ways to see the need to hold a pep rally about it? Perhaps not a few Christian men would benefit from paying attention to such exemplars in their very midst.

> *May the God of peace himself sanctify you entirely, and may your spirit and soul and body be kept sound and blameless at the coming of our Lord Jesus Christ. The one who calls you is faithful, and he will do this. (1 Thess 5:23-24)*

NINE
Cultivating Gentleness in the Midst of Aggression

You must understand this, my beloved: let everyone be quick to listen, slow to speak, slow to anger; for your anger does not produce God's righteousness. Therefore rid yourselves of all sordidness and rank growth of wickedness, and welcome with meekness the implanted word that has the power to save your souls. (Jas 1:19-21)

If we live by the Spirit, let us also be guided by the Spirit. Let us not become conceited, competing against one another, envying one another. My friends, if anyone is detected in a transgression, you who have received the Spirit should restore such a one in a spirit of gentleness. (Gal 5:25-6:1)

Football stadiums. Saturday morning cartoons. Workplaces. Music videos. Toy stores. Movie theaters. Living rooms and kitchens. Computer games. School classrooms. Novels. Friday night dates. Network news programs.

What do all these have in common? At least one thing: they are all primary venues for the staggering amount of violence—both real and fictional—that permeates our lives. Even if one argues that fictional violence merely reflects the violent society in which we live, one has to admit that such portrayals do little to offer other options for resolving conflict. Perhaps this is one reason why the following statistics suggest a problem of epidemic proportions:

□ The Center for Disease Control and Prevention estimates that one million people die each year in this country as a direct result of violence. Researchers also found that about three out of every four murders of children on the planet take place in the United States, which has more child homicide, suicide and gun-related deaths than any other of the world's twenty-six richest nations.

☐ Depictions of violence occur in over half of all television programming, with the average television viewer exposed to roughly 18,000 violent interactions per year.

☐ Workplace violence has shown a staggering increase in recent years, even though the apparent causes of this violence are usually relatively minor annoyances or offenses. (The same could be said about the recent outbreak of so-called "road rage" incidents.)

☐ Each year, nearly two million men in this country severely batter their wives.[1]

Although scholars and experts disagree about the precise relationship between the prominence of violence in the mass media and our cultural penchant for solving conflict violently, one thing seems clear: we are both the most violent society in the world and the one that immerses itself most deeply in portrayals of violence—a connection which, though difficult to demonstrate, hardly seems coincidental. But for Christians the issue need not be circumscribed so narrowly. For us the question is not merely whether media portrayals of violence encourage acts of violence, or whether it makes many viewers more aggressive or antisocial, or whether it only numbs us to the real effects of violence. For us the question is this: How do you cultivate gentleness in a culture like ours?

The Character of Gentleness
The eighth fruit of the Spirit listed by Paul is variously translated as gentleness, meekness or humility. This word—together with several others that are used throughout both Testaments—point to that strength of character required to ground one's relationships in something other than pride and power. In each case these words originally have their roots in economic and social realms, where one's lowliness is not merely a matter of inner attitude or disposition, but is open for all to view. Indeed, in the Old Testament the same word group *('ānî, 'ānāw)* often refers to the poor, the afflicted, the

humble, the meek and the lowly. Because the Old Testament is clear that Yahweh is the advocate of those who are exploited by the rich and the arrogant, over time, this word group came to be associated with not only the materially poor but also those who in humility rely on Yahweh alone. For example, God proclaims to Israel through the prophet Zephaniah that a day is coming when "I will remove from your midst your proudly exultant ones, and you shall no longer be haughty in my holy mountain. For I will leave in the midst of you a people humble and lowly. They shall seek refuge in the name of the LORD" (Zeph 3:11-12). Elsewhere in the Old Testament the meek and humble are promised that God will be their advocate, particularly when they are oppressed by the proud (Ps 10:17-18; 37:11; 147:6; 149:4; Is 11:1-4; 29:19ff.).

Arrogance, pride, haughtiness. These attributes characterize those who through power and strength of will attempt to secure their own future well-being. By so doing, they deny their need for God. Israel itself is often characterized as stubborn or "stiff-necked" (Ex 32:9; 33:3,5; 34:9; Deut 9:6, 13; 10:16; 2 Chron 30:6-8). The image is telling: not only does it suggest stubbornness but also a refusal to bow to another's authority. This image of ancient Israel as stiff-necked carries over into the New Testament as well. For example, in the disciple Stephen's speech before the council, he provoked his listeners not only by referring to ancient Israel's tradition of being stiff-necked but also by adding a telling connection, "You stiff-necked people, uncircumcised in heart and ears, you are forever opposing the Holy Spirit, just as your ancestors used to do" (Acts 7:51).

Opposing the Holy Spirit. Quenching the Spirit. These are dangers that must be avoided by anyone who desires to cultivate the fruit of the Spirit. In the above contexts these dangers arise on account of our stubborn pride and our desire to secure our own futures apart from God. Rather than placing our trust in ourselves and our own abilities, God calls us to humble ourselves and place our hope and trust in God and the kingdom that God is ushering in.

This kingdom is an upside-down kingdom, where God's order is restored by reversing or inverting the order routinely instituted by human beings. The kingdoms we construct almost always exalt the rich, the powerful, the proud and the aggressive. For those who have eyes to see, however, the reign that God is ushering in is of a quite different sort. For example, by humbly submitting to the will of God, Mary is placed in a position to see the in-breaking of God's reign:

> My soul magnifies the Lord,
>> and my spirit rejoices in God my Savior,
> for he has looked with favor on the lowliness of his servant.
>> Surely from now on all generations will call me blessed;
> for the Mighty One has done great things for me,
>> and holy is his name.
> His mercy is for those who fear him
>> from generation to generation.
> He has shown strength with his arm;
>> he has scattered the proud in the thoughts of their hearts.
> He has brought down the powerful from their thrones,
>> and lifted up the lowly;
> he has filled the hungry with good things,
>> and sent the rich away empty.
> He has helped his servant Israel,
>> in remembrance of his mercy,
> according to the promise he made to our ancestors,
>> to Abraham and to his descendants forever. (Luke 1:46-55)

Jesus also speaks of this inversion in the Beatitudes, where he insists that both the poor in spirit and the meek are blessed (Mt 5:3, 5). Significantly, the meek do not aggressively conquer the earth and subdue it; instead, they inherit it: it is given to them. And closely connected with this theme, a persistent refrain echoes throughout the New Testament: All who exalt themselves will be humbled, but all who humble themselves will be exalted (Mt 23:12; Lk 14:11; Jas 4:10; 1 Pet 5:6). Jesus underscores this point powerfully in one of his parables:

> He also told this parable to some who trusted in themselves that they were righteous and regarded others with contempt: "Two men went up to the temple

to pray, one a Pharisee and the other a tax collector. The Pharisee, standing by himself, was praying thus, 'God, I thank you that I am not like other people: thieves, rogues, adulterers, or even like this tax-collector. I fast twice a week, I give a tenth of all my income.' But the tax collector, standing far off, would not even look up to heaven, but was beating his breast and saying, 'God, be merciful to me, a sinner!' I tell you, this man went down to his home justified rather than the other, for all who exalt themselves will be humbled, but all who humble themselves will be exalted." (Lk 18:9-14)

Those who would follow this crucified Messiah must recognize that following him involves cultivating different sensibilities than those promoted by the dominant culture. Twice in the New Testament, Christians are urged to clothe themselves with humility and meekness. Both to the elders and to the younger believers Peter writes, "And all of you must clothe yourselves with humility in your dealings with one another, for 'God opposes the proud, but gives grace to the humble' " (1 Pet 5:5). Paul offers a similar admonition to the Colossians, "Clothe yourselves with compassion, kindness, humility, meekness and patience" (Col 3:12).

I have claimed that each fruit of the Spirit is a specific manifestation of love and that it does so by embodying a steadfast other-directedness. It should come as no surprise, therefore, that when Paul speaks of love to the Corinthians, he insists that love is not "envious or boastful or arrogant or rude" (1 Cor 13:4-5). In short, love is not focused on itself.

Love's other-directedness takes many different forms. For example, Timothy is instructed that "The Lord's servant must not be quarrelsome but kindly to everyone, an apt teacher, patient, correcting opponents with gentleness" (2 Tim 2:24-25). All of us have likely been corrected by people whose focus was clearly on themselves. They were correcting us, to be sure, but they seemed to be doing so primarily because they derived a degree of pleasure from being the ones to set us straight. Such correction is rarely marked by gentleness. In contrast, the person who is other-directed, who cares more about the one being corrected than about his or her own ego, can do so with a measure of gentleness, recognizing that the issue is one of love—of desiring what is best for the other—rather than one of control or power.

Indeed, there appears to be an intimate connection in Scripture between gentleness, meekness, humility, lowliness and even patience: each requires us to give up trying to exercise absolute control over the world. Because we believe that God's Spirit continues to be active in the world, we are freed from the necessity of clawing our way into positions of power in order that God's will might be done. We are freed from having to force our wills upon other people, freed from having to think too highly of ourselves, freed from having to think we are always right, freed from having to assert ourselves in order to get what is our due and freed from having to retaliate in order to secure justice. Even though Paul's words to the Romans have been quoted earlier, perhaps now we are in a better position than before to see how they hang together:

> Bless those who persecute you; bless and do not curse them. Rejoice with those who rejoice, weep with those who weep. Live in harmony with one another; do not be haughty, but associate with the lowly; do not claim to be wiser than you are. Do not repay anyone evil for evil, but take thought for what is noble in the sight of all. If it is possible, so far as it depends on you, live peaceably with all. Beloved, never avenge yourselves, but leave room for the wrath of God; for it is written, " 'Vengeance is mine, I will repay,' says the Lord." (Rom 12:14-19)

In several of the passages above, Christians are admonished that their speech ought to be marked by gentleness. James, more than any other New Testament writer, elaborates on this point, suggesting along the way the close connection between gentleness and wisdom. Although the entire third chapter is pertinent to our discussion, only the last half is quoted here:

> With [the tongue] we bless the Lord and Father, and with it we curse those who are made in the likeness of God. From the same mouth come blessing and cursing. My brothers and sisters, this ought not to be so. Does a spring pour forth from the same opening both fresh and brackish water? Can a fig tree, my brothers and sisters, yield olives, or a grapevine figs? No more can salt water yield fresh. Who is wise and understanding among you? Show by your good life that your works are done with gentleness born of wisdom. But if you have bitter envy and selfish ambition in your hearts, do not be boastful and false to the truth. Such wisdom does not come down from above, but is earthly,

unspiritual, devilish. For where there is envy and selfish ambition, there will also be disorder and wickedness of every kind. But the wisdom from above is first pure, then peaceable, gentle, willing to yield, full of mercy and good fruits, without a trace of partiality or hypocrisy. And a harvest of righteousness is sown in peace for those who make peace. (Jas 3:9-18)

I have argued throughout these chapters that the fruit that the Spirit desires to cultivate in our lives is rooted in the very character of God. We are called to love because God loves; we are called to be faithful because God is faithful and so on. But what about this fruit? In what sense is God gentle, meek, or humble?

The Hebrew word *'ānî* is never used with reference to God anywhere in the Old Testament. God is not poor, lowly and humble as we are. But it would be a mistake to assume from this that God is to be equated with power or brute force. If meekness is the strength to refrain from resorting to power and coercion, then certainly there is an important sense in which God is meek. This sounds odd to our ears, not least because we commonly associate meekness with weakness. But the God who is revealed in Jesus Christ is not weak, even if that God does not exercise power the way we tend to. God reveals the divine character most determinatively in Jesus Christ, whose life is characterized not by the exercise of brute force, power or coercion, but by self-sacrificing love. For those of us accustomed to thinking of God as "the power guy," this may be the most surprising feature of the God we encounter in Christ.

When John, in the book of Revelation, looks for the conquering Lion who can open the scroll and its seven seals, he sees instead a Lamb. The Lion is the Lamb, and the way of the Lamb is the way of the cross. Yet such surprises are not limited to the closing chapters of the Christian story. When we look for a king born of royalty, we find instead a baby wrapped in strips of cloth lying in a manger, born to a peasant girl of no account. When Jesus' time has come to begin his ministry and we look for him to put John the Baptizer in his place, we find instead a Jesus who humbly approaches John in order to be baptized by him. When we look for Jesus to take the world by storm, to win over those who have power, influence and prestige in order to advance his kingdom more efficiently, we find instead an itinerant preacher and healer who spends much of his time with the weak and outcast of society: children, lepers, prostitutes and tax-collectors. When we see Jesus rejected by the Samaritans, we look for him to do what his disciples wanted done—to rain down fire upon them—but instead he rebukes *us*. When we look for the conquering hero to make his move, to enter into the royal city on his white charger to signal to the people that the time has come to establish his kingdom, we find instead a Jesus who enters into Jerusalem astride a humble donkey. When we gather with him for the last time in that upper room, expecting to get our marching orders and to honor him by pledging our allegiance to him, we find instead that he honors us by washing our feet and by calling us his friends. When Jesus is arrested and taken before the authorities, we look for him to set those authorities straight, to proclaim proudly and defiantly that he is God's anointed one; instead we find him strangely silent, showing no need to justify himself. When we look for a deliverer who will crush the opposition by superior force, we find instead a servant-messiah who allows himself to be crushed and bruised for us. What kind of God is this?

We are often tempted to think of these details as little more than the frame around the picture we call Jesus' life. The picture itself—not the frame—is what is important, we tell ourselves, and because we assume that God is mostly about power and control, we construct a picture of Jesus out of those parts of the narrative that fit our assumptions: the miracles, his stinging rebukes of the religious authorities, the triumphant resurrection. Yet what if the surprising details mentioned above are not part of the frame but integral to the picture itself? What if these details reveal something about the very character of God?

Such a view, though perhaps strange to us, is not foreign to Scripture. Jesus instructs us to take up his yoke and learn from him because he is "gentle and humble in heart" (Mt 11:29). The New Testament testifies that God exalts Jesus because Jesus humbles himself. Thus this movement from humility to exaltation mentioned earlier is not just sage advice that Jesus proffers to the crowds; Jesus' own life embodies this pattern as well. If we are inclined to overlook this, the great hymn in Philippians drives the point home with clarity and beauty:

> Do nothing from selfish ambition or conceit, but in humility regard others as better than yourselves. Let each of you look not to your own interests, but to the interests of others. Let the same mind be in you that was in Christ Jesus,
>> who, though he was in the form of God,
>>> did not regard equality with God
>>> as something to be exploited,
>> but emptied himself,
>>> taking the form of a slave,
>>> being born in human likeness.
>> And being found in human form,
>>> he humbled himself
>>> and became obedient to the point of death—
>>> even death on a cross.
>
>> Therefore God also highly exalted him
>>> and gave him the name
>>> that is above every name,
>> so that at the name of Jesus
>>> every knee should bend,
>>> in heaven and on earth and under the earth,
>> and every tongue should confess
>>> that Jesus Christ is Lord,
>>> to the glory of God the Father. (Phil 2:3-11)

Finally, though Scripture is largely silent on this point, Christians throughout history have often suggested that we see evidence of a kind of humility, a kind of deference, within the Godhead itself. We see this most clearly with reference to the Spirit: the Spirit neither testifies to itself nor draws attention to itself; rather, the Spirit is self-effacing, bearing witness to the Son (Jn 14:26; 15:26; 16:13-15). Though Christian tradition has resoundingly affirmed that the Spirit is fully God, the Spirit does not exist to assert its proper rights to be worshiped and adored, but to serve as the Godhead's most determinative manifestation of other-directed love.

Obstacles to a Life of Gentleness

Those who desire to have the Spirit's fruit of gentleness cultivated in their lives must understand not only what gentleness entails but also the obstacles that their culture poses to such cultivation. Like each of the fruit discussed thus far, gentleness does not seem to grow "naturally"; indeed, several hardy and "aggressive" indigenous plants threaten to choke out the Spirit's fruit of gentleness. Although cultivating gentleness will not be easy, we can hope that if such fruit would grow to maturity in our culture, it would be noticed for no other reason than its relative rareness.

Fostering aggression and self-promotion. The dominant culture worships strength and power. Often, this strength is manifested through brute force and violence. For example, so-called action films—still one of the most popular genres among young men—usually portray their heroes as gun-toting vigilantes whose goal is to exact justice by violent means. The popularity of many video and computer games seems to be directly correlated to the high body counts they produce. Increasingly we observe that sports are as much about intimidation as they are about skill. We see sports figures who regularly get in each other's faces and who refuse to back down lest they be perceived as weak. We see more and more people who are decked out in "No Fear" T-shirts, not because they lack fear but because they want to project an aura of toughness and invincibility that proclaims: "Don't mess with me."

We are taught at an early age and in various ways that "only the tough survive." Nearly every day we hear of another hostile corporate takeover, and we are told that the business world is a "dog eat dog" kind of world where only the most aggressive, competitive and therefore "fittest" survive. (It seems ironic that so many Christians who are opponents of evolution have so few qualms with this form of social Darwinism.) Thus if we want to "get ahead" in the world, we will have to be assertive, ambitious and engage in self-promotion. Because we assume that everybody else is looking out for his or her own interests, we assume that the only way to succeed is to look after ours. Thus we are counseled to extol our own talents and to push ourselves to the front of the pack. Or as the old adage goes, since you cannot expect anyone else to toot your horn, you had better learn to do it yourself.

Because the dominant culture continues to associate strength and power with masculinity, the culture of aggression impacts young men decisively. Most young boys are socialized at an early age into believing that to be a "real man" they must flaunt their strength and act tough and "macho." Moreover, young boys are taught to hide their feelings (unless they are feelings of anger or rage) and to avoid crying in public, because such emotional displays are viewed as sure signs of weakness. For too long gentleness and tenderness toward others have been routinely regarded as "feminine" virtues and thus "unmanly." But men are not the only ones who eschew gentleness. Women who realize that they are competing for jobs and advancement in a male-dominated society have increasingly discovered that the only way to get ahead is to play by the cutthroat rules that characterize day-to-day life in many sectors of the business world.

One does not, however, have to be immersed in the world of popular culture or corporate boardrooms to see aggression and self-promotion at work. Many of us experience the impact of these "virtues" most regularly in such mundane activities as daily conversations with colleagues, acquaintances and even family and church members. How often, for example, do we find ourselves in the midst of an exchange that revolves entirely around put-downs, insults, one-liners and other forms of sarcasm and ridicule? In many forums such activity is regarded as sport or entertainment. Most of us have likely been on the giving and receiving end of such comments enough times to realize that they usually involve a subtle (or not-so-subtle) form of self-promotion. In desiring to draw attention to myself, I degrade or humiliate another person, wrongly assuming that if I have diminished another person, then I have inevitably exalted myself in the eyes of other people.

Although we rarely consider this kind of practice to be violent when we are the perpetrators, the fact that many of our own deepest wounds have been exacted at the tip of a seemingly harmless barb suggests otherwise. Even more telling is how frequently we injure in this way those we claim to love the most. This, of course, is no accident. A relationship of mutual intimacy and vulnerability always reveals the weaknesses in another person's armor. That we would then turn around and exploit that knowledge by aiming an acerbic and humiliating dart precisely at that point reveals much about how deeply we have drunk at the well of aggression and self-promotion.

Such examples remind us how difficult it is, once having imbibed at this well, to be "selectively" aggressive or self-promotional. Many sincere people, for example, insist that although they would have no qualms about using violence to protect their families from harm, they would never consider using violence against their own family members. Yet when violence is considered as a viable option for dealing with conflict, we should not too readily assume that we will always discriminate judiciously among possible objects of our violence. In other words, it may be more difficult than we imagine living out our insistence that violence is appropriate in some contexts but not in others. That aggression and violence may not be able to be turned on and off like a light switch may help account for the overwhelming statistical evidence that the most dangerous person in the life of a child or wife is "the man of the house."

Aspiring to positions of power. In the midst of a dominant culture that promotes aggression and self-promotion, it seems only "natural" that we would also be encouraged to grab and exploit for our own benefit whatever power we are capable of seizing. How often have we been told that we must grasp for power and influence in order to "make a difference"? If you want to get anything done, we are told, if you want to make an impact, you have to be in a position of power to do so; otherwise, you are doomed to ineffectiveness and, ultimately, failure. Hence, people who want to make their mark on the world will have to make their peace with doing so by using the world's ways, which are usually the ways of power and coercion.

This lesson is perhaps taught most determinatively in that arena we call politics (understood here in its more popular and narrow sense). At an early age we are told repeatedly that the president of the United States is the "most powerful man in the world." Presumably this is an awe-inspiring thing and explains why he commands our respect and that of others around the world. If we want other ways to gauge how important we believe the "political" sphere to be, we need only note the staggering amount of time, energy, media coverage and money devoted to it. How many times have we heard in our lifetimes that if you want to make a real difference in this society, you must be engaged in passing legislation, lobbying congress, electing officials or running for office yourself? This, we are told, is where the action is.

Yet politics is not the only venue that encourages us to aspire to positions of power. After all, most of us do not aspire to be president of the United States (many of us wouldn't want the job if it were given to us). Because power as humans exercise it almost always involves the capacity to coerce people to do things they might not otherwise do, we learn relatively early in life that it's more fun to get others to do what we want them to do than it is to do another's bidding. Although for many of us this lesson may have first been learned when our parents put one of us "in charge" while they were briefly away, the lesson was reinforced over and over again at schools, playgrounds, churches and jobs. All of us have been in situations where those in authority "lorded their positions" over us; that is, they took inordinate pleasure in reminding us that they were in charge, that they exercised power over us. People who repeatedly find themselves in this position can be forgiven if they grow tired of such antics and long for something different. Sometimes they seek to be self-employed so they can "be their own boss." Other times they start their own company or work their way to the top of their present one, so that when they say "jump," it will be their subordinates who are expected to ask "how high?"

What does all of this have to do with gentleness and humility? Nothing, and perhaps that is the point. Although our society unapologetically fosters aggression and self-promotion in many conspicuous ways, some obstacles to a life of gentleness and humility are less obvious. These more subtle ones, I suspect, are the ones that are most invisible even to many Christians, at least if the level of discussion among Christians is any indication. What subtle effect on the cultivation of gentleness and humility, for example, is produced by a mindset that assumes that one can only make a real difference in the world if one is in a position of power, if one is in a position to set the agenda? How does such a mindset encourage us to think about those in our society who are not now (and will likely never be) so positioned? Finally, how does our ambition, our single-minded desire to ascend to the top, encourage us to treat those we pass up along the way? With gentleness and humility? Not likely.

Cultivating Gentleness

Christians are called to be the people of God in the midst of the world. God's purpose in calling us to a life formed by the Spirit is not to parade our lives before others in order to draw attention to ourselves, win their praise or even convince them to be "better" people. Instead, God calls us to be the body of Christ in order that we might be a light to the nations, showing them something of the character of God. What resources does the church have for cultivating a life of gentleness in the midst of a society marked by aggression and self-promotion?

Altering our posture through prayer. One of the Desert Fathers once said, "Prayer is the seed of gentleness and the absence of anger." Why might this be so? At least two reasons come to mind. First, Christians have observed for centuries that though we find it quite easy to speak harshly about people to one another, it is much more difficult to rail against those who have wronged or angered us when we speak of them to God. Indeed, Jesus instructed us to love our enemies and pray for those who persecute us not because he assumed that such prayer would transform *them* into lovable people, but because he believed that in praying for them a transformation might take place in *our* hearts (Mt 5:44-45). According to Jesus, it is by loving and praying for our enemies that we become children of our Father in heaven. Praying for other people—especially our adversaries—has a tendency to soften our hearts toward them and encourages us to treat them more gently, as other fallible creatures made in the image of God.

This leads directly to the second reason: if we believe that prayer brings us into God's presence, then we should enter into prayer and God's presence with a profound sense of humility. This is why so many Christians across the ages believed that it was appropriate to kneel for prayer. Christians did not believe that such kneeling helped God hear their prayers, but that it helped remind them of who they were before God. Yes, we come boldly on account of Christ, but we also come in humility, with a healthy sense of our own shortcomings and unworthiness. When we do so, the shortcomings of our neighbors appear in a different light than they do when we stand self-righteously before God and give thanks that we are not like other people.

The Christian faith has long underscored the need for Christians to acknowledge regularly their own sinfulness. Although this has already been mentioned in the earlier chapter on goodness, here we see how remembering our own sinfulness can provide a powerful impetus to treat others with gentleness. Once again we have Jesus for our example. When he is confronted by the angry—and self-righteous—crowd who have brought him a woman deserving of capital punishment, Jesus neither joins in the frenzy nor rebukes her accusers harshly. Rather, he bends down quietly, writes in the dust and then speaks, "Let anyone among you who is without sin be the first to throw a stone at her" (Jn 8:7). Jesus goes back to writing in the dust, the crowd slowly disperses, and Jesus finally sends the woman on her way with instructions not to sin again.

Like this woman's accusers, I am often tempted to lash out at another human being when I allow myself to "think higher of myself than I ought." In that moment of anger and self-righteousness I am too easily persuaded that I am somehow "better" than this other person is. In contrast if I were to remember that I am very much like other people—especially when it comes to my sinfulness and need for God's grace—then I might be more likely to respond in gentleness, offering this other person the same grace that I have been freely offered. This intimate connection between the grace we have received and the way we treat other people—not least in the way we speak about and to them—is summed up well in the letter to the Ephesians:

> Let no evil talk come out of your mouths, but only what is useful for building up, as there is need, so that your words may give grace to those who hear. And do not grieve the Holy Spirit of God, with which you were marked with a seal for the day of redemption. Put away from you all bitterness and wrath and anger and wrangling and slander, together with all malice, and be kind to one another, tenderhearted, forgiving one another as God in Christ has forgiven you. Therefore be imitators of God, as beloved children, and live in love, as Christ loved us and gave himself up for us, a fragrant offering and sacrifice to God. (Eph 4:29—5:2)

Learning to yield. What marks the Christian life as a life of the Spirit is not that Christians never have conflict but that Christians negotiate conflicts differently. The apostle Paul, for example, was frustrated by many of the Corinthian Christians, but rather than be harsh with them, he appeals to them "by the meekness and gentleness of Christ" (2 Cor 10:1). Christians will have conflicts with other Christians about matters that matter, but when we do, we should not assume that we are always right and that those who think or act differently than we do are wrong. Such presumption is only possible if we have forgotten our own standing before God and one another. We need to yield to other points of view by listening carefully to one another. We need to yield by entertaining the possibility that we may be mistaken. And we need to yield to one another when it becomes clear that we are in error. As the passage from James quoted earlier affirms, the wisdom that is from above is not only gentle but also "willing to yield" (3:17).

Such yielding and admission of error is not a sign of weakness. Indeed, given how rarely public officials willingly admit their mistakes (which always seem to happen in the passive voice: "mistakes were made"), we might conclude that many people find it quite difficult. I suspect Christians are no different in this respect. Yet we do have the resources to be different, because we have been freed from having to insist that we are always right. When we find ourselves disagreeing with other people, we need not be combative in pushing our point of view. Instead, we are free to state humbly what seems to us—from our finite, limited and sinful perspective—to be the case, leaving what comes from that, or even whether others find it persuasive, up to God.

Of course, this willingness to yield and to leave the results up to God has implications far beyond the way that we deal with conflicts and arguments. Too often we believe that we control—and are therefore ultimately responsible for—our own destiny. As a result, we are often only too willing to engage in acts of self-promotion, believing that such promotion is the only kind available. But Christians are called to tell and live a different story, a story where God invites us to positions of honor rather than our securing them by running over other people. As noted earlier, central to the narrative of Scripture is the notion that God exalts those who humble themselves. Jesus insists that someday a great reversal will take place, a reversal where the first will be last, and the last will be first (Mt 19:30; 20:16; 23:11; Mk 9:35; 10:31;

Lk 13:30). In God's kingdom those who were thought to be of no account are exalted by God, while those who were secure in their own self-attained positions find that they have been stripped of their self-importance and rank. Such stories should remind Christians not to place too much stock in the world's pecking order. God promises to humble someday those who grab for positions of honor and power and who refuse to humble themselves. It should seem odd for Christians to be caught up in the same struggle for power and control that characterizes so much of contemporary life.

This leads us to consider another way in which the church should model a different politics, a different way of ordering our lives together. With respect to gentleness and humility, this difference involves not "lording" our positions over each other (Mt 20:25; Mk 10:42; Lk 22:25; 1 Pet 5:3). Whatever it means to be in a position of authority in the church, it should mean something very different from the models we encounter elsewhere. Jesus insists that those who are most highly esteemed in God's kingdom are servants (Mt 20:26; 23:11; Mk 10:43), a model which Jesus himself embodied (Mt 20:28; Mk 10:45). Although the church is beginning to talk more about "servant leadership," we likely need more concrete examples of it.

Hanging out with those of "no account." Having been reminded that we should not trust the world's (and too often the church's) way of reckoning who and what is important, we are set free to engage those around us in different ways. For example, once we are no longer preoccupied with establishing and maintaining our own status and position of power, we need no longer cut ourselves off from those whose lack of status in the world's eyes threatens to impede our rise to the top. This connection between humility and hospitality to those of "no account" is seen clearly in Luke's gospel, where Jesus' parable about the inadvisability of scrambling for the honorable seats at wedding banquets is followed immediately by these comments:

> When you give a luncheon or a dinner, do not invite your friends or your brothers or your relatives or rich neighbors, in case they may invite you in return, and you would be repaid. But when you give a banquet, invite the poor, the crippled, the lame, and the blind. And you will be blessed, because they cannot repay you, for you will be repaid at the resurrection of the righteous. (Lk 14:12-14)

All acts of hospitality, as forms of gift-giving, create and sustain relationships. Jesus reminds us that we are too often tempted to use hospitality as a means to further our own selfish ends. In contrast, God's hospitality, which Christians are called to emulate, is not a hospitality of calculation intended to advance one's own fortunes or status, but a hospitality overflowing with grace. Rooted in humility and gentleness toward "the least of these," such hospitality serves as a channel of God's grace to all involved, reminding them of their equality before God. As Paul reminded the Romans, we should "not be haughty, but associate with the lowly" (Rom 12:16).

Though such acts of hospitality often (and rightly) involve a meal, Christians should also be willing simply to be with those whom society considers of "no account." Similarly, though there will be times when we will be called to serve them, we must also be ready to receive from them. What might those of "no account" have to offer us? We should, of course, be prepared to be surprised, because like many good gifts, they come unexpectedly. Yet given what was said above about the character of God's upside-down kingdom as revealed in the life and ministry of Jesus, we should be prepared to encounter none other than Christ himself. In the Gospels, Jesus identifies himself not only with the "least of these" in the well-known passage in Matthew (25:31-46) but also with other powerless and seemingly inconsequential people:

> Whoever receives this child in my name receives me, and whoever receives me receives him who sent me; for he who is least among you all is the one who is great. (Lk 9:48)

> Truly I tell you, unless you change and become like children, you will never enter the kingdom of heaven. Whoever becomes humble like this child is the greatest in the kingdom of heaven. Whoever welcomes one such child in my name welcomes me. (Mt 18:3-5)

Children. Jesus suggests that we need to be more like them, especially when it comes to humility. The disciples assumed that Jesus should be attending to more "important" matters. How do we tend to think of children?

Or more importantly perhaps, how often do we choose to be in their presence, believing that in so doing we might be transformed? Much of the public discourse in our society might lead one to believe that children occupy a central place, and perhaps they do. But perhaps many people, not least of all some politicians, simply find it expedient to cast themselves as the champions of children and their futures. Too often, it seems, we have a lot of people who want to speak for and about children, but far fewer who want to speak to them, and even fewer still who want to listen to them.

What might children teach us if we listened? Although it would be a mistake to predict ahead of time (because this would suggest that we need not really listen), perhaps one of the lessons they might teach us is how thoroughly we have adopted the world's ways of looking at life. One of my students, for example, when pondering what it means to be gentle, commented that she could still remember watching the Olympics on television as a young girl when, to her horror, one of the runners fell down, writhing in pain, and none of the other runners stopped to see if she was okay. Why, we might ask, are none of us adults horrified at this?

Many of us fail to consider the possibility that our ambition might have a "dark side" because we have already convinced ourselves that we are only aspiring to these positions of power and influence in order to do good, in order to make a difference in the world. What could possibly be wrong with wanting to make a difference? These are important and complex matters, yet we might begin by reflecting on a crucial story from the life of Jesus. The temptation narratives stand as a consistent reminder that Christians can never be content with simply making a difference, but must also concern themselves with the *kind* of difference they make, which is inevitably inseparable from the way that difference is brought about (Mt 4:1-11; Lk 4:1-13). Jesus is not so much tempted to do evil as he is tempted to take the expedient course—to take that route that would undermine his mission by affecting it through means contrary to its character. In the end Jesus turns his back on the audacious, flashy, attention-getting and crowd-pleasing strategy that is offered him in order to carry out his mission in gentleness and humility.

God has given the church resources by which it might cultivate gentleness and humility. Often, these resources are no further away or more difficult to find than the nearest child or other person of "no account." Such people remind us of God's order, an order where the proud, haughty and arrogant are brought low, and the lowly, humble and gentle are exalted. Such people remind us that the Messiah we worship and follow surprised his contemporaries by the "other-directedness" of his life, an other-directedness that included the gentle reaching out to those we left by the side of the road in our race to construct our own kingdoms.

Reflection Questions and Practical Suggestions

☐ Reflect on the lives of those people you know whom you regard as gentle or humble. In what specific situations have you seen their gentleness or humility? For example, do they tend to react differently than you do when they are criticized or misunderstood? Consider speaking with them at some point about how they have come to respond with gentleness and humility.

☐ Begin now to make a habit of praying for people who misunderstand, disappoint, irritate or attack you. Realize up front that such a habit will be difficult to cultivate. Most of us secretly (and even sometimes, not-so-secretly) relish an opportunity to be justifiably angry with them. If we choose to let some of that anger go by speaking to God—rather than other people—about them, we may find that God softens our hearts toward them, which is often the first step in treating them with gentleness and humility.

☐ Reflect on your habitual posture for prayer. Although God certainly hears our prayers regardless of our physical posture, we should not thereby assume that our bodily posture in prayer is unimportant. Often we hesitate to kneel because we well realize what such kneeling communicates. Where else, for example, in our culture would we ever find ourselves kneeling before someone else in an act of deference and humility? Perhaps our reticence about kneeling suggests that we are capable of being no less stiff-necked than ancient Israel.

☐ If you do not already do so, consider praying the psalms on a regular basis. If you need a guide, consider using the Book of Common Prayer, which cycles through the psalms each month. Praying the psalms, as the church has done for many centuries, offers us an opportunity to express the full range of human emotions before and to God. The psalms are a wonderful vehicle for expressing reverence, gratitude and delight. But they can also serve as a vehicle for expressing some of our rawer emotions as well. For example, many psalms ring out with anger toward the psalmist's enemies and even toward God. Praying these regularly might remind us that there is little point in pretending that we do not feel such anger; the problem comes when we refuse to bring this anger and the one who has angered us before God.

☐ Devote some time to evaluating the stories that shape your imagination. Do any of these offer examples of gentleness and meekness? How often do we tell each other stories where conflicts are resolved by some means other than violent ones? As mentioned in several chapters, Christians need to have their imaginations enriched. Often our failure to respond gently and with humility is closely connected to the narrow range of options we believe we have in any given situation. Seek out examples from the church's history of Christians responding to their adversaries with gentleness and humility. Although Christians have often failed to so respond, there are plenty of examples when they did, and these stories might go a long way toward reshaping our imaginations as we seek to respond to others with gentleness. We would also do well to cut down on our intake of gratuitously violent "entertainment," since such entertainment tends both to trivialize violence and to stunt our imaginations as we seek to respond to people with gentleness and humility.

☐ As a step toward greater gentleness, seek to resolve conflicts without inciting further violence. Following the model of Jesus, be willing to absorb violence and anger rather than multiply and perpetuate it. In any conflict seek first in a spirit of humility to identify your own faults and the ways in which you have contributed to the problem. For example, if you find yourself in the midst of an argument with a spouse or friend, try to resist the temptation to attack the other person should you be criticized. Even if you think the criticism is unfair (and most all of us do in the heat of the moment), do your best not to respond in anger.

☐ Reflect on those times when you've been "in charge." In what ways were you tempted to "lord it over" others? Why do you think you were tempted to act this way? Look carefully around you for examples of servant leadership that you can model. Don't get discouraged if such people are hard to find, but remember that true servant leaders are often difficult to spot because they're not attempting to draw attention to themselves.

□ Devote some time to reflecting on the people you choose to "hang out" with and your reasons for doing so. All of us can probably think of times in our lives when we desired to be associated with certain people because we believed that this association would raise our status in the eyes of other people. Conversely, we can likely remember attempts we made to avoid certain people because we feared that being associated with them would "reflect poorly" on us. These attitudes stem not only from a misguided desire to be viewed as "important" by those whom the world deems so but also from a willingness to view other people as little more than status symbols to be used for our own benefit. Neither is rooted in the other-directedness that should mark the life of the Christian.

□ Consider what it might mean for us to desire that our relationships reflect something about the kingdom of God rather than our own insecurities. Jesus devoted time and energy to those of "no account" as a visible demonstration of the expansiveness of God's love. Who do you tend to ignore or exclude? Pray that God will empower you to reach out to them in humility and gentleness, not condescendingly or as a way of drawing attention to yourself but as a testimony to the in-breaking of God's kingdom at that time and place.

□ Finally, set aside some time to think seriously about the notion of ambition. In cultures like ours where ambition is widely regarded as a highly desirable virtue, Christians need to ask whether those who follow Jesus should regard ambition as a desirable character trait. Can Christians be ambitious in our society without succumbing to the world's skewed notions of success, advancement and status? If so, then what content remains when we use the word? Or in other words, what would be the purpose or goal of such ambition if it was not to climb to the top of the world's pecking order?

Cultivating gentleness and humility in cultures like ours will not be easy. In fact, the task will be made all the more difficult once we realize that many around us will often understand our gentleness, meekness and humility as weakness. We must not, however, let this discourage us. Although we earnestly hope that having the Spirit bear these fruit in our lives will have a positive impact on those who taste this fruit, there's no guarantee that it will. But as suggested earlier, perhaps we are called to surrender, in a spirit of gentleness and humility, the notion that we are responsible for what God does with this harvest of the Spirit's fruit.

> *I, therefore, the prisoner in the Lord, beg you to lead a life worthy of the calling to which you have been called, with all humility and gentleness, with patience, bearing with one another in love, making every effort to maintain the unity of the Spirit in the bond of peace. There is one body and one Spirit, just as you were called to the one hope of your calling, one Lord, one faith, one baptism, one God and Father of all, who is above all and through all and in all. (Eph 4:1-6)*

TEN

Cultivating
Self-Control
in the Midst of
Addiction

As for what fell among the thorns, these are the ones who hear; but as they go on their way, they are choked by the cares and riches and pleasures of life, and their fruit does not mature. (Lk 8:14)

For we ourselves were once foolish, disobedient, led astray, slaves to various passions and pleasures, passing our days in malice and envy, despicable, hating one another. But when the goodness and loving kindness of God our Savior appeared, he saved us, not because of any works of righteousness that we had done, but according to his mercy, through the water of rebirth and renewal by the Holy Spirit. (Tit 3:3-5)

Over the years the Olympic Games have become an important fixture of our corporate life in the United States. Although some citizens keep a watchful and (often) prideful eye on the medal counts, most seem attracted for other reasons. For many there is the irresistible lure of determining the "best in the world." Others are drawn by the human drama that inevitably unfolds around the Games. Over and over again we find ourselves profoundly moved by stories of men and women who have overcome tremendous obstacles in order to participate and excel. Still others are drawn primarily because of their deep respect for those who have pursued this Olympic dream so single-mindedly. Although many of us at some point in our lives may have fantasized about being Olympic athletes, we recognize that these athletes did not achieve this level of excellence without considerably more dedication and discipline than most of us can muster.

Athletics seem to be one of the few areas in our society where we encourage and honor self-discipline and self-control. If sports have a redeeming value in our society, it is in the potential that they have for training us to be disciplined, to exercise control over both mind and body. The hope, of course, would be that this practice of self-control would influence other areas of our lives. Although many athletes testify that this has indeed happened in their own lives, there are no guarantees. One need only be a casual follower of sports to think of examples of prominent athletes who have enormous difficulty controlling their tempers or their appetites for gambling, drugs or illicit sex. Many are well known for their outbursts of violence both on and off the playing field, and one widely idolized sports hero is reportedly addicted to competition itself.

Of course, athletes are not the only persons in our culture who are expected to exercise discipline and self-control, nor are they the only ones who find themselves battling addictions. Are there specific features of our society that impede the cultivation of self-control and encourage addiction? And equally important, does the popular understanding of self-control in our society today coincide with what Paul seems to have had in mind?

The Character of Self-Control

Most wisdom traditions have recognized how easily human beings become enslaved to their passions. For example, Buddhism has taught for millennia that the root of all human suffering and dissatisfaction is unbridled desire. A similar sentiment is expressed by the writer of Proverbs, who employs the image of a walled city: "He that hath no rule over his own spirit is like a city that is broken down and without walls" (Prov 25:28 KJV).

Although wisdom traditions have generally agreed that unconstrained passion and desire threaten human well-being, they have not always agreed about how best to address this threat. Buddhism recommends that unhealthy cravings be extinguished, often by means of meditation on the transitory character of all life. Other wisdom traditions have recommended the exercise of what we today commonly call "self-control." However, we should be cautious here because this common English translation of the Greek word for this concept *(egkrateia)* is relatively recent and may actually lead us to miss (if not undermine) the radical challenge that Paul is mounting to the popular ethics of his day. To see this we must understand the important role the concept of *egkrateia* played in Greek thought prior to the writing of the New Testament.

Egkrateia was widely praised by the Greeks long before the time of Paul. In fact, ancient Greek philosophers such as Socrates considered it to be the foundational human virtue. Xenophon, a follower of Socrates, summarized well his teacher's views on the subject:

> Shall not every man hold self-control *[egkrateia]* to be the foundation of all virtue, and first lay this foundation firmly in his soul? For who without this can learn any good or practice it worthily? (*Memorabilia* 1.5.4-5)

For the Greeks, virtue could not be learned if one was continually overcome by one's passions and desires. To take up the life of virtue, therefore, required that one begin by bringing one's own desires under control. Hence, the first and foundational virtue for all others was *egkrateia* (variously translated as "temperance," "continence," "moderation" or, most recently, "self-control"). As sensible as such an argument seems, even Plato was readily aware that this seemed to involve a paradox if not a contradiction. In brief, the paradox is this: when we speak of self-control or self-mastery, who is "the self" that is being controlled or mastered, and who is "the self" that is controlling or mastering? Isn't it in both cases the same "self"? Or as Plato writes in *The Republic*,

> Isn't the phrase "self-mastery" absurd? I mean, anyone who is his own master is also his own slave, of course, and vice versa, since it's the same person who is the subject in all these expressions. (*Republic* 430e-431)

Plato goes on to argue that if we can make any sense out of this expression at all, it must mean something like this: a person's noble and less noble aspects are often at war with each other about which will rule a person's life. When the nobler part brings the less noble part under subjection, we say that a person exhibits self-mastery or discipline. When the less noble part wins out, we say that the person lacks these virtues. For Plato the nobler aspects of humanity are always associated with rationality; moreover, only a limited number of citizens are capable of exercising these rational capacities in order to bring pleasure and desires under control. These elite few, by virtue of their ability to exercise discipline and self-mastery, deserve to rule the republic.

In much of Greek thought, therefore, the virtuous person was the self-directed person, while the weak and despised were those who had little or no control over their passions. To be driven by passions and desires was to be driven by those enticements and pleasures that were external to the self; a person so driven, therefore, was always under the control of another. For the Greeks, who highly valued their freedom, the highest ideal was to master one's desires so that one was free to enjoy them rather than be enslaved to them.

Given the central role that *egkrateia* played in Greek philosophical thought and ethics, what is most striking about its usage in the New Testament is its relative infrequency. The word *egkrateia* only appears three times (Acts 24:25; Gal 5:23; 2 Pet 1:6) and its cognates only three more (1 Cor 7:9; 9:25; Tit 1:8). One might be tempted to conclude that this human problem to which *egkrateia* was the recommended solution was unknown to the New Testament writers, but this is hardly the case. Numerous times in the New Testament writers allude to the problem of "licentiousness" or "lasciviousness" (Mk 7:22; 2 Cor 12:21; Gal 5:19; Eph 4:19; 1 Pet 4:3; Jude 4). Although neither word is a common part of our everyday vocabulary, both point to the willingness to abandon oneself to one's passions and desires. Moreover, the New Testament includes numerous references to our disordered affections and desires. These are referred to variously as "lusts," "desires," "lusts of the flesh," "passions of our flesh," "fleshly desires," "worldly passions" or "inordinate affections" (Mk 4:19; Rom 7:5; 13:14; Gal 5:16, 24; Eph 2:3; 1 Tim 6:9; 2 Tim 2:22; 3:6; Jas 1:14-15; 4:1-3; 1 Pet 2:11; 4:2-3; 1 Jn 2:16). Much like their Greek counterparts, the New Testament writers seem to agree that "people are slaves to whatever masters them" (2 Pet 2:19).

If the New Testament writers rarely appeal to that concept *(egkrateia)* that was at the heart of so much Greek ethics, I believe it was because they sensed that a new power had been made available to them through Christ. This power was not of their own making, nor was it a power inherent in the human person. Instead, this power was intimately bound up with Jesus Christ and made possible a new way of life, a way that could only be described by contrasting it with the old way of death. Indeed, this death of the "old self" liberates us from that self-imposed bondage created by our disordered desires, freeing us to live in God's likeness.

> We know that our old self was crucified with him so that the body of sin might be destroyed, and we might no longer be enslaved to sin. (Rom 6:6)

> You were taught to put away your former way of life, your old self, corrupt and deluded by its lusts, and to be renewed in the spirit of your minds, and to clothe yourselves with the new self, created according to the likeness of God in true righteousness and holiness. (Eph 4:22-24; cf. Gal 2: 19-20; Col 3:1-10)

This suggests that whatever the New Testament writers may have meant when they employed the concept of *egkrateia,* we should not too quickly assume that they meant "self-control," which in our day means something akin to control *of* the self, *by* the self, *for the sake of* the self. At this point we should also remind ourselves once again that Paul's list of the Spirit's fruit not only comes after a lengthy list of "the works of the flesh" but is also framed by two admonitions. In the first, Paul exhorts the Galatians to "live by the Spirit" and "not gratify the desires of the flesh" (5:16). In the second, he notes that "those who belong to Christ Jesus have crucified the flesh with its passions and desires," so that those who live by the Spirit should also be guided by the Spirit (5:24-25).

So if Paul likely does not mean what his contemporaries meant when they employed the term *egkrateia,* can we surmise what he might have meant? I believe we might get a hint when we consider Paul's extended discussion of his apostolic ministry in 1 Corinthians 9. Here we find that Paul contrasts exercising *egkrateia* with running "aimlessly" (1 Cor 9:25-26). In other words, Paul argues that athletes exercise *egkrateia* because they have a clearly defined purpose or goal. Such people cannot afford to be distracted by every passion or desire that comes along. If we combine this insight with the radical suggestion in Galatians that *egkrateia* is first of all a fruit of the Spirit's work and not of our own, then we might suggest that its meaning (in at least these two instances) is something akin to "control of the self by the Spirit for the sake of the gospel."

I do not believe that Paul placed *egkrateia* at the end of his list strictly by chance. Although he continues to use a word with wide currency in his day, his placement of it at the end of this list suggests a *dis*-placement. Rather than see self-control (understood as self-mastery) in the way that many of his contemporaries did—as the foundation for all other virtue—Paul's reconfiguration suggests that "the self" no longer occupies center stage. As we have noted, each fruit of the Spirit that Paul has listed to this point is decidedly other-directed; moreover, each has also been a reflection of God's own character. Yet *egkrateia*, as commonly understood, was decidedly self-directed, and such a "virtue" is nowhere in Scripture predicated of God's character. Is this final fruit an exception to the pattern established to this point? I don't believe so.

To suggest that Paul is an advocate of *egkrateia* as a form of self-mastery for the sake of the self would be to believe that Paul concludes his list in a way that runs counter to all that he has commended thus far. In contrast to such a view I believe Paul placed this highly regarded virtue at the end of his list in order to underscore the radical orientation of the Christian life. In so doing Paul not only stripped this virtue—and "the self"—of its previously foundational character but also imbued this word with new meaning. "The self" and the passions that threaten to drive it to excess are not robbed of their power and bondage by a further and more determined exercise of the human will or human reason. Instead, Paul seems to suggest that when our lives are other-directed (toward God and neighbor) in the ways they must be if we are truly to embody the fruit of the Spirit, "the self" and its twisted desires cannot remain at center stage. In sum, the desires of the self are most determinatively ordered not when we strive most diligently to bring the self under control but when we use our freedom in the Spirit to become servants of God and our neighbors (Gal 5:13). Understood in this way, this final fruit, by being other-directed and reflecting God's own other-directedness, does not contradict the pattern but reinforces it. In other words, if the Spirit brings to harvest these first eight fruit, this final fruit will also be among the harvest.

Given the potentially misleading character of our contemporary notion of self-control, we would do well to find a different way of naming this final fruit of the Spirit. We do not seem to have a suitable word in current English usage that does not bring with it a good deal of unhelpful baggage. Nevertheless, in an attempt to remind us of the problems of speaking about self-control, I have rendered Paul's notion of *egkrateia* with a word that carries slightly less baggage: *continence.* By choosing a word that is not compounded with *self,* I hope to remind readers that even though Paul does employ the popular Greek concept of *egkrateia,* he effects a radical transformation of its meaning by suggesting that this new life in Christ is animated not by the demands of the self but by the other-directedness of the Spirit.

Obstacles to a Life of Continence

We live in a society characterized by excess, addiction and attempts at self-mastery. Although we may joke about being "addicted" to such things as chocolate or romance novels, beneath our jokes an uneasiness often lurks. When we are honest with ourselves, each of us realizes that we are capable of indulging in addictive behaviors. Thus while we may often find ourselves looking down our noses at those trapped in lives of addiction, most of us can remember times in our own lives, past or present, when we ourselves were enslaved to such single-minded and reckless pursuits.

To get an idea of the scope of the problem, one need only explore the enormous resources this society dedicates to the treatment of addictions. A cursory search of the Internet reveals that twelve-step programs are available for those addicted to alcohol, narcotics, overeating, sex, work, debt, marijuana, cocaine, nicotine, gambling and even emotions! The study and treatment of addictions is also becoming increasingly institutionalized and professionalized. To combat addictions we now have research institutes, international symposia, social-scientific journals and addictive recovery institutes staffed by "certified rational addictive therapists." Even when we attempt to control our addictions, we are often driven to excess. Some people have even argued recently that people are becoming addicted to twelve-step programs. Whatever the merits of that argument, much about the contemporary situation remains embarrassing, even shameful, as we swing from one excess to another. For example, while one billion people around the world each year suffer from the effects of malnutrition, we live in a country where roughly three-fourths of our citizens are overweight, one-third are clinically obese and over thirty billion dollars a year are spent trying to lose weight. Where else in the world are so many resources dedicated simultaneously to our self-indulgences and the eradication of their harmful effects?

Is there something about our society that thwarts the development of continence, that indeed nourishes this kind of excessive and addictive behavior? In many ways, what is said below echoes much of what has been voiced in previous chapters. This should not be surprising, for if the final eight fruit of the Spirit are best understood as further specifications on the first fruit of love—and these fruit are characterized by their other-directedness—then a life marked by disordered passions will be a life that bears little of this Spirit's fruit. In short, a life dedicated to the pursuit of pleasure (or its eradication) is by definition a life focused on self; it cannot, therefore, at the same time be a life focused on the other, whether that other be God or neighbor.

Pursuing happiness. As already noted, in our society we are promised not only the freedom to pursue happiness but also the freedom to define what constitutes happiness. For many people happiness is equivalent to experiencing pleasure. Thus for many the pursuit of happiness is easily transformed into the pursuit of pleasure. This tendency, coupled with the pride that many people take in being driven about everything they do, offers up a fairly straightforward recipe for excess and addiction. In a culture where freedom is widely understood as freedom from restraint, the combination of being driven and yet having little guidance about what it is good to be driven about encourages people to become enslaved to their own private pursuits of pleasure.

Controlling the self (by the self, for the sake of the self). In a society as preoccupied with self and self-gratification as is ours, it is understandable that discussions about the right ordering of our desires and appetites rarely come up. Discussions about disordered desire arise most often with respect to recognized addictions, when it becomes apparent that a person's bondage has become self-destructive (or destructive of those personal relationships deemed important to and by the self). In a society where the individual is routinely exalted for its unlimited potential, it comes as no surprise that when the subject of disordered desire does arise, it is often framed in terms of self-control or self-discipline (understood as self-mastery). A welcome exception to that rule are various twelve-step programs, which require the person in recovery to admit both their powerlessness and their need to depend on a power outside themselves. However, a recent backlash against such programs by those who believe that the self and its own resources are all that is necessary to overcome addiction suggests that belief in self-mastery is alive and well.

In addition to discussions about how best to deal with addictions, our culture also circulates numerous stories about the benefits available to the self through self-mastery. Indeed, our society has long valorized self-mastery, insuring that it has a deep hold on our national psyche. The stories passed down to us about the Puritans always emphasize their Protestant work ethic, which was fueled by their industry, thrift and self-discipline. The public schools in this country, from their very beginnings in the late nineteenth century, saw it as their task to instill, among other virtues like obedience and respect for property, self-control and self-discipline. Most of us have a ready repertoire of stories of people who learned such lessons well and "made good." Furthermore, anyone who has read Benjamin Franklin's well-known autobiography will remember that he delineates thirteen virtues he desires to pursue, beginning with temperance (understood as "Eat not to dullness; drink not to elevation"). Franklin is quite clear that if he is to master these virtues, he will have to do so one at a time and that it only makes sense to start with temperance because such will provide him with the "coolness and clearness of head" necessary to master the rest. With such a history of self-mastery as our legacy, it seems appropriate that the first chapter of William J. Bennett's widely praised collection of stories *The Book of Virtues* is dedicated to "self-discipline."

The cumulative impact of this legacy is likely most visible, however, not in our literature but in our own attitudes. Who in our society do we most admire? Do we really admire those whose lives are characterized by genuine continence, those whose passions we discern are rightly ordered? Or do we find ourselves admiring most those who have purportedly mastered or disciplined themselves for the sake of some chosen goal, such as an Olympic medal, an NBA contract, a bigger house or a slimmer waistline? As a former athlete I well remember the frequent injunctions (offered by others and me) to exercise self-discipline and self-control—by which was meant the control or discipline of the self for my own future benefit.

Someone might object at this point, arguing that the exercise of such self-control or self-discipline is certainly to be preferred over the exercise of self-indulgence. Although I would certainly agree, I would still insist that we not confuse the exercise of such self-control or self-discipline with what Paul identifies as the final fruit of the Spirit. When it comes to nurturing that fruit, our culture's notions of self-control and self-discipline—exercised for the sake of the self—are likely to be serious obstacles.

Indeed, by wrongly assuming that Scripture advocates self-control as a form of self-mastery, Christians have often zealously championed self-control. In so doing, these well-meaning Christians have assumed that people (including Christians) can be trained to be masters of their own unhealthy desires and passions. By wrongly believing that we are individually equipped to deal with these problems by ourselves, we have unwittingly cut ourselves off from the very resources God has entrusted to us for our common benefit. Perhaps even worse, by encouraging people to "pull themselves up by their own bootstraps," we have set them up not only for likely failure but also for the enormous guilt that accompanies failing at something one had been assured one could do if one simply applied oneself diligently.

Moderation in all things. Paradoxically, another possible obstacle to the cultivation of continence is the maxim "Moderation in all things." In a culture that exhibits excess at nearly every turn, it is surprising how often this injunction is invoked. A cursory Internet search found a number of churches that even list "moderation in all things" as one of their core doctrines. What is most instructive, however, is not simply that this maxim is invoked but when. Often it is not with reference to food, drink or work but with reference to our deepest convictions. In our society few epithets sting as deeply as being labeled a "fanatic," and so many people have adopted as a kind of general principle this maxim written six centuries before Christ by a pagan named Theognis: "moderation in all things."

Although there are undoubtedly many areas of our lives where such advice is certainly prudent and wise, it is not clear how such a maxim is to be applied to the Christian life itself. Taking this maxim as a guide to all of life encourages many people to believe that the Christian life—like all pursuits—is fine in moderation, but one should avoid taking these matters too far or too seriously. So, for example, when confronted with Jesus' call for us to love our enemies (which might presumably preclude us from killing them), it is not uncommon for Christians to reply that they simply cannot adopt such an "extreme" position. Of course, they are right: this is an extreme position, if by *extreme* we mean a position not held or practiced by the majority of people. But surely Jesus was aware of this when he called us to love in this way. On what basis and by whose authority do we allow the pagan Greek maxim "moderation in all things" to trump the words and call of Jesus?

As a result of our uncritical adoption of this maxim, many of us are addicted to "balance," or more precisely, to mediocrity and lukewarmness. Too often we have used phrases such as "moderation in all things" to avoid the hard demands of the gospel. Perhaps the church at Laodicea, referred to in the book of Revelation, had a similar problem. Jesus criticizes them for their lukewarmness and warns them that because they are neither hot nor cold that he is about to spit them out of his mouth (Rev 3:14-17). Like the church at Laodicea, we want to be "balanced," by which we mean not overly committed to any one thing or person. To stray from this middle path—at least in the eyes of the wider society—is to risk becoming a fanatic. Yet would anyone who read the Sermon on the Mount for the first time suspect that Jesus was an advocate of "the balanced life"? Jesus does not call us simply to moderate the tyrannical demands of the self; rather Jesus calls us to a cross, where our old self is called to die. The Spirit-animated Christian is not one whose life is characterized by a modicum of selfish desires and flights of self-indulgence but one whose passions are oriented toward loving God and neighbor. The tragedy is that our lives are often marked by excess with respect to those things about which we are called to continence, while we are quick to moderate (or be lukewarm about) those things about which we should be passionate. For example, if I want to orient my entire life around my favorite college football or basketball team, adjusting my schedule to attend all home and away games, spending my days memorizing statistics and talking strategy with fellow "fans" (a word from the same root as *fanatic*), some people may consider me slightly eccentric, but most will admire my devotion. Such behavior is accepted, even encouraged, in our society. If, however, I choose to orient my life around a two-thousand-year-old community brought into existence by a Jewish carpenter, I am likely to be regarded as a "religious fanatic" who needs to learn the virtues of moderation and balance. Given the present shape of our society, therefore, it is not likely that living as God would have us live in the midst of it will appear "balanced." In fact, I suspect that living the Christian life faithfully in the United States will look suspiciously like fanaticism to a lot of people, including many Christians.

"Cultivating" Continence

If my argument to this point seems plausible, then such an argument would also seem to have a bearing on how we open ourselves up to having this fruit cultivated in our lives. Stated bluntly: we cannot actively cultivate continence, because such a strategy of self-mastery would likely only empower and further entrench the very self that first needs to die. If our lives come to bear the fruit of continence, it will not be because we have strained to control and direct our passions and our desires. Rather this fruit will be one of the natural byproducts of the Spirit's work in our lives. That is, when the Spirit produces the other eight fruit in our lives, it will also produce the fruit of continence, because the other eight already require a displacement of the self in order to thrive.

This does not mean, however, that nothing we do will have an impact on whether this fruit develops. I have insisted throughout these pages that the single most important venue for cultivating the fruit of the Spirit is the community gathered for worship. Here the gathered church receives its most important lessons in being other-directed. What are some of these lessons?

First, good worship might help us develop a sounder theology of pleasure. Such a theology will help us to recognize and guard against our tendency to turn inward, to pursue that which brings pleasure to the self alone. With this tendency in view we see how engaging in and reflecting on worship offers us an important resource. We worship God because God is worthy of our worship and because Scripture and tradition teaches us that God takes pleasure in our worship. Worship therefore is first of all focused on that which is pleasing to God. Yet if God has created us for worship, then we should not be surprised if we find ourselves deriving pleasure from that for which we've been created. The same, I believe, holds for the pleasure we receive in serving our neighbors. Although such pleasure is not our goal, we need not deny the experience of pleasure that comes both from desiring what God desires and from acting on those desires.

Hence worship—rightly understood and practiced—shapes and reorients our desires. In gathering together in the presence of the God who created us, we listen again to the grand story of "God with us," a story that both frees us from the necessity of spinning our own stories with ourselves at the center and frees us to locate our lives afresh within God's story. In so gathering we do our best to quiet the voices of our own agendas, our own desires, our own strivings—in order to hear afresh what God desires.

At its best, worship should also engage more than our ears and our minds. Unfortunately, much Protestant worship embodies a certain asceticism, a certain denial of the importance of the body, particularly of those senses other than hearing. Most of us well realize that much of the pleasure we enjoy in this world comes through our senses: the sight of a crimson sunset, the sound of young children laughing, the smell of freshly baked bread, the sweet taste of early corn, the warm embrace of a dear friend. Such pleasures are surely God's good gifts. Most of us would also admit that temptation often gains its initial foothold in our lives through those same senses, that our selfish and unholy desires are often shaped by the traffic we allow on those sensorial avenues. Yet how often are we encouraged to direct all our senses to the things of God? That this rarely happens stems from our assumption that there are only two ways to regard the senses and the pleasures they make possible. One option is to pursue pleasure for its own sake, which always entails pursuing pleasure for the sake of the self alone. The other option is to deny the goodness of the body and its attendant pleasures and to seek, therefore, to minimize the role of the body in worship and to extinguish all our desires by engaging in some form of strict asceticism. The first option enslaves us to our own pursuit of pleasure; the second option denies the goodness of the body and pleasure. Although these two options appear to be polar opposites, they actually share at least one common assumption: that our bodily senses and the pleasures that come through them can serve no higher purpose than our own selfish indulgence.

For the Christian, neither option is viable. If we really are the temple of the Holy Spirit, then surely that Spirit is capable of sanctifying all of us and not just part of us. What we need, it seems, is a more sacramental view of the body. Just as bread and wine are transformed into more than bread and wine in the Eucharist, thereby sanctifying part of God's good creation for a higher purpose, so full-bodied worship ought to facilitate the offering of all we are—including our bodies—to God as a sign of God's re-creative and transforming work. Authentic worship of the God who created us as embodied beings and who will resurrect us as embodied beings at the last day ought to engage our material senses and make possible the sanctification of what we see, hear, smell, taste and touch. God calls us to be holy because God is holy, but such holiness involves not a denial of our embodiedness but a sanctification of it. Full-bodied worship ought to serve as a powerful reminder that the body is not always an impediment to a life of the Spirit but may also be a vehicle for God's redemptive and sanctifying purposes. Those Protestants unaccustomed to full-bodied worship might need to reflect seriously on the potential resources that lie hidden beneath what might seem like strange practices of our brothers and sisters in other Christian traditions. Is it possible, for example, that the Orthodox Christian who regularly kisses an icon of Christ might be less likely to engage in unholy kissing than those who believe their lips are only an avenue for human pleasure? Similarly, is it possible that those who raise their hands to God in worship might be less inclined to raise those same hands to strike a child or spouse?

In addition to a theology of pleasure and a sacramental view of the body, Christians who want to understand how continence takes root in our lives would also do well to recover a theology of moral formation. Christians and non-Christians alike have understood for centuries the important role that habits play in shaping us to be the people we are. In light of this it is fascinating that recent research on brain chemistry suggests that there is a physical-material impulse to engage in behavior for which we have established neural networks. In other words, we may be closer to offering a physiological explanation for how habits work to direct our behavior. If so, then we may discover a deep connection between this physiological explanation and Paul's words in Romans that resonate so deeply with all of us: "For I do not do the good I want, but the evil I do not want is what I do" (Rom 7:19).

Such work should remind us once again that we are fully embodied beings, not disembodied minds or souls that drag around a body like a ball and chain. Moreover, such work has important implications for how we help those in our midst who are enslaved to certain desires. In such cases it hardly seems prudent to foster self-mastery, since most people readily admit to being at war with themselves. What is possible, however, is the establishing of new habits. This obviously takes time and so should be attempted with the help of others who can offer encouragement and accountability while one continues to labor under the bondage of previous habits.

It is within such a context that Christians might rediscover one appropriate use of fasting. Rightly understood, fasting is neither a form of asceticism or renunciation for its own sake nor a denial of the legitimate place of pleasure in our lives. The Christian doctrine of creation stands as a constant reminder that God's creation is good. The problem is not with what God has made but with the ways we so consistently twist it to our own destructive purposes. As a result, temptation rarely takes the guise of doing something "purely evil"; more often, it comes as an offer to take God's good gifts and twist them to our own less-than-good purposes. For example, food is a good gift of God, but when we eat excessively in order to avoid dealing with the stresses and conflicts in our lives, we twist God's good gift. Similarly, human speech is a good gift of God, but when we use our tongues to sow discord and tear down one another rather than to encourage and build them up, we twist God's good gift. The practice of fasting from food or speech, therefore, is not taken up because food or speech are evil but because we often need to be reminded of their proper places in our lives.

When we as Christians find ourselves trapped by our self-inflicted addictions, we might consider the benefits of fasting, not as an exercise in self-mastery but as an attempt to carve out space for God and neighbor. Ideally, fasting should be a last resort, for if we focus our energies on being other-directed and cultivating the other fruit of the Spirit, our attention will not easily turn to servicing the otherwise tyrannical demands of the self. The problem, of course, is that many of us have served ourselves for so long that we find it difficult to say yes to God and neighbor without first saying a definitive no to self. In such cases, a fast may prove helpful. Fasting, in this instance, is an exercise in learning to say no. But fasting alone is not enough, for it is quite possible to learn to say no to self without saying yes to God and neighbor. In such cases, we may find ourselves in a situation similar to the one described in the Gospels: an unclean spirit is driven out, but because the "house" remains empty, seven more unclean spirits return and take up residence (Mt 12:43-45). We must always be mindful that fasting is not an end in itself; fasting is an attempt to break the bondage to self in order to free us for others. If, for example, I choose to fast from watching television, I might do so not because I believe television is evil or because I desire an opportunity to feel self-righteous about my self-discipline. Instead, I might do so because I have come to realize both that hours spent watching television usually isolates me from those I am called to serve and that those hours spent watching regularly instill within me certain self-serving desires that impede such service.

As helpful as such a fast might be, it bears repeating that fasting, although a potentially useful resource for the Christian, should be used cautiously. Fasting that is undertaken as a form of self-mastery can easily reinforce the self-centeredness that often fosters addictions in the first place. This potentially self-defeating feature of fasting has long been recognized. For example, Isaiah warned his listeners that their fasts were unacceptable to God because they sought to please God by their self-centered fasts while oppressing and being unjust to their neighbors (Is 58:3-14). Perhaps this is why fasting, when mentioned in Scripture in a positive way, is often linked with prayer (Neh 1:4; Mk 9:29; Lk 2:37; Acts 13:3; 14:23; 1 Cor 7:5). Both activities involve not a stifling or extinguishing of one's own will (by an act of one's will!) but a willingness to bend one's will to God's will.

Taken together, therefore, prayer and fasting is not so much an exercise in self-denial as it is an exercise in cultivating awareness. Too often we unwittingly nourish our addictions because we so clutter our lives with busyness that we have little time or energy left to reflect on the direction of our lives. For such people, learning to say no to those behaviors in which we habitually and (often) unthinkingly engage to our own (and others') detriment may be the only way to create the reflective space to say yes to God and neighbor.

Reflection Questions and Practical Suggestions

☐ Have you ever had what you would consider to be an addiction? As you reflect back on that experience, how would you explain your coming to be addicted? As you struggled to overcome that addiction, did you ever experience the frustration that accompanies being at war with yourself? Have you ever felt guilty for not doing a better job of exercising "self-control"? How might Paul's displacement of self-mastery offer you a different way of thinking about these matters?

☐ Reflect on the way your own church tradition formed you to think of pleasure. How has it formed you to regard your body? Of the role of your body in worship? Ask several Christians you respect from various traditions of worship and spirituality how they think about these matters, including the rationale within their traditions for thinking of these matters in these ways.

☐ Are you ever tempted to deflect the gospel's "extreme" demands by retreating behind our culture's motto of "moderation in all things"? Which demands do you find most problematic? In what sense do you find them extreme?

☐ Devote some time to reflecting honestly and prayerfully on the orientation of your life. To what extent do you believe your life is other-directed? To what extent is your life taken up with the service of self? One way to get at this is to make a list of your current goals and aspirations. As you write down your list, be honest. List not only those goals of which your are proud but also those that are less noble and more self-serving. After you have completed your list, consider carefully how you can come to desire these things. Remember that every culture forms its participants to desire some things rather than others. With this in mind, reflect on the ways in which your desires have been shaped not only by the powerful cultural practices discussed throughout this book but also by other cultural practices as well.

If we agree that God's deepest desire is for us to be transformed into the image of Christ, consider whether the pursuit (or the attainment) of your desires listed above is likely to foster or undermine God's greatest and ultimate desire. After you have been as honest with yourself as you know how to be, seek out some trusted friends who know your desires well and with whom you can discuss these matters further. Ask specifically if they see any areas of your life where your desires and affections seem disordered. Give them permission to speak the truth to you in love, particularly on those points where their assessment of your life differs from your own assessment.

Odds are good that you will identify at least some areas in your life where your desires are disordered or misplaced. Rather than seeking to bring those desires "under control" by a further exercise of your own will, consider whether this disorder is not at least partially attributable to an inadequate harvest of the other fruit of the Spirit. If so, consider taking positive steps to do what is in your power to cultivate and nourish those fruit, steps which will of necessity require you to take your focus off of yourself. In the long run such an approach may do much more to nourish continence in your life than any direct attempt to exercise "self-control."

☐ If you do choose to fast in order to break the bondage of an addiction, keep in mind the potential dangers articulated in this chapter. At the very least, be sure that such a fast is coupled with prayer, linked to a plan to replace this activity with one more other-directed and monitored with the aid of another

Christian who can help you discern whether the fast is being used by God to create the space for further and more constructive action.

> *Brace up your minds for action, therefore, and be alert, and fix your hope fully on the grace that will be coming to you when Jesus Christ is revealed. As obedient children, do not shape your lives by the passions that controlled you in your previous ignorance; instead, as the One who called you is holy, so you yourselves should be holy in all your conduct; for it is written, "You shall be holy, because I am holy." (1 Pet 1:13-16 Modern Language Bible)*

CONCLUSION
Hoping
Against Hope

The fruit of the Spirit is love, joy, peace, patience, kindness, goodness, faithfulness, gentleness and self-control. There is no law against such things. And those who belong to Christ Jesus have crucified the flesh with its passions and desires. If we live by the Spirit, let us also be guided by the Spirit. (Gal 5:22-25, amended).

If we are called by God to holiness of life, and if holiness is beyond our natural power to achieve (which it certainly is) then it follows that God himself must give us the light, the strength, and the courage to fulfill the task he requires of us. He will certainly give us the grace we need. If we do not become saints it is because we do not avail ourselves of his gift.
—Thomas Merton

The analysis in the preceding pages is neither the definitive nor the final word on the subject. Indeed, if I am correct about the kind of discernment that the church must undertake in every place and time, there can be no definitive or final word. Every generation in every culture must take up the hard work of discerning the opportunities for and the obstacles to embodying the gospel faithfully in that place and time. The present study has focused on only some of the formidable obstacles that the dominant culture within the United States presents to communities of Christians who desire to be the body of Christ for the world. My aim has not been to offer an exhaustive catalog of obstacles, but to offer a model of Christian discernment. My reason for doing so is simple: the challenges that any culture presents to faithful embodiments of the gospel will always be changing. Thus what is most needed is not simply a ready-made list of obstacles, but a method of identifying them as obstacles and for discerning a way forward. Unfortunately, Christians in this country have considered our cultural soil to be conducive to embodying the gospel for so long that we have in large part lost our skills of discernment. Without such skills the church will not be able to distinguish an obstacle from an opportunity. But the opportunities are real enough as well. I hope no one who has read through these pages could fail to sense that the church is uniquely poised to offer up to the peoples of our land a much different fare than that to which their palates have grown accustomed. Whether we take advantage of that opportunity is, of course, another matter.

From my own limited perspective, I do not see how the church can overcome the formidable obstacles or take full advantage of its opportunities without engaging in something like the process of discernment that I have attempted here. For this reason I would be content if readers disagreed with many of the details of my analysis and recommendations, but agreed that the kind of discernment I have done here is the sort of serious reflection that the church ought to be doing. Rather than trying to convince such readers that my analysis is correct, I would rather encourage them to engage in the kind of analysis that I have done from the perspective of their own peculiar situation and context. This is not to suggest that these details do not matter, but quite the opposite. Because these details matter immensely to the ways we embody the gospel, discernments must always carry a distinctively local flavor. This is why I suggested at the beginning of this study that by the time we were through, the reader would likely know more about my own specific context, perspective and blind spots than anything so general or universal as "American culture." The perspective offered in these pages has been forged through my own interactions with Christians and the dominant culture of this nation, and though it certainly bears my own idiosyncrasies, this is because I am the one who has undertaken the analysis. Other efforts at discernment will inevitably bear the character of their authors as well.

Those readers who have resonated with at least parts of my analysis may still have come to the end of the book feeling overwhelmed, perhaps even paralyzed. The task before the church is incredibly daunting. Where should we begin? Is there any reason even to try? Why not just give up and throw ourselves upon the mercy of God? Isn't the church either already dead or beyond recovery?

One of my favorite children's stories is *The Cherry Tree,* written by Daisaku Ikeda.[1] This story, set in post-war Japan, tells of two children who one day stumble upon an old man who is attempting to nurse back to life a barren, aged and war-damaged cherry tree. At first the children are puzzled by the man's devotion to a tree that already appears to be dead. When they inquire about this, the old man explains:

> It's true she hasn't blossomed since before the war. But one day, with a little kindness and patience, she may again. Not in my lifetime perhaps, but one day! I'm sure of it.

The children, inspired by the old man's devotion and hope, agree to join him in his efforts to nurse the tree back to life. They work hard, but much of their time is spent waiting and hoping.

And then one day a single pink petal appears, followed in due time by a rapturous display of fruit-producing blossoms.

The church, I believe, could learn much from this simple story. Most importantly, the story could remind us that we are called to devote our lives to nurturing this tree called the church, even when the tree seems dead and even when we have no guarantees that we will see in our lifetime a bountiful harvest of the Spirit's fruit. We may or may not see the church bear abundant fruit in our generation. We may or may not see the reign of God manifested more fully in our day. But we must not give up hope that God will do what God has promised to do. In effect, we find ourselves in a position similar to the one occupied by those saints enumerated in Hebrews 11. After recounting the ways in which their lives embodied faith, the author of the epistle writes:

> Yet all these, though they were commended for their faith, did not receive what was promised, since God had provided something better so that they would not, apart from us, be made perfect. (Heb 11:39-40)

Two things are striking about this passage. First, none of these exemplars of faith received what God promised, yet they remained faithful. Like the old man in *The Cherry Tree*, their faithfulness was not contingent on their seeing, in their own day, that for which they longed. Second and perhaps even more striking, the completion and perfection of God's promise—a promise these men and women of faith longed to see fulfilled—will not be brought about apart from us. This, it seems, is why we find ourselves "surrounded by so great a cloud of witnesses" (Heb 12:1). They have run their legs of the relay and have passed the baton to us. The race is far from over and they remain in the stands, cheering us on—not least because they know their promised reward will not be secured apart from us. Is it really thinkable that we who find ourselves on the track, though tired and even perhaps lagging behind where we would like to be, would simply take off our running shoes and head home once it became clear that the race would extend beyond our lifetimes and that we could not be assured that we would be ahead by the time we passed from the scene?

We can readily admit that in many places the church is not offering the kind of embodied witness to the gospel of Jesus Christ that the church is called to offer—a fact born out by the impoverished character of the Spirit's fruit available in those locales. Nevertheless, we have not been promised that we will see in our day the promised reign of God come in all its fullness, nor have we been asked to usher in that reign on our own. Instead we have been asked to cooperate with God in bearing fruit that reflects the character of that reign as a foretaste of what is to come. We would do well, therefore, to seek to be faithful in those small things to which God has called us. Only then might God entrust us with more weighty matters (Lk 16:12).

Thus despite the church's present plight, I see no reason for pessimism or panic. I remain confident that God will do what God has promised to do, and I call my brothers and sisters in Christ to remain confident as well. Like Abraham, we find ourselves "hoping against hope" (Rom 4:18), choosing not to let the pitiful condition of our body dissuade us from believing that God will ultimately accomplish all that God has set out to do. My aim in these pages, therefore, has not been to be alarmist; rather, my aim has been to call the church to serious reflection and faithful embodiment. If our faith and hope are ultimately in God and not in ourselves, there is no reason to sell the family farm. We must continue to hope, like the gardener in Jesus' parable (Lk 13:6-9), that God will be merciful to us and will grant us one more season to produce the Spirit's fruit.

Yet we must also not presume upon God's grace. The church, like Israel, has been called to mission, and if we refuse to accept that call of being a "light to the nations," we might find Jesus' words to ancient Israel echoing in our own ears: "Therefore I tell you, the kingdom of God will be taken away from you and given to a people that produces the fruits of the kingdom" (Mt 21:43). It would be presumptuous of the church to assume that the word of judgment spoken to Israel—a word spoken for her ultimate good—could not also be spoken to the church. May the church in our day set our hope on God and our hand to the plow as we seek to work with God to bring to fruition all that God has promised.

> *For this reason I bow my knees before the Father, from whom every family in heaven and on earth takes its name. I pray that, according to the riches of his glory, he may grant that you may be strengthened in your inner being with power through his Spirit, and that Christ may dwell in your hearts through faith, as you are being rooted and grounded in love. I pray that you may have the power to comprehend, with all the saints, what is the breadth and length and height and depth, and to know the love of Christ that surpasses knowledge, so that you may be filled with all the fullness of God.*
>
> *Now to him who by the power at work within us is able to accomplish abundantly far more than all we can ask or imagine, to him be glory in the church and in Christ Jesus to all generations, forever and ever. Amen. (Eph 3:14-21)*

Notes

Chapter 1: Dying on the Vine?

[1]Raymond Williams, *Keywords: A Vocabulary of Culture and Society*, rev. ed. (New York: Oxford University Press, 1983), p. 87. I am indebted to Williams's account for much of what follows.
[2]William J. Bennett, *The Book of Virtues: A Treasury of Great Moral Stories* (New York: Simon & Schuster, 1993), p. 11.

Chapter 2: Cultivating Love in the Midst of Market-Style Exchanges

[1]Stephen F. Winward, *Fruit of the Spirit* (Grand Rapids, Mich.: Eerdmans, 1981), p. 26.
[2]Mother Teresa, as quoted in Malcolm Muggeridge, *Something Beautiful for God: Mother Teresa of Calcutta* (San Francisco: Harper & Row, 1971), p. 65.

Chapter 3: Cultivating Joy in the Midst of Manufactured Desire

[1]C. S. Lewis, *Surprised by Joy* (New York: Harcourt Brace & World, 1955), p. 168.
[2]Evelyn Underhill, *The Fruits of the Spirit, Light of Christ and Abba* (London: Longmans, Green, 1956), pp. 11-12.
[3]Augustine *Confessions* 10.22, trans. R. S. PineCoffin (New York: Penguin, 1961), pp. 228-29.
[4]Karl Barth, *Epistle to the Philippians* (Richmond, Va: John Knox Press, 1962), p. 120.
[5]John Kavanaugh, *Following Christ in a Consumer Society*, rev. ed. (Maryknoll, N.Y.: Orbis, 1991), p. 34.

Chapter 5: Cultivating Patience in the Midst of Productivity

[1]Augustine *Confessions* 11.14, trans. R. S. PineCoffin (New York: Penguin, 1961), p. 264.
[2]Alister E. McGrath, *The Genesis of Doctrine* (Oxford: Basil Blackwell, 1990), p. 105.
[3]Kosuke Koyama, *No Handle on the Cross* (Maryknoll, N.Y.: Orbis, 1977), p. 19.
[4]Kosuke Koyama, *Three Mile an Hour God* (Maryknoll, N.Y.: Orbis, 1980), p. 7.
[5]Henri J. M. Nouwen, *Making All Things New: An Invitation to the Spiritual Life* (HarperSan-Francisco, 1981), p. 74.

Chapter 6: Cultivating Kindness in the Midst of Self-Sufficiency

[1]*Johnson City Press*, July 24, 1994, p. 1.
[2]Martin Luther, *The Freedom of a Christian*, in *Martin Luther: Selections from His Writings*, ed. John Dillenberger (Garden City, N.Y.: Anchor, 1961), pp. 74, 75, 76.

Chapter 9: Cultivating Gentleness in the Midst of Aggression

[1]The above statistics come from the following sources: Sandra Arbetter, "Violence: A Growing Threat," *Current Health* 21, no. 6 (February 1995): 6-12; *Pittsburg Post-Gazette*, March 31, 1997, p. A10; *Government and Television: Improving Programming Without Censorship*, hearings before the Subcommittee on Oversight of Government Management, Restructuring; and the District of Columbia of the Committee on Governmental Affairs, United States Senate, 105th Congress, first session, April 16 and May 8, 1997; *Boston Globe*, October 26, 1998, p. A18.

Conclusion: Hoping Against Hope

[1]Daisaku Ikeda, *The Cherry Tree*, trans. Geraldine McCaughren and illus. Brian Wildsmith (New York: Afred A. Knopf, 1991).